Enchanting a
Disenchanted World

TITLES OF RELATED INTEREST FROM PINE FORGE PRESS

Exploring Social Issues Using SPSS for Windows95/98 Versions 7.5, 8.0, or Higher *by Joseph Healey, John Boli, Earl Babbie, and Fred Halley*

Social Prisms: Reflections on Everyday Myths and Paradoxes *by Jodi O'Brien*

This Book Is Not Required: An Emotional Survival Manual for Students, Revised Edition, *by Inge Bell and Bernard McGrane*

Media/Society: Industries, Images, and Audiences, 2nd Edition *by David Croteau and William Hoynes*

Crime and Everyday Life: Insight and Implication for Society, 2nd Edition *by Marcus Felson*

Building Community: Social Science in Action *edited by Philip Nyden, Anne Figert, Mark Shibley, and Darryl Burrows*

Race, Ethnicity, Gender, and Class: The Sociology of Group Conflict and Change, 2nd Edition *by Joseph F. Healey*

Riddles of Human Society *by Donald Kraybill and Conrad Kanagy*

The McDonaldization of Society, Revised Edition *by George Ritzer*

Sociology for a New Century: *A Pine Forge Press Series*
Edited by Charles Ragin, Wendy Griswold, and Larry Griffin

An Invitation to Environmental Sociology *by Michael M. Bell*

Schools and Societies *by Steven Brint*

The Gender Lens: *A Sage Publications/Pine Forge Press Series*
Edited by Judith A. Howard, Barbara Risman, Mary Romero, and Joey Sprague

The Gender of Sexuality *by Pepper Schwartz and Virginia Rutter*

Enchanting a Disenchanted World: Revolutionizing the Means of Consumption

George Ritzer

PINE FORGE PRESS
Thousand Oaks • London • New Delhi

For information:

Pine Forge Press
A Sage Publications Company
2455 Teller Road
Thousand Oaks, California 91320
sales@pfp.sagepub.com

SAGE Publications Ltd.
6 Bonhill Street
London EC2A 4PU
United Kingdom

SAGE Publications India Pvt. Ltd.
M-32 Market
Greater Kailash I
New Delhi 110 048 India

Production Editor: Wendy Westgate
Production Coordinator: Windy Just
Production Assistant: Stephanie Allen
Designer/Typesetter: Janelle LeMaster
Cover Designer: Ravi Balasuriya

Printed in the United States of America

99 00 01 02 03 10 9 8 7 6 5 4 3 2 1

Library of Congress Cataloging-in-Publication Data

Ritzer, George.
    Enchanting a disenchanted world: Revolutionizing the means of
consumption / George Ritzer.
        p.   cm.
    Includes bibliographical references and index.
    ISBN 0-7619-6101-1 (cloth: acid-free paper)
    ISBN 0-7619-8511-5 (pbk.: acid-free paper)
    1. Consumption (Economics)—United States.   2. Consumption
(Economics).   3. Marketing—United States.   4. Marketing.   I. Title.
    HC110.C6 R58   1998
    339.4'7'0783—ddc21   BOOK   98-40128
                                  $27.49

To Dylan Tyler Ritzer

Falling in love all over again

◆◆◆

ABOUT THE AUTHOR

George Ritzer is Professor of Sociology at the University of Maryland, where he has been named a Distinguished Scholar-Teacher and has won a Teaching Excellence award. He has chaired the American Sociological Association's section on theoretical sociology and its section on organizations and occupations. He has been scholar-in-residence at several international think tanks and has lectured throughout the world. He is best known for his work in metatheory: *Sociology: A Multiple Paradigm Science* (1975/1980); *Toward an Integrated Sociological Paradigm* (1981); and *Metatheorizing in Sociology* (1991). He is also well known for his work in the application of sociological theory to everyday economic phenomena, especially those relating to consumption: *The McDonaldization of Society* (1993/1996); *Expressing America: A Critique of the Global Credit Card Society* (1995); and *The McDonaldization Thesis* (1998). His work has been translated into many different languages; there are a dozen translations of *The McDonaldization of Society* alone.

ABOUT THE PUBLISHER

Pine Forge Press is a new educational publisher, dedicated to publishing innovative books and software throughout the social sciences. On this and any other of our publications, we welcome your comments, ideas, and suggestions. Please call or write to:

Pine Forge Press
A Sage Publications Company
2455 Teller Road
Thousand Oaks, CA 91320
805-499-4224
E-mail: sales@pfp.sagepub.com

Visit our World Wide Web site, your direct link to a multitude of online resources: www.pineforge.com

CONTENTS

PREFACE

As a consumer, you can do many things today that you could not do a few decades ago, including

♦ Shopping in an immense, brightly lit, colorful mall with several hundred shops many of them part of well-known chains and with literally millions of goods and services from which to choose.

♦ Spending a day or more in an even bigger and more dazzling megamall that encompasses not only shops but also an amusement park.

♦ Gambling the day (and night!) away in a casino that not only is an enormous hotel but also includes a shopping mall and an amusement park on the grounds of the complex.

♦ Whiling away a week on a deluxe, 100,000-ton cruise ship that offers the expanse of the sea and the beauty of tropical islands and also hotel-like facilities, a casino, a mall, a health spa, amusements, and many other places to spend money.

♦ Eating in a "themed" restaurant, part of an upscale chain, where the setting, the accoutrements, the staff, and the food bring to mind a tropical rain forest or the world of rock music.

♦ Vacationing at a theme park where the restaurants and everything else—attractions, costumes, employees' utterances—portray such themes as life in the future, life in other parts of the world, or animals of the world.

Enchanting a Disenchanted World: Revolutionizing the Means of Consumption is concerned with the development of these settings, and many others like them, in the last half century. A revolutionary change has occurred in the places in which we consume goods and services, and it has had a profound effect not only on the nature of consumption but also on social life.

One of the concepts used to describe the settings of concern in this book is *means of consumption*. These settings, as means, allow us to consume a wide range of goods and services. But as you will see, these places do more than simply permit us to consume things; they are structured to lead and even coerce us into consumption.

Another important concept presented in this book is *cathedrals of consumption*, which points up the quasi-religious, "enchanted" nature of these new settings. They have become locales to which we make "pilgrimages" in order to practice our consumer religion.

These new means of consumption have helped to entice us to consume far more than we ever did in the past; we have been led in the direction of hyperconsumption. We are also being led to consume differently than we did in the past. For instance, we are now more likely to consume alone, to purchase many different kinds of goods and services in one locale, and to buy many of the same things and consume in many of the same kinds of places as most other people. In fact, because our cathedrals of consumption are actively being exported to the rest of the world, people in many other countries consume as actively as we do and obtain many of the same goods and services.

The new means of consumption have been so successful with the public that other social settings—ballparks, universities, hospitals, museums, churches, and the like—have begun to look quite dated and stodgy. Thus, those who control these other types of settings are rushing to emulate the cathedrals of consumption. For example, universities increasingly have "theme" dorms, fast-food restaurants, souvenir shops, and video arcades. Students and parents are more likely than ever to be treated like consumers who need to be lured to a particular university and "enchanted" so they will stay there for the duration of the college years. Similarly, a modern baseball stadium offers far more than just a baseball game. Sometimes the game seems like a minor distraction from the other attractions on the stadium grounds: theme restaurants, food courts, swimming pools, hotels, exploding computerized scoreboards, and numerous souvenir shops. We are more likely to be treated as consumers than as fans in such a setting; in turn, we are more likely to view baseball stadiums in the same way we view shopping malls and theme parks.

The result of these changes is that consumption pervades our lives; we are increasingly consumed by consumption. We frequently find ourselves in settings devoted to consumption. Even our homes have become means of consumption, penetrated by telemarketing, junk mail, catalogs, home shopping television, and cybershops. We get little respite from the pressure to consume.

Of course, most of us are enthusiastically a part of the consumer society and are eager to visit the cathedrals of consumption and to obtain what they have to offer. We frequent those settings that offer the greatest spectacle. But we easily grow bored. Thus consumption settings, from fast-food restaurants to Las Vegas casino–hotels, compete to outdo one another and to see which one can put on the greatest show. The result is increasingly spectacular displays and a continual escalation of efforts to lure consumers.

Ironically, when these efforts at enchantment are successful, they draw large numbers of consumers necessitating rationalization and bureaucratization. Thus the cathedrals of consumption grow increasingly disenchanting to the jaded consumers they have been designed to attract. A sizable portion of this book is devoted to the contrary pressures that enchant and disenchant consumers.

It should come as no surprise to you that this new world of consumption exists. Many of you spend a great deal of time in such settings. However, you may not have recognized how closely consumer enchantment and disenchantment are related, how the principles used to design cathedrals of consumption are being employed in locales that we do not often think of as devoted to consumption, and how these principles are helping to create a social world increasingly dominated by consumption. In this book you are invited to take a close look at the sometimes radical effect the new means of consumption have had on the way we think and live.

ACKNOWLEDGMENTS

Many people deserve thanks for their help with this book. A special thanks goes to my research assistant of many years, Jan Geesin, and to my long-term indexer (and even longer-term son), Jeremy Ritzer. I wish to acknowledge and thank Paul Baker at Illinois State University, who reviewed an early version of this book. I am grateful to developmental editors Dretha Phillips (Washington State University) and, especially, Alan Venable. Alan worked through two drafts of this book, and his incisive comments and critiques have made it far better. All the blame for the failings in this book belongs to the president of Pine Forge Press, Steve Rutter. Seriously, Steve has been a good friend and a hard taskmaster, insisting that this book be as good as it can be. He read and critiqued it himself on several occasions, and he provided the assistance needed to help make it better. His help has been so immense that I would give him part of the royalties were he not such a tough negotiator that I think I have already agreed to pay him a royalty on each book sold.

1

A TOUR OF THE NEW
MEANS OF CONSUMPTION

Consumption plays an ever-expanding role in the lives of individuals around the world. To some, consumption defines contemporary American society, as well as much of the rest of the developed world. We consume many obvious things—fast food, t-shirts, a day at Walt Disney World® and many others that are not so obvious a lecture, medical service, a day at the ballpark. We consume many goods and services that we must have in order to live and many more that we simply have come to want. Often we must go to particular settings to obtain these goods and services (although, as we will see, more and more of them are coming to us). This book is concerned with those settings: shopping malls, cybermalls, fast food restaurants, theme parks, and cruise ships, to name a few. We will be concerned with the issue of why we go to some places rather than others, and we will also deal with the ways in which these settings contribute to the high and increasing level of consumption that characterizes society today.

Unlike many treatments of the subject of consumption, this is *not* a book about the consumer[1] or the increasing profusion of goods and services.[2] Rather, it is about the almost dizzying proliferation of settings[3] that allow, encourage, and even compel us to consume so many of those goods and services. The settings of interest will be termed the *new means of consumption*. These are, in the main, settings that have come into existence or taken new forms since the end of World War II and that, building on but going beyond earlier settings, have dramatically transformed the nature of consumption. Because of important continuities, it is not always easy to clearly distinguish between new and older means of consumption,[4] but it is the more contemporary versions, singly and collectively, that will concern us.[5]

In order to get a better sense of the new means of consumption, let us first look at Walt Disney World and the larger Disney operation of which it is part.

DISNEY'S WORLD

Building on late 19th- and early 20th-century efforts, including world exhibitions (and fairs) and Coney Island in New York, Walt Disney and his company created a revolutionary new type of amusement park: the theme park. The first of the theme parks, Disneyland, opened in southern California in 1955.[6] It was followed by Disney World in Florida in 1971, Tokyo Disneyland in 1983,[7] and Euro Disney in 1992. The Disney theme parks (even the initially financially troubled Euro Disney) have, of course, been enormous successes, in great part because they built on and greatly expanded the bases of the success of the early amusement parks. This includes entertainment for the masses, great spectacles, use of technology for consumption rather than production, the commercialization of "fun," and the offer of a safety valve where people can expend their energies without threatening society. In addition, Disney systematically eliminated the "seedy" and risque elements that characterized and played a major role in the decline of many amusement parks in the first half of the twentieth century. Although visitors who arrived at earlier amusement parks felt a sense of looseness, even danger, tourists who arrive at Disney World know and take comfort in the fact that inside the gates lies a tightly regulated world.

Disney transformed the world of amusement parks by, among other things, cleaning them up, creating far more "moral" order than most of the early parks ever had, and making the amusement park acceptable as family entertainment.[8] Disney offered a self-contained, controlled environment free from the kinds of problems that had undermined earlier parks. It pioneered the order and constraint that is characteristic of virtually all contemporary theme parks.[9] Although the primary appeal of early amusement parks such as Coney Island was that they offered visitors "a respite from . . . formal, highly regulated social situations,"[10] the main attraction at Disney World is just such tight regulation.[11] To put it another way, although parks such as Coney Island provided "a moral holiday,"[12] Disney World created a new morality emphasizing conformity to external demands.

Disney World is highly predictable. For example, there are no midway scam artists to bilk the visitor. There are teams of workers who, among their other cleaning chores, follow the nightly parades cleaning up debris—including animal droppings—so that visitors are not unpleasantly surprised should they take an errant step. There is no sexual titillation of the kind that characterized many early amusement parks. The park is continually cleaned, repaired, and repainted; there is nothing "seedy" about Disney World. The steep admission charge, the high cost of eating, shopping, and so forth, as well as the costs involved in getting there have succeeded in keeping "undesirables" out. A Disney executive said, "Think of Disney World as a medium-sized city with a crime rate of zero."[13] As a result of this sanitation of the park experience, Disney parks have become a favorite destination for middle-class families and many other people as well.

The heart of Disney World is the Magic Kingdom (a telling name given, as you will see, our interest in this book in enchantment) and its seven "lands." The trek through Disney World begins and ends in Main Street, U.S.A, which leads to the six other themed "lands"—the newly remodeled Tomorrowland[14] with, among other things, a roller-coaster-like space adventure on "Space Mountain" (sponsored by FedEx), Fantasyland with the recent addition of the "Legend of the Lion King" (sponsored by Kodak), Adventureland with the long-running "Jungle Cruise," Frontierland anchored by such traditional favorites as "Country Bear Jamboree," Liberty Square with the "Haunted Mansion," and Mickey's Toontown Fair with Minnie's and Mickey's Country Houses.

Epcot Center has the General Motors exhibit encompassing the new Test Track thrill ride.[15] Reminiscent of world fairs, the World Showcase has pavilions featuring a number of exhibits from nations including China, France, and Morocco.

Another set of major attractions at Disney World is Disney-MGM Studios. The Hollywood Boulevard/Echo Lake Area features the "Star Tours," which involves a thrill ride inspired by Star Wars. On Dalmatian Avenue one will find the "Disney-MGM Studios Backlot Tour." New York Street/Backlot features "Jim Henson's Muppet*Vision 3D" movie (sponsored by Kodak). Sunset Boulevard has as one of its two attractions "Beauty and the Beast—Live on Stage." One of Animation Courtyard's two attractions is "Voyage of the Little Mermaid."

The latest addition to Disney World is Animal Kingdom, which opened in April 1998. It encompasses 500 acres, nearly five times the size of the Magic Kingdom. Many parts of the park are still under construction with a number of "lands" to be opened in the future. Already in existence is The Oasis, a lush jungle-like setting through which people enter Animal Kingdom and that includes a branch of the chain of Rainforest Cafe® theme restaurants. Safari Village includes the centerpiece of Animal Kingdom, the massive "Tree of Life." Several hundred hand-carved animals seem to grow out of the tree inside of which is a multimedia theater. Dinoland attempts to depict life as it existed millions of years ago and includes "Boneyard," a children's playground with equipment made out of what appear to be giant dinosaur bones. Africa includes a town, "Harambe," on the edge of a simulated savannah including natural landscapes and herds of animals indigenous to that continent; it also includes the "Kilimanjaro Safari" involving a trip through the countryside and a high-speed automobile chase across, among other things, a collapsing bridge over a "crocodile-infested" river.

Beyond the four theme parks, there are three water parks, a nighttime entertainment district, a shopping area, fourteen hotels, the town of Celebration, and the Disney Institute—all means of consumption in their own right.[16]

Disney has become a global presence not exclusively through its theme parks but also through its many other enterprises, such as its movies, television shows, and cable television network. Of greater relevance to the concerns of this book are the Disney stores that are found in innumerable shopping malls and on-line; Club Disney (entertainment centers for children); Radio Disney (a children's radio network); the new Disney Cruise Line; Disney's ownership of ABC, ESPN, the Anaheim Angels Major League Baseball team and the Anaheim Mighty Ducks National Hockey League team; the Disney Catalog; and even the Disney Credit Card. All of these are employed synergistically to sell one another in a tightly integrated system that ultimately sells the Disney name and yields huge profits. Disney theme parks are revolutionary in many senses, but perhaps above all they are part of a "selling machine" capable of marketing Disney to an unprecedented degree.

Disney's power is also reflected in the role it has played in the resuscitation of the area around Times Square and 42nd Street in New York City.[17] Prior to Disney's arrival, this area was all but dead as a commercial center, dominated by peep shows and street hustlers. In fact, *Rolling Stone* dubbed 42nd Street "the sleaziest block in America."[18] Many previous high-profile efforts to rebuild the area never got off the ground. But in 1993 Disney agreed to invest $8 million in the renovation of the New Amsterdam Theater to serve as a site for Broadway productions of Disney shows. In addition, a Disney Store was opened. Because of the luster of the Disney name, theme restaurants, a twenty-five-screen movie theater, a Virgin Mega-Store, Starbucks, and a hotel and entertainment complex soon followed. The result is that Times Square has been revived as a means of consumption and a business center and it may well serve to revivify other areas of New York City. For its part, Disney gained more stature and a theater as yet another means to sell itself and its products.

THE NEW MEANS OF CONSUMPTION

Disney World is of interest to us because it represents a model of a new *means of consumption,* or in other words the settings or structures[19] that enable us to consume all sorts of things. As a new means of consumption, Disney World has many continuities with older settings, as do many of the other new means of consumption. The predecessors to today's cruise lines were the great ocean liners of the past. Las Vegas casinos had precursors such as the great casino at Monte Carlo. Shopping malls can be traced back to the markets of ancient Greece and Rome. At the same time, these new means also exhibit a number of important and demonstrable differences.

The means of consumption are part of a broader set of phenomena related to goods and services: production, distribution, advertising,[20] marketing,[21] sales, individual taste,[22] style,[23] fashion.[24] Our concern is with the process leading up to, and perhaps including, an exchange of money (or equivalents such as checks, electronic debits to bank or credit card accounts, and so on) for goods or services between buyers and sellers.[25] This is often dealt with under the rubric of shopping,[26] but our interests are broader than that and include the consumer's relationship with not only shops and malls but also theme parks, casinos, and cruise lines, and other settings including athletic stadiums, universities, hospitals, and museums,[27] which surprisingly are coming to resemble the more obvious new means of consumption. In most cases an exchange occurs;[28] people do purchase and receive goods and services. This process may take place instantaneously or over a long period of time and may involve many steps—perception of a want, arousal of a desire by an advertisement, study of available literature (e.g., *Consumer Reports*), comparison of available options, and ultimately perhaps an actual purchase. Of course, the process need not stop there; it is not unusual for people to take things home, find them wanting, return them, and perhaps begin the process anew.

Many of the new settings have attracted a great deal of attention individually, but little has been said about them collectively. I undertake to analyze them not only because of their growing importance and inherent interest, but also because they have played a central role in greatly increasing, and dramatically altering the nature of, consumption. Americans, especially, consume very differently and we consume on a larger scale, at least in part because of the new means of consumption. Further, these settings are important beyond their role in the consumption process. Many of the settings considered here—for example, McDonald's,® Wal-Mart,® Disney—have become some of America's, and the world's, most powerful popular icons. My net is cast more widely than even Disney's reach to include discount malls, superstores, warehouse stores, Las Vegas casinos (which are increasingly Disneyesque), and so on.

Why should the readers of this book, most of them consumers, be concerned about the new means of consumption? In addition to the inherent interest of a major, often spectacular, social change in the realm of consumption, the new means of consumption are involved in a variety to developments that are designed to get more of us to spend time and money in consumption. Admittedly, most of us are eager to spend money in these settings. Others may feel that they are devoting too much time and money to consuming in these settings.[29] In either case, it makes sense to understand the ways in which those in charge of the new means of consumption are tempting us.

CATHEDRALS OF CONSUMPTION

The new means of consumption can be seen as "cathedrals of consumption"—that is, they have an enchanted, sometimes even sacred, religious character for many people.[30] In order to attract ever-larger numbers of consumers, such cathedrals of consumption need to offer, or at least appear to offer, increasingly magical, fantastic, and enchanted settings in which to consume. Sometimes this magic is produced quite intentionally, whereas in other cases it is a result of a series of largely unforeseen developments. A worker involved in the opening of McDonald's in Moscow spoke of it "as if it were the Cathedral in Chartres . . . a place to experience 'celestial joy.' "[31] A visit to Disney World has been depicted as "the middle-class hajj, the compulsory visit to the sunbaked city,"[32] and analogies have been drawn between a trip to Disney World and pilgrimages to religious sites such as Lourdes.[33] Book superstores such as Barnes and Noble® and Borders® have been called "cathedrals for the printed word."[34]

Shopping malls have been described as places where people go to practice their "consumer religion."[35] It has been contended that shopping malls are more than commercial and financial enterprises; they have much in common with the religious centers of traditional civilizations.[36] Like such religious centers, malls are seen as fulfilling peoples' need to connect with each other and with nature (trees, plants, flowers), as well as their need to participate in festivals. Malls provide the kind of centeredness traditionally provided by religious temples, and they are constructed to have similar balance, symmetry, and order. Their atriums usually offer connection to nature through water and vegetation.[37] People gain a sense of community as well as more specific community services. Play is almost universally part of religious practice, and malls provide a place for people to frolic. Similarly, malls offer a setting in which people can partake in ceremonial meals. Malls clearly qualify for the label of cathedrals of consumption.[38]

As is the case with religious cathedrals, the cathedrals of consumption are not only enchanted, they are also highly rationalized. As they attract more and more consumers, their enchantment must be reproduced over and over on demand. Furthermore, branches of the successful enchanted settings are opened across the nation and even the world with the result that essentially the same magic must be reproduced in a wide range of locations. To accomplish this, the magic has to be systematized so that it can be easily recreated from one time or place to another. However, it is difficult to reduce magic to corporate formulas that can be routinely employed at any time, in any place, and by anybody.[39] Yet, if these corporations are to continue to attract increasing numbers of consumers who will spend more and more money on goods and services, that is just what they must be able to do. Although such rational, machine-like structures can have their enchanting qualities (food appears almost instantaneously, goods exist in unbelievable profusion), they are, in the main, disenchanting; they often end up *not* being very magical. There is a tendency for people to become bored and to be put off by too much machine-like efficiency in the settings in which they consume. The challenge for today's cathedrals of consumption (as for religious cathedrals), is how to maintain enchantment in the face of increasing rationalization.

Although the new means of consumption will be described in terms of rationalization and enchantment (as well as disenchantment), it is important to recognize that they are not all equally rationalized or enchanting. Some are able to operate in a more machine-like manner than others. Similarly, some are able to take on a more enchanted quality than others. Disney World, a Las Vegas casino, or a huge cruise ship seem far more enchanted than the local McDonald's, Wal-Mart, or strip mall. In addition, specific settings may enchant some consumers and not others. For example, fast food restaurants and theme parks may enchant children far more than adults, although adults may be led by their children or grandchildren to participate—and to pay. Furthermore, enchantment tends to be something that declines over time as the novelty for consumers wears off. After nearly a half century of existence in the United States and proliferation into every nook and cranny of the nation, modern fast food restaurants offer very little enchantment to most adult American consumers. However, we should not forget that many adults found such restaurants quite enchanting when they first opened in the United States and they still do in other nations and cultures to which fast food outlets are relatively new arrivals. In sum, although we will describe the new means of consumption in terms of rationalization and enchantment, there is considerable variation among them, and over time, in their degree of rationalization and enchantment.

The terms *new means of consumption* and *cathedrals of consumption* will be used interchangeably in this book, both referring to the new settings in and through which we obtain goods and services. The idea of the new means of consumption emphasizes both that these settings are new and that they allow and encourage us to consume. The idea of cathedrals of consumption emphasizes that these settings are characterized by the enchantment needed to lure consumers, although disenchantment is an ever-present possibility as a result of the process of rationalization.

Two theories (a third will be added later) lie at the base of these conceptualizations of the new means of consumption. The first is the work of Karl Marx and his extension of his ideas on the means of production to the lesser-known, but central to us, conceptualization of the "means of consumption." The second is the theorizing of Max Weber who gave us the ideas—rationalization, enchantment, and disenchantment—that are fundamental to the conceptualization of the "cathedrals of consumption." I will offer a more detailed discussion of these and other theoretical ideas in Chapter 3, but before that I need to delineate more fully the major cathedrals of consumption.

OVERVIEW OF THE CATHEDRALS OF CONSUMPTION

We will review the cathedrals of consumption, beginning with fast food restaurants.

Franchises and Fast Food Restaurants

A large proportion of fast food restaurants are franchises. Franchising is a system in which "one large firm . . . grants or sells the right to distribute its products or use its trade name and processes to a number of smaller firms . . . franchise holders, although legally independent, must conform to detailed standards of operation designed and enforced by the parent company."[40] Franchising began in the mid-1800s,[41] and today, one out of twelve businesses in the United States is a franchise.[42] On business days a new franchise opens once every eight minutes; more than 8 million people work in the franchise industry.[43] A&W® was the first food service franchise, beginning operations in 1924; Dairy Queen® opened in 1944 and by 1948 had a nationwide chain of 2,500 outlets. Bob's Big Boy® started in the late 1930s and Burger King® (then InstaBurger) and Kentucky Fried Chicken® began in 1955. McDonald's was a successful hamburger stand in San Bernardino California owned by Mac and Dick McDonald before it was discovered by Ray Kroc; the first of the McDonald's chain opened in 1955. By the end 1996, McDonald's had 21,022 restaurants, with projections of 30,000 McDonald's outlets by the year 2000 or shortly thereafter. In addition to its expansion within the United States, McDonald's has become much more of an international presence in recent years. The other big player in the fast food business is Tricon Global restaurants. Spun off by PepsiCo in late 1997, Tricon owns three of the largest franchises—Pizza Hut®, Taco Bell®, and Kentucky Fried Chicken. Overall, Tricon has approximately 30,000 restaurant units and operates the largest fast food system in the world.[44] There are, of course, other important players in the industry, including Hardee's®, Wendy's®, and Domino's Pizza®.

Chain Stores

Related to the franchise is the chain store. The main difference is that chain stores have a single owner whereas many individual franchises are owned by independent entrepreneurs. The first true chain store was the supermarket chain A&P® (The Great Atlantic and Pacific Tea Company), which by 1880 encompassed ninety-five stores. Others were J.C. Penney® (begun in 1902) in the dry goods area and among the variety stores the five and dime store opened by Frank Woolworth in 1879 in Lancaster, Pennsylvania. Although many of these early chains have declined or disappeared, the chain store is still an important presence in American retailing. Examples include chains of supermarkets (Giant,® Kroger,® Safeway®), drug stores (Rite Aid®, Walgreens®, and CVS®, for example), department stores (J.C. Penney, Macy's®), as well as elite shops such as Valentino®, Ralph Lauren®, Calvin Klein®, and Dolce and Gabbana®.[45]

Catalogs

The roots of the modern catalog reach back to 1872 and its pioneer, Aaron Montgomery Ward. The catalogs of Ward's®, Sears®, and other mail order firms constituted significant ways of consuming from the late-1800s well into the 1900s. Catalogs have boomed in recent years.[46] Currently almost 14 billion catalogs are distributed annually by about 10,000 companies. The catalog industry now has approximately 377,000 employees. Each week the average U.S. home receives 1.7 catalogs. In 1996, almost 60 percent of the American population, about 113 million people, ordered goods from catalogs. Almost $48 billion was spent on catalog sales in 1990, and that has been growing by almost 7 percent a year since then.[47] Among today's leading catalogs are those from L. L. Bean®, Land's End®, and Victoria's Secret®.

Shopping Malls

The first planned outdoor shopping center in the United States, Market Square, was built in the Chicago suburb of Lake Forest in

1916.[48] It was followed in 1924 by another, Country Club Plaza, on the then-outskirts of Kansas City. The Highland Park Shopping Village in Dallas, built in 1931, represented the first time that storefronts were turned away from the public streets inward to a central area. There was a hiatus in the building of malls until the post-World War II suburban boom gave it new impetus. The first "dumbbell" mall, Northgate in Seattle, was built in 1947. It included "two department stores anchoring the ends of an open-air pedestrian mall, set in the middle of acres of parking."[49] More important, the first modern, fully enclosed shopping mall was Southdale Center in Edina, Minnesota, which opened in 1956. Enclosing the mall gave it a vertical dimension and served to make it more spectacular. Enclosed malls were also cheaper to build and created a synergy that increased business for all occupants. Shopping malls have since been built on the Southdale model, and they are considered one of the new means of consumption.

However, the formulaic pattern of shopping malls and the competition from newer means of consumption have caused the conventional mall considerable difficulty. Shopping time per trip to the mall is down to about 70 minutes compared to more than 90 minutes in the early 1980s. Some are warning that about 30 percent of existing regional malls either will be forced to close or will be converted to other purposes. Said the chair of one of the largest mall developers, Mills Corporation, "There is too much sameness in retailing. If you dropped a person into most malls, they would not know what part of the country they were in."[50] The result is a shift toward entertainment in shopping malls[51] as well as the development of different kinds of malls.

Of tremendous importance itself as a cathedral of consumption, the shopping mall has been of perhaps even greater importance in providing the groundwork for a variety of related developments. There is, for example, the development of increasingly large malls culminating in so-called mega-malls such as the West Edmonton Mall (opened in 1981) in Alberta, Canada, and the Mall of America in Minneapolis, Minnesota (opened in 1992). The largest mall built in the past five years is the 1.7 million-square foot Ontario Mills outside of Los Angeles with 200 stores and a 30-screen movie house.[52]

There is also the profusion of various kinds of specialty malls, especially the discount outlet malls that are so popular in resorts or as tourist destinations. The first outlets appeared in the 1920s attached to the mills of New England fabric companies. Later, the outlets took hold in association with the sewing factories in the Southeast. The first outlet centers are traceable to the opening of the Reading (Pennsylvania) Outlet Center in 1970. Larger outlet malls began to appear in the 1980s. The largest is Sawgrass Mills in Florida, which encompasses 1.9 million square feet, attracted 25 million customers in 1997, and is the state's second most popular tourist attraction (trailing only Disney World).[53] The outlet mall in tiny Manchester, Vermont (population 3,600) is the fifth largest contributor of sales tax revenue to the state: Its contribution grew from $1.1 million in 1993 to $6.5 million in 1996.[54] Today, there at least 350 outlet centers in the United States; it is now a $12 billion a year business.[55] Outlet malls have become a cultural phenomenon, destinations in their own right. People even take vacations or trips in order to go to outlet malls. For example, on a typical fall weekend with the changing foliage at its peak, one is likely to find long lines at Manchester's factory stores, but the nearby Appalachian Trail is apt to be nearly empty.[56]

Also of interest is the recent spread of shopping malls into other settings such as Las Vegas casinos, cruise ships, airports, train stations, and college campuses (especially in student unions). In fact, malls are so ubiquitous (and Americans spend so much time and money shopping) that one scholar describes the United States as "the world's biggest shopping mall."[57]

Electronic Shopping Centers

Worthy of special treatment is the advent of the "dematerialized" new means of consumption, the electronic shopping centers that are likely to undergo enormous expansion in the years to come. One variant is the television home shopping networks such as HSN® (Home Shopping Network) or QVC® (Quality, Value, Convenience).

Round-the-clock television retailing has grown enormously in the years since it was first broadcast on HSN in 1985; QVC followed a year later.[58]

Another variant is the infomercial, which is estimated to have done almost $2 billion in business in 1995.[59] These are ordinarily half-hour "shows" (typically broadcast late at night or on weekends) that are really extended advertisements for a particular product. They are included as a means of consumption because they usually offer telephone numbers that allow viewers to purchase the product by telephone and credit card.[60]

Cybermalls and other forms of on-line shopping are still in their infancy. The Internet was founded in 1988, based on earlier technologies such as Arpanet (founded in 1969 by the Pentagon for messages between defense labs and universities) and NSFNET.[61] Although fewer than 10 million households had on-line computer access in 1995, by 2000 that number is expected to grow to more than 43 million.[62] In 1996 alone, the proportion of Internet users who shopped on-line doubled from 12.5 percent to 25 percent.[63] Wal-Mart opened its on-line Internet center in 1996 with 2,500 items; in 1997 it announced an expansion to 80,000 items, or about the same number as in its regular stores.[64] At the moment, the big attractions are sites that offer stocks, computer equipment, "boy toys" (e.g., Sharper Image®), CDs, cassettes and videos, books, and other products such as flowers.[65] However, big growth may still be some years away. One estimate is that although retail business on the Internet (only a small part of which is through the cybermalls) will grow from $530 million in 1996 to $7.2 billion in 2000, it will continue to represent a steady 4 percent share of Internet business—the big growth areas will be business-to-business commerce and finance.[66] So far, cyber sales have been hampered by slow technologies and problems with ensuring the security of credit card numbers. However, in the longer term, it is likely that cybermalls and related forms of cyber-commerce will outstrip the shopping mall.

The case of Amazon.com® is an interesting one. In 1994, the company's founder, Jeff Bezos, then on Wall Street, noticed that the new World Wide Web was growing at 2,300 percent a year. He decided he wanted to do business on the Web and thought through a list of products that could be sold. He decided on books because of the large variety, the fact that no single merchandiser controlled the market, and because computers could help customers find what they wanted. He quit his job and headed for Seattle because it was a high-tech town and it provided him access to an important book distribution center. Thus a new means for consuming books was founded. By the middle of 1998, Jeff Bezos's shares in that company were worth approximately $2 billion.[67]

Also worth noting is the dramatic and controversial growth of gambling through on-line casinos such as World Sports Exchange and Casino Royale.[68] Already estimated to be a $200 million a year business, it is expected to grow to $1 billion annually by the year 2000. Like all of the cyber sites discussed, it is a threat to the more conventional means of consumption, in this case the casino (to be discussed shortly). The reason is clear from the following statement by a person who plays almost every day for two or three hours: "It's great. I don't have to leave the house . . . It's very private. There are no distractions, no dirty looks from the casino people if you win."[69] Much the same thing could be said by consumers of another important on-line business: pornography.

Discounters

Discount merchandising began to boom in the 1950s. Although such stores had predecessors (e.g., Korvette's®, K-Mart®), discount department stores have recently undergone enormous expansion.[70] Of great note is the Wal-Mart chain. For the fiscal year ending January 1, 1997, Wal-Mart's total sales were almost $105 billion; a 12 percent increase over the previous year. It and its major competitor, Target®, were both founded in 1962. As of May 1997 there were 2,302 Wal-Mart stores. In addition, Wal-Mart spawned Sam's Club—a chain of warehouse stores—that began operations in 1983 and now has 438 outlets. (Warehouse clubs are very basic retail operations with merchandise displayed in huge, bare settings, and they offer opportunities to buy in bulk. They advertise little and offer few services. Although the membership requirements are very loose, a membership charge of $25 to $35 is usually required.[71])

Another warehouse club, Costco Wholesale® was created out of a merger of Price Club (founded in 1976 by Sol Price) and Costco (created in 1983). As of March 1997, the company operated 272 warehouse stores (each between 70,000- and 160,000-square feet) in twenty-three states and five other nations. It had 25 million cardholders and employed almost 53,000 people (more than 40,000 in the United States). In fiscal year 1996, its revenues exceeded $19 billion. Like Sam's Club, Price Club/Costco is characterized by simple, warehouse-like settings. A limited range of low-priced and discount goods, including food, are sold. Price Club/Costco offers discounted goods, especially in large sizes and in packages of multiple items, so that consumers often end up purchasing more of a given commodity than they intended to purchase. Demonstrations and samples are abundant. Goods are laid out in such a way that customers often end up buying many things on a whim that they may not need or ever finish.

Also worth mentioning are supercenters that combine a grocery store, a drug store, and a mass merchandiser in one enormous setting. For example, a 200,000-square foot Wal-Mart supercenter is twice as large as a normal Wal-Mart and six or seven times the size of a typical supermarket.[72] Wal-Mart operates 354 supercenters; its first supercenter opened in 1988. Other important operators of supercenters are Fred Meyer in the West, Meijer in the Midwest, Target, and Kmart.

Superstores

Not to be confused with the supercenter is the superstore, which is arguably traceable to a 1957 ancestor of the current Toys 'R Us®.[73] The distinguishing characteristic of a superstore is that it carries an extraordinary number and range of goods within a specific retail category.[74] Toys 'R Us has all the toys one can imagine (and it controls

20 percent of the U.S. toy market); Circuit City® and Best Buy® offer a wide range of electronic gear; books are the specialty at Barnes & Noble and Borders; office supplies are abundant at Staples®, Office Depot®, and Office Max®, and the specialties of many of the rest— Sports Authority®, Baby Superstore®, Petsmart®, and so on—are obvious from the names. Superstores have evolved in a number of incredible directions: Garden Ridge® with its 4,000 varieties of candles; American Health Superstore® with 8,000 products including, among other things, twenty types of canes[75]; and Just for Feet and Sneaker Stadium® with their 4,000 varieties of recreational shoes, "In short, every kind of gear a foot sweats in."[76]

Superstores are sometimes called "category killers" because their enormous variety and low price tends to drive an earlier means of consumption, the small specialty shop, out of business.[77] And these superstores are growing rapidly. An incredible 80 percent of all new retail space in 1994 was occupied by superstores. They now account for one-third of retail revenue in the United States, up from virtually nothing little more than a decade ago. Although this enormous growth is likely to be punctuated by a number of notable failures, we can safely anticipate the continued expansion of superstores.

The new means of consumption discussed to this point are the kinds of settings that most of us frequent on a regular basis. There is a whole other set of new means of consumption that are more unusual. They relate more to tourism, or extraordinary vacations, than to day-to-day activities; they involve attempts to escape the mundane.[78] In fact, they are part of a general trend toward viewing tourism as a type of consumption.[79]

Cruise Ships

Cruise ships have a long history. The great ocean liners of the late 1800s and early 1900s are certainly important predecessors. However, the modern cruise ship can be traced to the maiden voyage of the cruise ship *Sunward* in Florida on December 19, 1966.[80] A major boon to the cruise business occurred in 1977, when the television series "Love Boat" made its debut. The show took place on ships of the Princess Line® and made that line famous. It also served to popularize the cruise. The Carnival® line began operations in 1972 and soon thereafter came to emphasize the "Fun Ship."

In recent years, both cruise ships and the idea of a cruise have been revolutionized. In the early years of the industry, people took cruises in order to get from one location to another; the cruise was seen as a novel way of getting to interesting locales. Now the ships themselves, as well as the entertaining experience of the cruise, are the main reasons for taking a cruise. There are significantly more cruise ships, and cruises are far more frequent. Although the cruise lines carried only about one-half million passengers in 1970, by 1995 that number had increased ten-fold to 5 million passengers.[81] Through most of the 1980s and 1990s, the number of cruise passengers grew at a rate of 7.6 percent per year.[82] There are many more cruise destinations now and a much wider variety of types of cruises (gay, family, nature, and so on). Cruises have become far more affordable (cruise lines are now even offering financing).

The cruise ship itself has been transformed. Ships of the 1970s tended to be small, uncomfortable in inclement weather, with tiny cabins, no television, and limited menus. Although there is a wide variety of cruise ships, the most popular have become much larger and more spectacular. They also have come to encompass a number of other means of consumption such as casinos, night clubs, health spas, shopping malls, bars, and so on. Each of these plays a role in making the modern cruise ship a highly effective means for getting people to spend large sums of money and consume an array of services and goods.

Casinos

Like amusement parks and cruise ships, casinos (often coupled with hotels) have a lengthy history. The modern casino can be traced to the founding of the Flamingo Hotel® by gangster Bugsy Siegel in Las Vegas in 1946.[83] There had been casinos in Las Vegas prior to this time, but the Flamingo was the first of what was to be the ever-accelerating development of spectacular casino–hotels. In its early years, Las Vegas relied on income from gambling, and other potential money makers (hotel rooms, food, shows, and so on) either were loss leaders or marginal producers of income. In more recent years, Las Vegas has reinvented itself and become more oriented to family entertainment. Although gambling is still an important source of revenue, the other facets of the business of casino–hotels are also designed to make lots of money. The modern casino–hotel is a highly effective means of promoting gambling, the Las Vegas experience, and the activities and paraphernalia that go with them.

Modern Las Vegas hotels make money by offering as many as 5,000 or 6,000 rooms at operating margins around 25 percent. The city as a whole has more than 100,000 hotel rooms. The casinos are enormous and spectacular, offering an increasingly large number of ways to gamble. And these casinos are huge money makers for the house with operating margins on table games (blackjack, for example) of roughly 25 percent and of more than 50 percent on slot machines, the true cornerstones of the modern casino.[84] The Mirage Hotel–Casino® alone has operating profits of $200 million per year. Whatever last small bills and coins a departing visitor might not yet have spent are apt to be taken by the slot machines at Las Vegas's McCarran Airport or in state line casinos for those who are leaving by automobile.

Las Vegas casinos have also, in one way or another, been transported to much of the rest of the United States. The most notable examples are the casinos in Atlantic City, on Native American reservations, and in many other settings (including, in Canada, the West Edmonton mega-mall). Tunica County, Mississippi, "long known as one of America's most wretched backwaters," has almost overnight become a gambling mecca with nine casinos and 50,000 visitors a day as of this writing.[85] In just five years, it went from the poorest to the richest county in Mississippi. Other examples of the spread of the casino influence include the previously discussed on-line casinos as well as race tracks that have poker rooms or slot machines.

Entertainment Aimed at Adults

The Las Vegas casino model has had other kinds of influences. For example, there is a chain of adult-oriented entertainment centers known as Dave and Buster's® (the first one opened in 1982; there were nine at the end of 1996), which look like miniature casinos; the chain is seen as a possible harbinger of "the Las Vegasification of America."[86] In fact, one of the co-owners said, "By virtue of its scale and the adult concept . . . yes, we're like Las Vegas."[87] They are large (in one case, 50,000 square feet), have bars, restaurants, pool tables, and a large number of modern games (video games and virtual reality games such as virtual skiing and car racing) and traditional arcade games (skee ball, for example). One can win tickets redeemable for prizes. There is even a small casino, although gambling for money is not permitted. Servers deliver food and drink to the play areas from the restaurant and two bars.

Reflective of the Vegas influence, Dave and Buster's is itself also representative of the growing number of new means of consuming adult-oriented entertainment. Another is Q-Zar,® which involves a fifteen-minute game of laser tag played by two teams with up to twenty players on each team.[88] Many shopping malls are moving toward offering more entertainment like that found at Dave and Buster's. Other new entertainment-oriented chains include Gameworks® (the first opened in Seattle in 1997) and Viacom Entertainment Stores®.

Eatertainment

Another contemporaneous example of the trend toward emphasizing entertainment are chains of themed restaurants (often called "eatertainment"), which have grown dramatically in recent years (although some have run into trouble lately). Theme restaurants "typically combine lackluster food, designs that resemble theater sets and entertainment ranging from costumed waiters to museums of memorabilia."[89] The pioneer in this realm, Hard Rock Cafe®, was founded in London in 1971. Although a British creation, it took as its mission the introduction of "good, wholesome American food" to the English. By 1995 there were more than forty Hard Rock Cafes in many of the world's major cities. It is interesting to note that it is not the food but products with the Hard Rock Cafe logo that are generally coveted by visitors and tourists. According to one observer, "Most people who wear the t-shirts never even sit down to have a meal there; they simply walk into the apparel stores to look at and purchase Hard Rock buttons, caps and sweatshirts. What in the world compels these people to buy memorabilia from a restaurant in which they have never eaten?"[90] In fact, with the wide array of merchandise (including $300 leather jackets) now available sporting the Hard Rock Cafe logo,[91] the wearing of anything with that logo gives the wearer almost instant international recognition. As Thorstein Veblen argued long ago, "Esteem is awarded only on evidence," and for many today esteem is derived from the Hard Rock logo on a t-shirt.[92]

A similar chain is Planet Hollywood®, which openly admits that it "operates movie-themed restaurants in the Hard Rock Cafe 'eatertainment' vein."[93] Instead of rock memorabilia, Planet Hollywood offers movie memorabilia. It does not try to conceal the fact that its hamburgers are "high-priced." And it proudly states that the sale of t-shirts and other souvenirs accounts for 40 percent of all of its sales.

Among other such chains that have recently opened, or will soon open, are The Apple Cafe® (a cyber cafe from Apple Computer), Bubba Gump Shrimp Co.® (based on the movie *Forrest Gump*), Club Kokomo® (inspired by the Beach Boys's song), Marvel Mania® (comic-book theme), Motown Cafe® (inspired by the music and stars of Motown records), and so on.[94]

OTHER MEANS OF CONSUMPTION

The cathedrals of consumption are important not only in themselves but also for their influence on other parts of society. A surprising number of settings are emulating the new means of consumption in one way or another.

Athletic Facilities

A variety of modern athletic facilities such as golf clubs, tennis clubs, ski resorts, and fitness centers can all be seen as new means for consuming athletic activities. The new professional athletic stadiums can be described in a similar fashion, witness in baseball the Baltimore Orioles's Oriole Park at Camden Yards, the Cleveland Indians's Jacobs Field, and the Atlanta Braves's Turner Field. Although these new stadiums often resemble earlier versions, and even seek to copy them in many ways, they also have a number of innovations. For example, they all feature spectacular computerized scoreboards; they have all become more adept at extracting money from those who use their services (e.g., high-priced suites of box seats at baseball and football games; food courts that resemble those found in shopping malls; elaborate souvenir shops). As a stock prospectus for the Cleveland Indians Baseball Company put it: "Fans at Jacobs Field are offered a customer-focused experience in an attractive, comfortable environment featuring a variety of amenities, concessions and merchandise options."[95] Although these athletic facilities have a long history, the more modern forms are far more oriented to, and effective at, serving as means for the consumption of athletic services (and goods).

Luxury Gated Communities

Like the new athletic stadiums, luxury gated communities often seek to resemble, and even copy, traditional communities. Unlike the majority of these early communities, these new communities have opted to wall themselves off from the outside and to privatize their streets.[96] Consumed in these spectacular settings are expensive homes and a rich and luxurious lifestyle including golf courses, tennis clubs, fitness facilities, and so on. Almost *de rigueur* in these communities are expensive home furnishings, landscaping, and automobiles. (In the exclusive and expensive gated communities of Boca Raton, Florida, the high-priced Lexus® is known as the "Boca Chevy.")

Educational Settings

Administrators are coming to recognize that their educational campuses need to grow more like the other new means of consumption to thrive. The high school has been described as resembling a shopping mall.[97] The university, too, can be seen as a means of educational consumption. These days most campuses are dated, stodgy, and ineffective compared to shopping malls, cruise ships, casinos, and fast food restaurants. To compete, universities are trying to satisfy their students by offering, for example, "theme housing"—dorms devoted to students with shared special interests.[98] As universities learn more and more from the new means of consumption, it will be increasingly possible and accurate to refer to them as "McUniversities."[99] A related and important trend, still in its infancy, is the growth of the virtual university, especially the Western Governors University being put together at the initiative of the governors of thirteen states in the western United States.[100] It will be increasingly difficult to dis- tinguish such dematerialized universities from cybermalls.

Medicine and Hospitals

A similar point can be made about medicine and hospitals.[101] We already have "McDoctors" (drive-in, quick service medical facilities) and there are many indications that we are moving in the direction of "McHospitals." Examples of the latter trend include expensive suites that look more like hotel than hospital accommodations, more and more "in-and-out" procedures, and so on. HealthSouth®, a chain of mainly outpatient rehabilitation and surgery centers, is seeking to copy McDonald's and offer low-cost, efficient and accessible health care throughout the United States. Its chair says, "I felt we could brand health care in 50 states, and no matter what city you were in, you could have consistent treatment."[102] HealthSouth uses sports stars to increase its visibility, puts its logo on jogging suits and gym bags, and is in the process of creating a catalog of HealthSouth products. It also is having discussions about co-branding athletic shoes and nutritional drinks. Another company official says, "We hope to be right up there with the Cokes and Nikes."[103]

Museums and Charities

Even museums are coming to look more like shopping malls.[104] (Blurring the distinction are largely mall-based commercial chains such as the Museum Shop® and the Nature Company®.) The Metropolitan Museum of Art houses what amounts to a small department store and has more than a dozen satellite stores in malls selling books and museum-made products. The Louvre not only has its shops but also an underground shopping mall with high-end boutiques such as Chanel and Yves Saint-Laurent.[105] The National Gallery of Art in Washington, D.C., has been described in the following terms:

> The huge skylighted atrium is surrounded by promenades connected by bridges and escalators; individual galleries open off this space, placed exactly where shops would be in the mall. Potted plants, lavish use of marble and brass, and, in the neon-lit basement concourse, fountains, shops, and fast-food counters make the resemblance even more striking.[106]

The former chair of Neiman Marcus® said, "I was in the Metropolitan [Museum of Art] recently, and I was flabbergasted when I saw the size of their store. They are selling everything from rugs to jewelry."[107] He might have been less flabbergasted had he known that the roots of the modern museum are, in part, in the World's Fairs and Expositions.

In addition, to raise money, charities are now using catalogs and 800-numbers to allow recipients to order, among other things, a rabbit and two chicks for a Rwandan family, prenatal care for women in Bangladesh, and a small business loan for a Haitian woman.[108]

Mega-Churches

We can bring this discussion full-circle by pointing out that although the cathedrals of consumption have a quasi-religious character, religion has begun to emulate those cathedrals. Here is one description of the result:

> Megachurches are huge steel and glass structures with acres of parking . . . at their fanciest [they] feature aerobics classes, bowling alleys, counseling centers, and multimedia bible classes where the presentation rivals that of MTV. On Sunday morning, big screens project Scripture verses and the lyrics to pop-style religious songs so that everyone in the congregation can see and follow along.[109]

Said one expert, "They're the biggest movement going in the Protestant Church."[110] Another commented, "They are what I call the Wal-Mart-ization of American Religion."[111] Similarly, the pastor of a large Baptist church has sought to make his services "fun" and to that end urged his staff to study Disney World.[112]

CONCLUSION

This chapter has been devoted to introducing the twin concepts of new means of consumption and cathedrals of consumption. I have also introduced the reader to the major types and examples of such means. Chapter 2 offers insight into the wider context and implications of the cathedrals of consumption, as well as their impact on the way Americans and, increasingly, much of the world consumes.

2

THE REVOLUTION IN CONSUMPTION AND THE LARGER SOCIETY

This chapter is devoted to several interrelated issues. First, we will examine the issue of why there is a rise in the new means of consumption. Second, we will analyze the role that the cathedrals of consumption play in generating hyperconsumption. Third, we will discuss the fact that the new means are not only affecting how much we consume but the way in which we consume. Fourth, we will see that the means of consumption are having a similar effect in many other areas of the world.

WHY NOW?

The creation of means of consumption is nothing new. However, the pace seems to have accelerated dramatically since the end of World War II. People want and can afford more goods and services. The means of consumption have proliferated to give people what they want, to create new wants, and, in the process, to allow those who satisfy those desires to profit. But why have so many people come to want so much more? One reason is that many people have more resources, and they are eager to spend much of it on personal consumption. There is also an enormous amount of money invested in advertising designed to create those wants and to induce people to consume. Ewen traces the development of modern advertising to the 1920s and to the realization on the part of owners and managers that it was no longer enough to control only workers.[1] Consumers had come to play too important a role in capitalism to allow them to make decisions on their own. The result was the growth of modern advertising designed to "help" people make those decisions. This represented an early step in the movement from a production to a consumption society.

Today, it is clear that we have moved much further in that direction; in fact, American society is now better characterized by consumption than production. That is, as more and more basic production is taking place in other nations, especially in developing nations, consumption has assumed center stage in American society. Although advertising has certainly proliferated enormously, other mechanisms for controlling consumers can be identified. The new means of consumption are the most important of these controls. Their development after World War II supplemented the efforts, begun in the 1920s in advertising, to control consumers. People are lured to the cathedrals of consumption by the fantasies they promise to fulfill and then kept there by a variety of rewards and constraints. The idea is to keep people at the business of consumption. This is nowhere clearer than in the case of credit cards,[2] which lure people into consumption by easy credit and then entice them into still further consumption by offers of "payment holidays," new cards, and increased credit limits. The beauty of all of this, at least from the point of view of those who profit from the existing system, is that people are kept in the workplace and on the job by the need to pay the monthly minimums on their credit card accounts and, more generally, to support their consumption habits.

The Economy

There are, of course, many other factors involved in the growth of the new means of consumption. The booming economy—especially the dramatic expansion in the 1990s, as reflected in the startling upturn in the stock market and a minuscule unemployment rate—has left large numbers of people with unprecedented amounts of disposable income. For such people, consumption, especially shopping,[3] has become a major form of recreation. Increasingly, many people have the time to spend their large incomes. For example, many are retiring earlier even as their life expectancy is increasing. The result is many years of the life cycle in which the focus, to a large extent, is on consumption. And because of the booming economy, an increasing number of retirees have the wherewithal to be active consumers.

The growth of the new means of consumption also has been fueled by the increasing reality that corporations, including those that own the new means of consumption, are driven by the stock market in which it is not good enough to maintain a high level of profitability; profits must show a substantial increase from one year (or even quarter) to the next. This creates a continually expanding need to lure people into the marketplace more frequently and more actively and to keep them there longer. Old customers need to be retained and new customers recruited. The new means of consumption offer more new goods and services in increasingly fantastic settings, an irresistible combination to many people. The new means of consumption both lure more people out of their homes to consume *and* allow them to consume more even while they are at home. The fantastic settings represent key sites where more of people's resources are extracted *and* more of their future income is captured as credit card or other consumer debt.

There is a confluence of interests: People want, or at least are led to think that they want, all of those goods and services. The new means of consumption require consumers to want those things and in increasing quantities. The same is true of manufacturers. Bankers and the executives of credit card companies also have vested interests in increased consumption because that means rising debt and growing income from servicing that debt.

The Growth of the Youth Market

More teenagers and young children than ever before are involved in the economy as consumers. As Ellen Goodman put it, "The marketplace has turned kids into short consumers."[4] Young people now have much more money and play a larger role in family decisions about consumption, with the result that many of the new means of consumption cater to them directly (fast food restaurants and theme parks) or indirectly (amusement parks in mega-malls, superstores such as Toys 'R Us, Blockbuster Video®).

Take the role that McDonald's and Disney, alone and in concert, play in hooking children on consumption.[5] Both clearly recognize that their present and future depend on attracting young children.[6] Of course, children grow up to be adult consumers, many of whom eventually will have children of their own and begin the cycle anew.

In recent years children and adolescents have become increasingly important consumers in their own right (e.g., a line of cosmetics aimed at children, CDs targeted at adolescents), and they play a central role in bringing adults into a number of the new means of consumption. Take toys. In the past, toys were play versions of adult tools (the toy hammer), taught adult skills (erector sets, doll houses), or involved shared interests in gadgets (electric trains).[7] The 1930s witnessed the first toys that were not play versions of adult objects and that appealed directly to children, among them toys derived from the early Disney characters. By the 1950s, toys such as Barbie® and G.I. Joe® were being marketed directly to children through television advertisements. Today, adults know little or nothing of many toys—X-Men, Sing and Snore Ernies, for example—"because they are part of a distinct children's culture that is marketed directly to children on television and at the movies."[8] Children must make their toy interests known to adults so that adults can make the purchase. Or adults can surrender completely, give the children money, and allow the children to make purchases on their own.

Technological Change

The chasm between children's toys and adults has led to a new technology: a computerized, nationwide toy registry at Toy 'R Us. Children are given hand-held scanners, a recent technology, and wander down the aisles zapping the bar codes on toys that catch their fancy. A computerized wish list is produced for the child that can be accessed at any Toys 'R Us store in the United States. (Toys 'R Us is not the only chain using gift registries. So do Home Depot, Crate and Barrel, Pottery Barn, and Sears.) Toy registries are great aids to adults ignorant of the world of children's toys, but they put even more power in the hands of children in determining consumption, and they bolster the increasingly powerful position of Toys 'R Us.

It is probable that technological change is the most important factor in why it is that we are now witnessing the ascendancy of the new means of consumption. Automobiles and superhighways enable us to use shopping malls, superstores, fast food restaurants, and so on. The national highway system was developed in the 1950s, expediting the development of Disneyland and Disney World, Las Vegas, Atlantic City, and, more recently, Tunica County, Mississippi. The commercial jet airplane arrived in 1952; its development through the

1950s and beyond allowed resorts and cruise lines, to say nothing of airports and their attendant malls, to prosper. Television, first nationally broadcast in 1946, was necessary for the emergence of television home shopping and infomercials. The advent of express package deliverers such as UPS®, Federal Express®, DHL®, and the like has revolutionized the ability of consumers to obtain commodities. By increasing the speed and efficiency of package delivery, these carriers played a major role in making possible a number of the new means of consumption. Cybermalls, home television shopping, as well as catalog shopping all depend on such delivery services for quick, low-cost delivery.

No technological change is more important in this context than the building of the first high-speed computer in 1946. Virtually all of the new means of consumption would be impossible, at least in their present forms, without the computer. Far-flung chains and franchises could not operate without computers to keep track of sales, inventories, shipments of goods, and so on. The national toy registries described previously depend on the computer and related new technologies such as the hand-held scanner. Modern amusement parks, cruise ships, and gambling casinos depend on computers for a variety of tasks.

New Facilitating Means

Many of the technological changes discussed in the preceding section (the computer, highways, and so on) facilitate the operation of the new means of consumption, but are not themselves such means. The recent development of new facilitating means has contributed greatly to the rise of the new means of consumption.

A major example is the credit card.[9] The credit card is *not* itself a means of consumption. It is not a setting or a place of consumption, of course. The goods or services that we desire are not to be found in the credit card. But the credit card is a mechanism that facilitates our ability to use various means of consumption. It is possible to bring large sums of cash, or for that matter even gold ingots, to the shopping mall, but consuming at a mall today is expedited if we use a credit (or debit) card. In the case of more recent means of consumption such as home shopping television and the cybermall, we are even less likely to use other facilitating means such as cash; the use of the credit card is virtually mandatory. Indeed, much of the future of on-line shopping depends on the ability of vendors and credit card companies to guarantee the safety of disseminating credit card numbers through the Internet. The key point is that the credit card is a *facilitating means* that makes it possible for people to obtain what they want and need from the cathedrals of consumption.

Although most of the new means of consumption could exist without credit cards, it could be argued that their explosive growth has depended on the credit card. The arrival of the modern credit card beginning in the 1950s is more or less simultaneous with the appearance of many of the new means of consumption.

There are other different types of facilitating means. Within the financial realm, cash, installment loans, personal checks, and travelers checks preceded credit cards as important facilitators and continue to be important today because we are still a long way from a cashless and checkless society. Of the newer facilitating means of this type, in addition to credit cards there are debit cards, smart cards, ATM (automatic teller machine) cards, as well as ATMs themselves.

The Internet, itself a facilitator, is giving rise to other new financial facilitating means.[10] For example, there is need for a technology that will allow people to spend small sums of money, say 25 to 50 cents, on the Internet for things such as "individual news articles, pictures, video-game plays, computer software, recipes, jukebox selections—or odds on the third race at Belmont."[11] The credit card industry is not set up to handle such small transactions, so several companies, including CyberCash Inc., are in the process of creating such a system. CyberCash's system is called Cybercoin, and it will allow Internet sites to charge for things they heretofore have been giving away free or permit them to charge small fees for visiting Web sites. The system works by giving the user an electronic "wallet," which is filled periodically by transferring funds from a bank or credit card account to

CyberCash's bank account. CyberCash collects a small fee on each transaction (as do the merchant's and the consumer's banks). Cumulatively, these small purchases will amount to big business on the Internet, but they are individually too small to process through the credit card system.

Even more important facilitators of consumption are the media and their ever-present advertisements. The new means of consumption, indeed almost all aspects of consumption, could not function were it not for the advertisements that are the lifeblood of the traditional media and are fast becoming central to the Internet as well. Although the facilitators of consumption are clearly of great and increasing importance, I will have little more to say about them in this book, the focus being mainly on the new means of consumption themselves.

In any case, we should acknowledge that the distinction between means of consumption and facilitating means is not as clear-cut as it first appears. Although there are some pure facilitating means (e.g., money and credit cards), some phenomena can be simultaneously facilitators and means of consumption. For example, the contemporary airport facilitates the consumer's ability to fly to such places as Disney World and Las Vegas, but it is simultaneously a means for consuming airline tickets and, as it grows more and more like a shopping mall, many other goods and services as well. Rather than get into these complexities, I will largely ignore pure facilitating means and in those cases where a setting performs a dual function, focus on it as a means of consumption.

CHANGES IN HOW MUCH WE CONSUME

American consumerism is not a new phenomenon. Concern about it dates back nearly 200 years.[12] By the end of the nineteenth century,[13] according to Leach, the "cardinal features of this culture were acquisition and consumption as the means of achieving happiness; the cult of the new; the democratization of desire; and money value as the predominant measure of all value in society."[14] The means of consumption of the day—large department stores, mail-order houses, dry goods shops, chain stores, banks, hotels and restaurants, dance halls, theaters, and amusement parks—played a key role in generating and supporting mass consumption.[15] Some of these have since declined in importance. Others are still important, and are joined by the new cast of characters that are the subject of this book.

Leach discusses the concept of *consumptionism,* coined by the journalist and political philosopher Samuel Strauss in 1925. According to Strauss, consumptionism involved a commitment to produce (and consume) more things from one year to the next. All other values were subordinated to emphasize one's standard of living. The concept of consumptionism involved an emphasis on the pressure that business interests placed on people to consume. Previously, business had sought to give consumers what they wanted. Now business shifted to an emphasis on compelling consumers to want and "need" the things that business was producing and selling. Traditions were being abandoned in the search for the new in goods and services. Business was interested only in "standardization, mass production, and mass distribution" and consumers were seen as little more than "'units in mass' or as 'mass consumers.'"[16]

There is little question that the United States is increasingly characterized by what now could be termed *hyperconsumption,*[17] and that most Americans are increasingly obsessed by consumption.[18] According to Juliet B. Schor, Americans spend three or four times as much time shopping as Western Europeans. Of the total land area of the United States, about 4 billion square feet is devoted to shopping centers, which works out to sixteen square feet of shopping area per capita. And most important, "The average American is consuming, in toto, more than twice as much as he or she did forty years ago."[19] On a per capita basis, Americans are apt to consume more of virtually everything than people in most, if not all, other nations of the world. Examples include television sets, VCRs, computers, microwave ovens, automobiles and the energy needed to keep them running. In the realm of services, Americans are the world leaders in the consumption of medical, psychiatric, legal, and accounting services. It is not just that they consume more of everything, but more varieties of most things are available to, and used by, American consumers than those of most other nations. To take just one example, the number of toys on the shelves of Toys 'R Us often stuns visitors to the United States. (As we will see, Americans are eager to see the rest of the world join them in hyperconsumption.)

At its broadest level, hyperconsumption[20] is a highly democratic form of consumption involving the vast majority of the population. The amount of money available to individuals for consumption varies enormously, but virtually everyone today is a consumer to some degree. The poor have fewer resources than the rich, most ethnic and racial minority groups have much less to spend than members of the majority, children fewer means than adults, and so on, but all are enmeshed in the consumer culture. Even those who live on the streets survive off the discards and charity of that wildly affluent culture.[21] This is not to deny the immense impact of factors such as race, class, gender, and so forth on consumption (see Chapter 7), but it is virtually impossible for anyone in the United States today to avoid being deeply involved in, or at least touched by, the culture of consumption.

Those with lots of resources may buy high-priced originals, and those with modest means may buy inexpensive imitations, but all are buying. Beyond the purchase of luxury goods (or cheap simulations of them), everyone must consume the basics (food, for example) needed to survive, although here, too, there is likely to be great variation in the prices paid for, and the quality of, the goods obtained. America is characterized by mass consumption because all but a handful of the population is actively involved in one way or another as consumers. The mass character of consumption also means that the occupations of large numbers of people are implicated in the culture of consumption. Many millions of people work in fast food restaurants, shopping malls, superstores, gambling casinos, cruise ships, and the like.[22]

There is yet another sense that mass consumption is characteristic of American society: People are apt to spend most, if not all, of their available resources on consumer goods and services. In fact, in many cases it is no longer enough to spend all available resources, one is enticed to go deeply and increasingly into debt.[23] Various data support this contention. For example, the rate of personal savings as a percentage of disposable income dropped from 6.2 percent in 1992 to 3.8 percent in 1997.[24] Only slightly more than half of all American households indicated in 1995 that they had any savings at all. Those in the world's other advanced economies manage to save two to three times what Americans save.[25] Conversely, Americans are far more likely to be in debt, and the average level of indebtedness is much greater. Huge and ever-increasing sums of money are owed on home mortgages, car loans, and credit card balances.[26] Many find themselves unable to repay their debts as reflected, for example, in the increases in credit card delinquencies and bankruptcies.[27]

Within a few decades, the United States has gone from a society that emphasized personal savings to one that focuses on debt. Banks have, to a large degree, shifted from the business of inducing people to save to luring them into debt. In 1997 Americans received 3.1 *billion* pieces of mail imploring them to sign up for a credit card.[28] The profits from servicing debt, especially credit card debt, are much higher than those derived from savings. Easy and extensive credit has played a key role in making America's modern mass consumer society possible and that, especially in the form of credit cards, is being exported to many parts of the world.

Schor adds to the idea that there are problems associated with hyperconsumption by contending that

> the new consumerism has led to a kind of mass "overspending" within the middle class . . . large numbers of Americans spend more than they say they would like to, and more than they have. That they spend more than they realize they are spending, and more than is fiscally prudent. And that they spend in ways that are collectively, if not individually,

self-defeating. Overspending is how ordinary Americans cope with the everyday pressures of the new consumerism.[29]

However, Schor argues that public opinion polls demonstrate that in spite of the increase in consumption and in material possessions, Americans seem no happier than previous generations. According to one who has given up the rat race, "The more you have, the more you spend, and the more you go into debt."[30] The increased demand for consumer goods forces people to devote long hours to work in order to pay for those goods, what Schor calls the work-and-spend syndrome. This focus on consumption means that many people forgo the option of exchanging less work and more leisure time for fewer goods and services.[31]

The Role of the Cathedrals of Consumption

Advertising, credit card companies, and the consumers themselves play important roles in hyperconsumption, but our focus is on the part played by the new means of consumption in this phenomenon. In addition to contributing to the general atmosphere of consumptionism, the cathedrals of consumption lead in various ways to higher levels of consumption.[32] Most important, they are designed artistically and scientifically to lure people into consumption.[33] For example:

♦ In Las Vegas casinos, the few remaining nickel slot machines are usually placed in hard-to-get-to corners where gamblers will be forced to pass by the lure of greater payoffs from higher cost one-armed bandits in order to get to them.

♦ In airports, wherever possible, gift shops are located on departing passengers' right as they head to the gate with fast food restaurants on the left. The reasoning is that passengers are more likely to cross the aisle in order to get food; they might pass up the gift shop if it is not conveniently placed on the right.

♦ At the Gap®, the much sought after denims are positioned at the back of the store, forcing customers to pass by all of the other goods in order to get to them.

♦ In Disneyland and Disney World, the visitor enters and exits through a minimall, Main Street, so that purchases can be made both on entering and leaving.

♦ In shopping malls, the number of exits are often deliberately limited to keep people in the mall; escalators tend to be placed at the end of corridors to force people to walk their length; "fountains and benches are carefully positioned to entice shoppers into stores."[34]

♦ At warehouse stores such as Sam's Club® and Price Club, goods are sold in large quantities or multipacks so that people often end up buying more than they intended. Said one Price Club customer, "Look, you just see it and then you use it. I don't need 24 batteries, but, oh well, it's here and it's cheap and I'll use it—eventually."[35] In addition, consumers are channeled past long rows of seemingly bargain-priced nonfood items before even getting to the food area. Many of these items find their way into customers' carts.

♦ Direct-mail marketers seek to prevent us from throwing their "junk mail" directly into the trash by, for example, making it look like government mail, like it was delivered by a courier service, or by personalizing it by making it look as if it was handwritten.[36]

Although an older means of consumption, supermarkets continue to be important and are especially revealing in terms of the techniques used to lead customers to do what is desired of them:[37]

♦ The flower (or bakery) section is often the first one encountered in a supermarket. It is designed to tickle consumers' sensations, produce a positive image for the market, and weaken consumers' resolve.

♦ The best place to display food is at the head and foot of each aisle. Food displayed in those places ("end caps") can easily double or triple in sales. More generally, sales increase for items displayed at eye level or at the beginning of an aisle.

♦ Foods oriented to children are usually placed lower on shelves. This allows children not only to see the products, but also to pick them up and plead with a parent to purchase them.

♦ Dairy is generally on one side, produce on the other, with meat in the back. In order to get all the basics, customers must work their way through much of the store and its array of merchandise.

♦ Stacking cartons of merchandise in the aisles can slow shoppers down and cause them to peruse the shelves more. They also present a warehouse image that conveys a sense of bargain pricing.

There are many such examples, but the central point is that means of consumption (both new and old) are structured in such a way as to induce people to buy more than they intended.[38]

The novelist Émile Zola saw the department store as a "selling machine."[39] It is clear that the new means of consumption are far more sophisticated and effective selling machines than their predecessors. In addition to the devices described, innovations such as drive-through windows, computerized inventory control and cash registers, adjacent and enormous parking lots, shop at home, and credit cards have all served to greatly enhance the ability of the "machines" to sell. However, the new means of consumption have done more than simply sell more things better.

CHANGING THE WAY WE CONSUME

The new means of consumption have also greatly altered the *way* we consume.

One-Stop Shopping

Many innovations aim at one-stop shopping. For those who want a wide range of goods at discount prices, Wal-Mart and its supercenters combine the discount store with a supermarket so that a shopper can get his or her food and other goods on one trip. For shoppers who want an even wider range of discounted merchandise, one stop at the discount mall should work. If, instead, consumers want a huge variety of a particular product (such as sneakers, candles, electronics, and so on), a single trip to a superstore should do the trick. For those desiring a huge number of shops and department stores in one place, there is the shopping mall. For consumers who want all those shops as well as a wide range of entertainment, the mega-mall is the place for them. For all those who want to have a world of goods and services at their fingertips without leaving home, all they need do is open their catalogs, turn the channel to the Home Shopping Network, or switch on the computer and enter cyberspace and its cybermalls. For vacationers who want to go to just one place and have a complete vacation experience, a cruise, a trip to Disney World, or a visit to Las Vegas will work quite well. By seeming to offer everything we could want under one roof, or in one setting, the new means of consumption have altered the nature of the experience of shopping and vacationing by making them more efficient.

Destinations

As noted earlier, many of the new means of consumption are so all-encompassing, or more generally so attractive and appealing, that consumers set out with the specific intention of going to them. For example, while in the past vacationers may have set out for the warmth of Florida, many now head directly for Disney World. Clearly, not only Disney World but also Las Vegas and cruises have become such vacation destinations. All of the other new means of consumption have become destinations for more day-to-day outings—Circuit City when we want electronics, Toys 'R Us when we want toys, Price Club when we want a bargain, and so on. Not all of the new means of consumption seek to be all-encompassing, but all do seek to be destinations.

Do-It-Yourself

Doing more things ourselves is another major change in the way we consume, brought about by the new means of consumption. Many cathedrals of consumption ask that the consumer do many things that in the older means of consumption were done for them. In older shops clerks fetched goods for us, we now spend a great deal of time retrieving what we want in supermarkets, superstores, mega-malls, and so on. In fast food restaurants we are asked not only to wait on our tables, but to clean up after ourselves. In using the ATM, we are doing work formerly performed by bank tellers.

Altered Social Relations

The new means of consumption have profoundly altered the nature of social relations. In earlier means of consumption, there tended to be more in-depth, face-to-face relationships among and between consumers and those who served them. They tended to get to know one another quite well, and the social character of consumption could be as important, if not more important, than that which was consumed. In the new means of consumption, face-to-face relationships have been reduced (e.g., at the drive-in window of a fast food restaurant) or eliminated completely (e.g., in cybermalls, on home shopping networks, etc.). Those that remain tend to be superficial. Few people today go to the new means of consumption for the social relationships that they offer. Rather, they go to get what they want as quickly and impersonally as possible.

In fact, the new means of consumption are better characterized by interaction with things than with people. On the one hand, the new means seek to maximize the unmediated contact between consumers and goods and services. On the other hand, a significant part of the success of the new means is the fact that they are constructed so that people will interact with, gaze on, the cathedrals of consumption and derive satisfaction from that relationship. This is especially true of the more extraordinary cathedrals such as cruise ships, Las Vegas casinos, and Disney World. Interaction with people, at least in the realm of consumption, is gradually being replaced by interaction with things, both great and small.

Consumers are supposed to be actively involved in consuming the means of consumption and their goods and services; and most of the time they are. But other kinds of behaviors are encouraged by the cathedrals such as sitting, gazing at the setting, watching other people, and wandering about. All of these can be done in the company of other people, but they also lend themselves well to being done alone.

Speed, efficiency, self-service, and limited interaction get to the heart of many of the new means of consumption. This should come as no surprise, because these are largely American innovations and therefore reflect American values.

CHANGING THE WAY OTHERS CONSUME

The new means of consumption are being rapidly and aggressively exported. However, in many places around the world speed, efficiency, a do-it-yourself mentality and limited interaction are devalued. Those in other nations are led to consume more and more like Americans. In many countries this poses a profound threat to indigenous culture. At the minimum, it poses the danger of a global standardization and homogenization as more people around the world consume in the primarily American new means of consumption and obtain goods in much the same way Americans do. It also involves increased consumption around the world and threats derived from that to global resources, the environment, and so on.

Although we will focus on the exportation of the new American means of consumption to the rest of the world, it goes without saying that there is a simultaneous exportation of American-style products and the lifestyle they bring with them. Even if they are manufactured elsewhere, these products (Nike® shoes is a good example) reflect American culture and have American logos. Mattel® is scheduled to introduce in Japan a line of clothing fashioned after the attire of its iconic Barbie doll. The company is relying on the fact that the Barbie doll itself is already beloved in Japan. Said one young Japanese woman: "I'm incredibly happy that the Barbie brand is coming . . . I will buy some for sure."[40]

How America consumes is likely to have a profound impact (these days quite quickly) on most other developed nations. This is the case in part because American-based corporations are intent on, and aggressive about, exporting American consumer goods and the American way of consuming them. In most of the world's developed nations (and in many less developed ones) potential customers are bombarded by American products and advertisements. (I see this process as better described by the term *Americanization* than *globalization*:[41] the latter would indicate more of a multidirectional relationship among many nations.[42]) Many of those being assailed in these ways are far from hostile to the blitz. Indeed, all indications are, at least in the realm of consumption, that the days of the "ugly American" are long past. Judging by their popularity and proliferation, virtually every new incursion of American goods and services and the American way of consumption appears quite welcome.[43]

In fact, many people from around the world travel to the United States to shop in the new means of consumption and to purchase American goods:

> Strolling past the Saks Off Fifth outlet, Dress Barn and a camera store in the vast corridors of the Potomac Mills discount mall in Dale City, Va., three college students from France smiled with anticipation as they spotted a shop that sold athletic wear.
>
> When they emerged with their purchases, including the New York Yankees baseball caps that were high on their list, one student . . . said, "Now that we've seen the tourist sights, we can go home."[44]

It is little wonder that the American cathedrals of consumption are so eager to export the American way of consuming.

The current worldwide acceptance and popularity of American cathedrals of consumption stands in stark contrast to, for example, the situation in the 1940s, when a major commotion took place in France over the threat posed by the exportation of Coca Cola® to the wine-loving French cafe culture. Quite a bit of heat was generated over what came to be known as "Coca-colonization."[45] In the end, Coca Cola gained a foothold in France that led neither to the disappearance of that nation's beloved cafes nor the wines consumed in them and virtually everywhere else in France, but the initial reaction was telling.

Although much of the world now seems enamored of the American way of consuming, that is not to say that controversy has completely disappeared. For example, a similar, albeit less heated, version of the "Coca-colonization" debate occurred over the opening of Euro Disney outside Paris. As a result of adverse publicity stemming from the "McLibel" trial in London,[46] McDonald's has become a prime target of a number of health, environmental, and other groups.[47] There have also been periodic objections to the opening of McDonald's in, for example, the older parts of the world's great cities.[48] Although such protests continue to occur, in the main they are quite muted and are overwhelmed by the evidence of wide-scale acceptance of, indeed excitement over, American consumer exports.

Although the aggressive exporting of American consumer culture is one factor in its worldwide acceptance, another key is the absence, with the fall of Communism, of any viable worldwide alternative to the American model. Whatever its problems in practice, Communism served as an alternative world–historical model around which people could rally against American capitalism and its model of consumption.[49] Today, all that remains for those opposed to these things is opposition based on local considerations. Such local forms of resistance to the American mode of consumption are apt to continue in some locations, but they are not likely to offer a serious impediment.

Much of the worldwide opposition to American economic practices has focused on the exportation of American production theories and methods. Although the exportation of the American mode of production certainly continues, it is increasingly being supplanted in importance by the exportation of the American way of consuming. This parallels a similar shift within the United States.

A Growing International Presence

There is much data to support the idea that the new means of consumption are a growing international presence. Take the case of McDonald's. In 1991, a little more than a quarter of its restaurants were outside the United States; by 1996, more than 40 percent of its sites were overseas. In 1991, McDonald's restaurants were found in

59 nations; by 1996, they were in 101 nations. The percentage of overseas outlets will continue to grow (about 80 percent of new restaurants in 1997 were built outside the United States). System-wide sales increased from $12.4 billion in 1986 to $31.8 billion in 1996. Less than a third of system-wide sales came from outside the United States in 1986, but in 1996 that proportion had grown to nearly one-half, with sales in the United States (approximately $16 billion) exceeding international sales by less than 1 billion dollars.[50] One observer offered a broader perspective on the exportation of the American means of consumption:

> Tool around Australia: the regional malls sprouting along its highways look more than a bit familiar. Walk Brazil's streets: a sign says Chocolate, but the store feels like Ann Taylor, the R. L. Polo store mimics Ralph Lauren and Bill Brothers bears a strong resemblance to Brooks Brothers. Tour Bangkok: the Big C Superstores are the image of Wal-Marts.[51]

Examples of the influence of the American means of consumption on other cultures are legion:

♦ Canada has been invaded by superstores and almost all other new means of consumption. Said a consultant, "We haven't seen the end of the U.S. invasion."[52]

♦ Israel has now acquired a McDonald's, but it also has Domino's and Kenny Rogers' Roasters®. Then there is the Gap, Tower Records®, Hard Rock Cafe, and most recently Planet Hollywood.[53]

♦ Among many other American new means of consumption, home shopping TV has recently come to Russia.[54]

♦ A second American-style shopping center (the first had opened three weeks earlier), Polus Center, opened in Budapest, Hungary, in late 1996. Lines were long and people waited half an hour to enter the stores. Five percent of the city's population, 100,000 people, showed up for the mall's first weekend. The mall includes 100 stores, a multiplex movie theater, a skating rink, and nineteen bars and restaurants. The anchor of the mall is a huge "hypermarket" combining a supermarket and a discount center. Similar malls are under construction throughout central and eastern Europe—Czech Republic, Poland, Slovakia, Romania, Ukraine, and Croatia. Said a teenager working in his family's clothing store in the Polus Center, "Finally, we have something really Western in this boring country."[55]

♦ Wal-Mart and Sam's Club arrived in China in late 1996, and several other superstores are there as well, although these stores have done little more than establish a beachhead. They must adapt to a variety of differences between China and the United States. For example, the Chinese typically live in small apartments, which "means that huge American-sized packages and cases are out; smaller, compact sizes are in."[56] Customers usually walk or bike to the store, which limits what they can carry home with them.

♦ Japan is seen as ripe for American-style shopping malls.[57] The largest of the current malls is small by American standards (seventy-nine mainly small shops and thirteen restaurants). One mall developer predicts that there will be fifty to sixty malls in Japan within the next two decades. Because of high prices at home, the Japanese spend large sums of money outside the country. This is seen as an indication that the Japanese consumer is sensitive to price and would be attracted to American-style innovations such as malls and discount stores.[58]

♦ In Hanoi, Vietnam, "Baskin-Robbins is here and expanding. TGI Friday and Kentucky Fried Chicken are scheduled to open their first outlets in Ho Chi Minh City next year. And McDonald's is reportedly on the way."[59] In the former Saigon, now Ho Chi Minh City, there is the Saigon Superbowl with its thirty-two-lane bowling alley, huge video arcade, eight-table billiard parlor, food courts featuring burgers and fries, twenty-plus store shopping mall featuring Baskin-Robbins® ice cream, as well as children and elders riding "the escalator over and over, amazed at the contraption."[60] The mall came to Ho Chi Minh City even before McDonald's, which opened in 1998.

♦ In Argentina and Brazil, a half-dozen water parks and amusement parks are under construction at a cost of about $1.5 billion. Large cities are being surrounded by shopping malls complete with multiplex movie theaters and game centers of various types. Theme restaurants such as Planet Hollywood are expanding, as are indigenous varieties such as Rock in Rio Cafe®. Said one developer, "Entertainment has graduated from a secondary theme to a central one in Latin America . . . We've learned you can make money from showing people a good time."[61] These developers are drawing on American models and American expertise.

♦ For their part, American developers are eager for new Latin American markets. Already, a major amusement park is within a two-and-a-half hour drive of *every* major American city. There is fear of a shakeout in the overdeveloped theme-restaurant market and similar problems confront other types of entertainment centers, and hence the attraction of the underserved Latin American market.[62]

♦ In Paris, "The Champs-Élysees is now an American mall, complete with Disney Store and Planet Hollywood."[63] And that grand boulevard has long had McDonald's and Burger King. More shocking is what has happened to Saint Germain des Prés. Once a quaint neighborhood known for its book shops and cafes, it is now being invaded by international shops such as Louis Vuitton, Georgio Armani, Dior, and Cartier. "It didn't matter that these companies were French (or Italian), they're still mega-corporations that are proud to have the same exact product on shopping streets in Hong Kong, Beverly Hills, Monte Carlo, Tokyo, London, New York, Bal Harbour and the other side of the Seine."[64] They are joining other less elegant chains such as Benetton®, Body Shop®, and the Gap, which are already there. Although locals are generally opposed to the luxury shops, they quietly whisper that, "It's better than McDonald's."[65]

♦ England already looks increasingly like the United States, at least as far as its means of consumption are concerned:

West Thurrock is probably the greatest bastion of American shopping culture in Great Britain.

There are familiar names, now recognizable to most Brits, such as Burger King and Toys 'R Us. There's a giant American-style supermarket.

And farther along the service road is something more unusual for Britain: a gargantuan, thoroughly American mall called Lakeside Shopping Centre, which offers a range of department stores, scores of smaller shops, parking for 12,000 cars, and the requisite food court with quick-service cuisine from many lands.

But it is the latest American-bred addition to this shopping tract that has brought national attention to modest West Thurrock: "Costco . . . arrived here late last year, opening the first warehouse membership club in Britain amid an onslaught of media fanfare."[66]

Not satisfied, a large factory outlet developer is looking into various
sites in England, largely because its American tenants such as Nike
and the Gap see European expansion as key to their continued
growth.[67] For their part, the English are attracted to the American
discounters for a very good reason—the high cost of American products in England.[68]

Many in other parts of the world not only are accepting of the
new means of consumption but are producing their own variants that
they are eager to export to the United States. For example, in Latin
America, the Rock in Rio Cafe has clearly taken a lead from American
theme restaurants with its "entry by monorail, walls with projected
imagery that changes the decor, and an indoor fireworks show every
night."[69] Its developer eventually plans to turn the tables and export
his theme restaurant to the United States: "Why import something
American when we can do it better ourselves. . . . After all, you can
export as much as you import in today's world."[70]

There was a time when American production was the envy of the
world, and others were eager to emulate its structures and methods.
Today, it is more America's new means of consumption that virtually
every nation around the world covets. Although there are certainly
foreign precursors of many of these means, there is something quin-
tessentially American about McDonald's, Disney, Wal-Mart, and the
Flamingo Hotel, and also about their respective founders Ray Kroc,
Walt Disney, Sam Walton, and Bugsy Siegel.

However, although the largely American cathedrals of consumption have made in-roads in many parts of the world, it is important
to remember that other nations retain means of consumption that are
distinctly their own. Tokyo has fast food restaurants, large discount
stores, and department stores, but it also has a profusion of small
shops and innumerable automatic vending machines "that dispense
not only soft drinks and cigarettes, but also beer and liquor, socks,
ties, women's stockings, coffee, hot noodles, magazines and . . . un-
believably, flowers and engagement rings."[71]

Pilgrimages to America

Merchants from many nations are making pilgrimages to the United States to study the means of consumption and see how they can be adapted to their cultures:

> The Mall of America is our Uffizi, Home Depot our Forum. The Gap, Nordstrom, Disney Stores, Sears, Crate and Barrel, Niketown, Barnes & Noble and Wal-Mart—these are our cathedrals. . . . Heading for shopping centers of all kinds—malls, strip centers, outlet mills, downtown stores and designer boutiques—travelers from overseas board buses, trains, planes and taxicabs for days at a time.[72]

There are regular tours of the new means of consumption organized for interested parties from many nations. Innumerable other foreign retailers come on their own in an effort to learn the secrets of America's new means of consumption.

Critics of the Trend

It is abundantly clear that many welcome the invasion of the largely American new means of consumption, but there are critics of this trend and especially its homogenizing impact:

> This view that the culture of consumerism is a type of generic culture . . . is buttressed by the spread of huge shopping centers. Remarkably alike in design and in content, these free-market temples sell the same clothes (Levis, Nike), serve the same food (Pizza Hut, McDonald's, Taco Bell) and show the same movies. From Santiago to Rio de Janeiro, Bogota and Mexico City, these centers in effect allow people to travel without leaving home and to feel at home even when traveling.[73]

The area around Kruger National Park in South Africa has a casino linked to a shopping mall. Considerable attention is being devoted to developing this area to attract more tourists, but the head of the tourist agency is obviously aware of the dangers of American-style development:

> The most successful or enduring cultural happenings internationally are not staged Disney-type events, with tourists as a spectator audience and with locals as actors. . . . They are living festivals such as the running of the bulls in Pamploma, the Carnival in Rio and Easter in Jerusalem . . .
>
> What better way . . . than to assist in the creation of ways for tourists to actually engage with living cultures by bringing travellers into our townships, villages and kraals. Why give them Disney when you can give them authentic Africa?[74]

There is no question that this exportation of the American means of consumption to the rest of the world involves a process of Americanization. There is a danger of backlash here, but McDonald's among others has sought to be "glocal"—that is, integrate the global with the local.[75] (This is also true of the Disney parks in Tokyo and outside Paris.[76]) McDonald's does this by using many local owners and by adapting its products to each local environment.[77] A good example is the McDonald's in Delhi, India. Given the Indian deification of the cow, this McDonald's sells the "Maharaja Mac" made from 100 percent mutton. Also on the menu because of the large number of vegetarians in India are "Vegetable McNuggets." Nonetheless, McDonald's has had opposition, especially from animal rights activists, one of whom said, "I am against McDonald's because they are the chief killers of cows in the world. . . . We don't need cow killers in India."[78]

In sum, there has been an explosion of the largely American new means of consumption not only in United States, but in many other parts of the world. They have brought with them many undoubted benefits such as lower prices and a cornucopia of consumer goods unheard of in human history. They have also brought a series of potential drawbacks not the least of which is the fact that people throughout the United States, and increasingly throughout the rest of the world, have become voracious consumers.

CONCLUSION

In addition to discussing why it is that we are now seeing the creation of so many new and important means of consumption, this chapter has dealt with the ways in which these means have altered the amount and way that Americans, as well as much of the rest of the world, consume. In the next chapter I will present a set of theoretical tools that will help to analyze the cathedrals of consumption.

3

SOCIAL THEORY
AND THE NEW MEANS
OF CONSUMPTION

This chapter is devoted to the three basic and interrelated theoretical perspectives that inform this book. The first is the approach of Karl Marx and neo-Marxian theory (including the early work of Jean Baudrillard, a theorist whose ideas will play a prominent role in this analysis). Marxian and neo-Marxian theory are the origins of the concept "means of consumption." In addition, that theory highlights the fact that the success of modern capitalism and the cathedrals of consumption is highly dependent on the control and exploitation of the consumer. The second perspective is Max Weber's work on rationalization, enchantment, and disenchantment. Rationalization helps to transform the cathedrals of consumption into highly efficient selling machines, thereby enhancing their ability to control and exploit consumers. However, rationalization tends to lead to disenchantment and, therefore, to cold, inhuman settings that are increasingly less likely to attract consumers. Weber saw little possibility of enchantment in the modern world, but the neo-Weberian, Colin Campbell, extended Weber's ideas to include the possibility of such enchantment. The work of Rosalind Williams and Michael Miller demonstrates that the early French department stores were *both* highly rationalized and enchanted "fantasy worlds." The theory of the relationship among rationalization, enchantment and disenchantment highlights the difficulties faced by the cathedrals of consumption in attracting and keeping large numbers of consumers. This is related to Marxian theory in the sense that in order to be controlled and exploited, consumers must be attracted, and continually return, to the cathedrals. Enchantment and rationalization help to bring large numbers of consumers to these settings, but their attractiveness to consumers is continually threatened by the prospects of disenchantment.

Marxian and Weberian theory are modern perspectives; the third theoretical orientation is postmodern social theory, especially ideas drawn from the later theories of Baudrillard. The ideas of the postmodern theorists are especially helpful in explaining how the new means of consumption overcome the problems associated with disenchantment and attain the reenchantment needed to continue to lure, control, and exploit ever-increasing numbers of consumers. We will see that, paradoxically, at least one of the postmodern processes leading to reenchantment ("implosion" into the home) is posing a profound threat to the nature, if not existence, of most of the new means of consumption. Consistent with the contradictory character of postmodern society, the new means of consumption are both bolstered *and* threatened by postmodern developments.

MARXIAN THEORY AND THE MEANS OF CONSUMPTION

The German social theorist Karl Marx developed his ideas in the 1800s in reaction to the Industrial Revolution and the early days of capitalism. Marx wanted to better understand the workings of capitalism, but he was most concerned with explaining the source of what he perceived to be its evils and helping to bring about the downfall of capitalism. In the more than 100 years since Marx's death in 1883, capitalism has undergone many changes and Marx's disciples have sought to use his theories as a base to analyze and criticize these changes. However, such theorizing had little effect on capitalism, which is now triumphant on the world stage. Furthermore, most of the Communist regimes that were erected, at least in part on a base of Marxian ideas, have collapsed. Given capitalism's unparalleled position of preeminence, some think it is more important than ever to analyze it from a Marxian perspective.

Animating Marx's original interest was his distress over the fact that the capitalists' ownership of the means of production allowed them to control and exploit the proletariat (the worker). In order to work, the proletariat had to have access to the means of production such as tools, machines, factories, and raw materials. Knowing this, at least subconsciously, the capitalists were able to pay them far less than they should have, given the value of what the workers produced. In fact, in the Marxian view, the proletariat deserved just about all of the money earned by the capitalists because all value is derived from labor.

Like most other modern theorists, Marx focused mainly on production—that is, he had a productivist bias. Given the realities that he was dealing with (the early days of the Industrial Revolution and capitalism) a focus on production in general, and the means of production in particular, was sensible. However, in recent years, to the degree that production and consumption can be clearly separated,[1] production has grown increasingly less important (for example, fewer workers are involved in goods production), especially in the United States, whereas consumption has grown in importance. In such a society, it makes sense to shift our focus from the means of production to the means of consumption.

Marx had a great deal to say about consumption, especially in his well-known work on commodities. Much less well known and visible is the fact that Marx (following Adam Smith, as he often did[2]) employed the concept "means of consumption."

Marx defined the *means of production* as "commodities that possess a form in which they . . . enter productive consumption."[3] The *means of consumption* he defined as "commodities that possess a form in which they enter individual consumption of the capitalist and working class."[4] Under this heading, Marx differentiates between subsistence and luxury consumption (Smith made a similar distinction). On the one hand are the "necessary means of consumption," or those "that enter the consumption of the working class."[5] On the other are the "luxury means of consumption, which enter the consumption only of the capitalist class, i.e., can be exchanged only for the expenditure of surplus-value, which does not accrue to the workers."[6] Basic foodstuffs would be subsistence means of consumption whereas elegant automobiles would be luxury means of consumption.

There is a logical problem in the way Marx uses the concept of the means of consumption, especially in comparison to the paired notion of means of production. The means of production occupy an intermediate position between workers and products; they are the means that make possible both the production of commodities and the control and exploitation of the workers. In contrast, the way Marx uses the idea, the means of consumption are not means but rather the end products in his model of consumption; they are those things (either subsistence or luxury) that are consumed. In other words, there is *no* distinction in Marx's work between consumer goods and what I term the means of consumption (for example, shopping malls and cruise ships).[7] To put it another way, in his work there is no parallel in the realm of consumption to the mediating and expediting role played by the means of production.

In this book I distinguish the means of consumption from that which is consumed. Fast food restaurants are different from the hamburgers we eat in them.[8] The means of consumption will be seen as playing the same mediating role in consumption that the means of production play in Marx's theory of production. That is, just as the means of production are those entities that make it possible for the proletariat to produce commodities and to be controlled and exploited as workers, the means of consumption are defined as those things that make it possible for people to acquire goods and services and for the same people to be controlled and exploited as consumers.[9]

The concept of the means of consumption appears, at least in passing, in various other places,[10] but most notably in one of Baudrillard's early works, *The Consumer Society*.[11] At this point in his career Baudrillard was still heavily influenced by Marxian theory, although he was to break with that approach in a few years en route to becoming today's preeminent postmodern social theorist. Baudrillard does not define the concept, but the way he uses it makes it clear that (unlike Marx) he is not conflating the means of consumption with the commodities to be consumed but is following the definition I am using. Baudrillard's paradigm of the means of consumption is the Parisian "drugstore":

> Any resemblance to an American pharmacy is tucked into one small corner. The rest of this amazing establishment is more like a mini-department store with everything from books to cameras, toys, French and foreign newspapers and magazines, clothing, and a booming takeout business in carved-on-the-spot sandwiches, salads, and soft drinks as well as caviar, pâté de foie gras, and elaborate picnic hampers. Le Drugstore's outdoor cafe offers what it claims is an "authentic" American menu.[12]

The Parisian "drugstore" is clearly a means of consumption in that it is a social and economic structure that enables consumers to acquire an array of commodities. Baudrillard goes on to talk about an entire community as the "drugstore writ large." In this context he describes a community, Parly 2, with its shopping center, swimming pool, clubhouse, and housing developments. The shopping center and at least a version of the kind of community described by Baudrillard (the elite gated community) are, as noted in Chapter 1, examples of the new means of consumption. Other examples discussed by Baudrillard are holiday resorts and airport terminals.[13]

Baudrillard was prescient in writing about the significance of these new means of consumption in the late 1960s. However, he did little with the idea and related phenomena. Furthermore, he erred in focusing on the Parisian drugstore because of its limited impact on the rest of the world. In fact, today that drugstore has been swamped by the importation of the kinds of means of consumption that occupy our attention: fast food restaurants, chains of all sorts, Euro Disney and so on. Nonetheless, Baudrillard's sense of the means of consumption is the closest in the literature to the way the concept is employed in this book.

Exploiting and Controlling the Consumer

Marx's theory, especially as it relates to the means of production, focuses on the control and exploitation of workers (the proletariat), as discussed previously. In twentieth-century capitalism, the focus shifted increasingly from production to consumption, resulting in a parallel shift from control and exploitation of workers to that of consumers. Consumers could no longer be allowed to decide on their own whether to consume, how much or what to consume, and how much to spend on consumption. Capitalists felt that they had to devote more time, energy, and money in an attempt to influence, if not control, those decisions. This idea is explicit in Baudrillard's early work. He views consumption as "social labor" and compares its control and exploitation to that of productive labor in the workplace. Capitalism has created a controllable and exploitable "consuming mass" to complement the control and exploitation of the "producing mass."[14]

The Marxian theory of the exploitation of workers was clear-cut because all value came from the workers. If they got anything less than everything, they were being exploited (when in fact they received barely enough to subsist).

In what sense can the consumer be said to be exploited? There are many ways to respond to this question. For example, advertisements are designed to lure people into buying things they might not otherwise consume. And it is the consumers who must ultimately pay for the cost of the advertisements as part of the purchase price of goods or services. In fact, as neo-Marxists Paul Baran and Paul Sweezy showed long ago, capitalists prefer competition on the basis of advertising campaigns (and other sorts of sales competition) to price competition because it enables them to keep prices high and to pass the costs of advertising campaigns on to consumers.[15] However, our focus is not on the way advertisements are used to exploit consumers, but on how the new means of consumption perform a very similar function.

At one level, the new means of consumption are set up to lead people to consume more than they intend and perhaps more than they can afford.[16] At another level, the sometimes astronomical cost of constructing and maintaining the cathedrals of consumption leads to high prices that are driven even higher by the desire of those involved in the cathedrals to reap large profits. Credit cards aid the ability of the new means of consumption to exploit consumers by leading them to buy more. Furthermore, credit cards are exploitative in themselves in the sense that people are lured into debt that many find it difficult to extricate themselves from and into paying usurious interest rates on balances that serve to stretch indebtedness out for years, if not decades. Consumers can be said to be exploited by the new means of consumption by being led to buy more than they need, to pay higher prices than need be, and to spend more than they should.[17]

It is true that it is far harder to argue that the consumer is exploited than it was for Marx to contend that the proletariat was exploited. The proletariat had no choice. If they wanted to work, they had to sell their labor time to the capitalist in exchange for access to the means of production and ultimately a subsistence wage. In contrast, the consumer appears to have the option of avoiding the new means of consumption and obtaining goods and services in other ways (e.g., making commodities themselves or using older means of consumption). However, the fact is that the proliferation of the new means of consumption is making it more difficult and less attractive for consumers to obtain goods and services in other ways. It is increasingly the case that if consumers want to consume, they *must* use ("labor" in) one of the new means of consumption. In a sense, consumers must give the capitalists their "consumption time" in exchange for access to the means of consumption. Consumers are then able to get goods and services only by placing themselves in a context in which they are likely to buy more, to pay higher prices, and to spend more money than they intended.

In a similar way, consumers are not *forced* to use credit cards. They could pay in cash and avoid many of the problems associated with credit cards. However, in the case of an increasing number of transactions through, for example, cybermalls or home shopping television networks, it is almost impossible to consume without credit cards. Even in the many cases that consumption can be accomplished in other ways, the credit card proves to be an irresistible lure.

So although the analogy between workers and consumers is far from perfect, there is a sense in which both have become "exploitable masses." With the proliferation of the new means of consumption, the choices open to consumers are declining. Although they may not be subject to much, if any, overt coercion, consumers are the objects of a variety of softer, more seductive controlling techniques. And such techniques are one of the defining characteristics of a postmodern society. Consumers can still choose venues other than the new means of consumption; they can opt not to pay exorbitant prices and not to buy things that are not absolutely needed; but at the same time we must not forget that enormous sums of money are spent on advertising and on the new means of consumption (among other sales mechanisms) to get people to buy and pay more. On balance, the evidence seems clear that this money is well spent and people often do what is expected of them.

Take the case of the lottery, a new means of consuming gambling that is traceable to Colonial America but which boomed in the 1970s and 1980s as a result of state government efforts to raise money.[18] Jackpots have reached astronomical levels and a wide array of new games have proliferated. Outlets that sell lottery tickets tend to be concentrated in poor areas and to target those with lower incomes and education. Heavy players may gamble as much as 10 percent or more of their annual income on the lottery. A great deal of money is spent in advertising lotteries and luring people into playing for the first time or to continue being regular players. Advertisements are clever and target specific groups such as low-income players who tend to prefer specific types of games such as Keno, the superstitious with the Lucky Numbers game, and the more affluent players with games based on themes, such as "Star Trek." Players are often ill-informed about payout percentages and the slim chances of winning. For all of these reasons, and more, it could be argued that the lottery is an exploitative means of consuming gambling.

Nevertheless, the analogy between the exploitation of workers and consumers is far from ideal. However, various neo-Marxists have offered us a different way of looking at the analogy between the capitalist's treatment of workers and consumers. They contend that the real focus in contemporary capitalism is no longer the *exploitation* of workers, but rather their *control*.[19] If control is the central concern as far as contemporary workers are concerned, then that must certainly be the case for consumers. We are on far firmer footing simply arguing that the new means of consumption concentrate on the control of consumers in order to get them to spend as much as possible. This allows us to skirt the bothersome issue of exploitation without losing any of the focus and power of our argument. And we can retain at least a partial theoretical footing in (neo-) Marxian theory.

WEBERIAN THEORY AND ENCHANTMENT, RATIONALIZATION, AND DISENCHANTMENT

German-born Max Weber (1864–1920) did his most important work in the three or four decades after the death of Marx. Although Weber shared Marx's interest in capitalism, he came to see it as just one of a number of developments that were unique to the Occident. Just as Marx believed that capitalism created a number of social advances, Weber noted the positive contributions of the Western institutions of interest to him. And like Marx, Weber was deeply concerned with the problems created by these changes. However, whereas Marx was a radical hoping for a revolution that would overturn capitalist society, Weber was much more pessimistic about doing anything about the problems associated with the distinctive set of Occidental institutions.

The key factors in Weber's theorizing are enchantment, rationalization, and disenchantment. His argument is that the modern process of rationalization in the Occident, as exemplified in capitalism and in the bureaucracy, has served to undermine what was once an enchanted (i.e., magical, mysterious, mystical) world. Rational systems in general, and the bureaucracy in particular, have no room for enchantment. It is systematically rooted out by rational systems, leaving them largely devoid of magic or mystery.

Rationalization

Weber delineated four different types of rationality and argued that rationality takes different forms in different social settings. *Practical rationality* is a mundane form in which people seek in their day-to-day activities the best means to whatever end they seek. *Theoretical rationality* is cognitive rather than practical and involves an effort to master reality through increasingly abstract concepts. *Substantive rationality* involves a choice of means to ends guided by, and in the context of, larger social values. *Formal rationality* involves a similar choice of means to ends, but this time guided by universally applied rules, laws, and regulations. It is formal rationality that is the distinctive product of the West.

In spite of Weber's effort to distinguish among these types of rationality, and to see them operating differently in various institutions, one emerges from a reading of his work with a clear sense that there is an overall trend in the West in the direction of the increasing domination of formal rationality—rationality as an "iron cage." This idea is clear, for example, in Weber's conclusion that socialism would not eliminate or reduce the possibility of such a future: "Not summer's bloom lies ahead of us, but rather a polar night of icy darkness and hardness, no matter which group may triumph externally now."[20] It is phrases like "polar night," "icy darkness" and "hardness" that convey such a disenchanted, frigid, nightmarish image when the new means of consumption are thought of in terms of Weber's theory of rationalization.

Authority Structures

The trend toward increasing formal rationalization is found in Weber's work on authority. Here Weber differentiated among three types of authority by specifying the way in which each is legitimated. *Traditional authority* exists when the leader rules on the basis of a claim to, and a resulting belief on the part of the followers in, the sanctity of age-old rules and powers. In the case of *rational–legal authority*, the leader rules and has the ability to issue commands on the basis of legally enacted regulations. Followers accept that right and those rules and therefore follow the leader's dictates. Finally, *charismatic authority* is based on the devotion of followers to the exceptional sanctity, exemplary character, heroism, or special powers (for example, the ability to work miracles) of the leader, as well as to the normative order sanctioned by the leader.

All three types have existed throughout history, but Weber argued that in the modern West we are witnessing the triumph of rational–legal authority and the progressive elimination of the other two types as legitimate bases of authority. For one thing, fewer people are inclined to accept the authority of someone (say, a king or queen) who rules on the basis of tradition. For another, as rational–legal authority becomes more firmly entrenched, it is less and less vulnerable to overthrow by charismatic leaders and their followers. As is the case for rationality in general, in the realm of authority formal rationality eventually comes to reign supreme.

The demise of tradition and especially charisma as ways of legitimating authority is of particular interest. Both traditional and charismatic authority can be seen as involving an enchanted relationship between leader and followers. In one case the enchantment comes from a belief in the way things have always been done, and in the other it comes from a belief in the leader's extraordinary qualities. Their demise implies the end of enchantment, at least in such a relationship. It is clear that the relationship between rational–legal leaders and followers is not enchanted; there is no mystery why some lead and others follow.[21]

It is also the case that Weber sometimes uses charisma in a broader sense to denote not just leaders but anyone with extraordinary abilities. Such individuals can be seen as enchanted, certainly in comparison to those who staff such rational–legal systems as the bureaucracy. In a rationalized world there is less and less room for such individual charisma, and therefore less room for enchantment.

Bureaucracy

The bureaucracy embodies Weber's thinking on rationality, authority, and the iron cage. First, bureaucracy is the epitome of formal rationality. As Weber put it, "From a purely technical point of view, a bureaucracy is capable of attaining the highest degree of efficiency, and is in this sense formally the most rational known means of exercising authority over human beings."[22] Second, bureaucracy is the organizational structure that is associated with rational–legal authority and its triumph over other forms of authority. Indeed, one of the key reasons that rational–legal authority wins out over the others is the superiority of its characteristic bureaucratic form in comparison to the organizations associated with traditional and charismatic authority. There really is no other option if the objective is mass administration. Third, the bureaucracy is itself an iron cage in terms of those who function in it. More generally, as more and more sectors of society come to be characterized by bureaucracies, they tend to form one enormous iron cage.

Although Weber praised the bureaucracy on a variety of grounds, he was also critical of its constraints on people. He described bureaucracies as "escape proof," "practically unshatterable," and among the hardest institutions to destroy once they are established. Along the same lines, he felt that individual bureaucrats could not squirm out of the bureaucracy once they were "harnessed" in it. Weber concluded,

> This whole process of rationalization in the factory as elsewhere, and especially in the bureaucratic state machine, parallels the centralization of the material implements of organization in the hands of the master. Discipline inexorably takes over ever larger areas as the satisfaction of political and economic needs is increasingly rationalized. This universal phenomenon more and more restricts the importance of charisma and of individually differentiated conduct.[23]

The bureaucracy, and formally rational structures in general, must be seen as objective structures that constrain people in very material ways. Rules, offices, hierarchies, and the like constrain people so that although they are enabled to do certain things, they are forced into doing others.

Capitalism

Weber conceived of capitalism as another formally rational system, and he offered an extraordinarily clear image of its material, cage-like character:

> Capitalism is today an immense cosmos into which the individual is born, and which presents itself to him, at least as an individual, as an unalterable order of things in which he must live. It forces the individual, in so far as he is involved in the system of market relationships, to conform to capitalist rules of action.[24]

The image that is being conveyed is well-reflected in the fiction of Franz Kafka, especially *The Trial*.

To greater or lesser degrees, most of the new means of consumption are objective structures[25] (often themselves bureaucratic structures or a part of larger bureaucracies) that exert constraint on those people who are lured into them. This constraint is important in itself, for its relationship to exploitation, and also because it makes possible the systematic extraction of enchantment from these structures.[26]

Disenchantment

Weber derived the notion that as a result of rationalization the western world has grown increasingly disenchanted[27] from Friedrich Schiller. It relates to the displacement of "magical elements of thought."[28] As Schneider puts it, "Max Weber saw history as having departed a deeply enchanted past en route to a disenchanted future—a journey that would gradually strip the natural world both of its magical properties and of its capacity for meaning."[29] Or,

> In the face of the seemingly relentless advance of science and bureaucratic social organization, he believed, enchantment would be hounded further and further from the institutional centers of our culture. Carried to an extreme, this process would turn life into a tale which, whether told by an idiot or not, would certainly signify nothing, having been evacuated of meaning.[30]

The theme of disenchantment recurs in many places in Weber's work, but especially in his sociology of that most enchanted of domains: religion.[31] For example, he saw a historical process of rationally and professionally trained (and, therefore, disenchanted) priests gaining ascendancy over magicians who acquired their positions through irrational means and who clearly have a more enchanted view of, and relationship to, the world than priests. Weber argued that in the modern world, "One need no longer have recourse to magical means in order to master or implore the spirits, as did the savage, for whom such mysterious powers existed."[32]

Prophets, who as a group are more enchanted than the priests, receive a personal calling and engage in emotional preaching. They are either the founders, or the renewers, of religion. Weber differentiated between ethical (e.g., Muhammed and Christ) and exemplary (e.g., Buddha) prophets. Ethical prophets believe that they have received a commission directly from God and they demand obedience from followers as an ethical duty. Exemplary prophets demonstrate the way to salvation to others by way of example. Both types are useful in creating a group of followers, but once they have succeeded in creating such a group, they tend to be replaced by the disenchanted priests who are far better than either type of prophet at the pastoral, day-to-day affairs of managing such a group. In the process, religion begins to lose its enchanted character and comes under the sway of the rationalized church that houses the priests. The priests derive their authority from their position within the church, whereas prophets derive theirs from their service to a sacred (and enchanted) tradition.

Weber also argued that the Protestants, especially the Calvinists, developed an idea system, "The Protestant Ethic," that helped give birth to the spirit of capitalism. Weber is here working at the level of ideas rather than material structures. Weber depicted a world that is, at least initially, enchanted. The Protestant Ethic sprang from the Calvinist belief in predestination. Believing that whether or not they were saved was preordained, the Calvinists looked for particular signs as a way of telling whether or not they were among the saved. The most important of those signs became economic success. The Calvinists came to work hard, and to reinvest profits in their businesses, to help ensure that they would, in fact, see the signs of their salvation. This was clearly an enchanted world. That is, the Calvinist was making decisions on the basis of mystical ideas ("signs," "salvation") rather than rational, matter-of-fact principles and procedures.

The capitalist economic system eventually lost all vestiges of enchantment and came to be a highly disenchanted world without room for ideas such as predestination and salvation. In fact, it became inhospitable to the Calvinists, indeed to all religions, because of the tie between religion and enchantment. There was little patience in the rationalized and disenchanted world of capitalism for such enchanted worlds as religion.

Enchantment

Weber's thinking on magicians, prophets, the Protestant Ethic, and charismatic and traditional leaders had a great deal to do with enchantment. However, his thinking on more recent developments, especially in the West, had much more to do with rationalization and disenchantment, enchantment having been largely driven out by the machine-like bureaucracy and rational–legal authority. A formally rational world is a disenchanted world. In a modern context it is not unusual to associate Weber with the imagery of disenchanted and rationalized iron cages, but it is unusual to link him to the idea of enchantment. However, such a connection has been made by Colin Campbell who has extended Weberian theory, at least as it relates to the Protestant Ethic thesis, in such a way that it is able to encompass the ideas of enchantment, dreams, and fantasies.[33]

The Romantic Ethic

In the *The Romantic Ethic and the Spirit of Modern Consumerism*,[34] Campbell does not contest Weber's basic argument about the central role of early Calvinism in the rise of capitalism, but merely contends that Weber did not take his analysis far enough. That is, Weber analyzed the Protestant Ethic up to approximately 1700, but it continued to evolve after that point and began to move in a very different direction. Although Campbell pointed out that there was more emotion[35] in early Calvinism than Weber recognized, he argued that later Calvinism became even more accepting of emotion. In other words, there were elements of enchantment in later Calvinism.

Although the early Calvinists required signs of success in order to help them to determine whether they were to be saved, later Calvinists sought evidence of their good taste. Good taste was linked to beauty and beauty to goodness. The Calvinist who demonstrated good taste simultaneously displayed goodness. In other words, pleasure-seeking came to be linked with the ideals of character. An easy mechanism for demonstrating that one had good taste was to show that one was in fashion. The later Calvinists grew "eager to 'follow fashion' and hence to consume 'luxury' goods with avidity."[36]

The later Protestant Ethic led, albeit unintentionally, to the spirit of modern *consumerism*. Defining this spirit was what Campbell called "autonomous, self-illusory hedonism." This hedonistic spirit stood in stark contrast to the asceticism of the early Protestants as well as of the spirit of modern capitalism. It also was individualistic and involved illusions, day dreams, and fantasies; in other words, it was a world of enchantment. The key is individual fantasies because, as Campbell pointed out, fantasies can be far more important and rewarding than reality. In fact, he argued that disappointment inevitably occurs when people are able to fulfill their fantasies, especially with a variety of consumer goods and services. Each time they venture forth into the marketplace, people delude themselves into believing that this time it is going to be different; the material reality is going to live up to the fantasy. These fantasies, rather than material realities, are crucial to an understanding of modern consumerism because they can never be fulfilled and are continually generating new "needs," especially for consumer goods and services.

Although Weber saw the spirit of modern capitalism leading to rationalized, disenchanted capitalism, for Campbell the spirit of modern consumerism leads to romantic, enchanted capitalism. Weber's capitalism is a coldly efficient world virtually devoid of magic, and Campbell's "romantic capitalism" is a world of dreams and fantasies. Although production is accorded central importance in rational capitalism, it is of secondary importance in romantic capitalism taking the form, for example, of the production of arts and crafts by Bohemians. What is of central importance for romantic capitalism (and for Campbell) is consumption. And, within the realm of consumption, Campbell accorded great importance to fantasies, especially the fantasizing of consumers. However, Campbell focused on the fantasies of individual consumers. In this book, I extend Campbell's work by focusing on the enchanted aspects of the new means of consumption. We will see that these are not only increasingly fantastic in themselves, but also are involved in generating fantasies about consumption among consumers.[37] Despite Weber's pessimism, enchantment persists. As Schneider puts it, "Enchantment . . . is part of our normal condition, and far from having fled . . . it continues to exist. . . ."[38]

I draw on both Weber and Campbell in my conceptualization of the cathedrals of consumption as not only rationalized and disenchanted, but also enchanted. Much the same thing could be said of the cathedrals associated with organized religions.

The French Department Store

Perhaps religious structures seem rather removed from our concrete concern with the enchanted and disenchanted aspects of the new means of consumption. Much closer is work on one of the major precursors of the new means of consumption, the French department store of the mid-1800s, especially Bon Marché in Paris. Rosalind Williams sees such settings as enchanted "dream worlds."[39] She has focused on such things as the use of decor to lure customers to the stores and to "imbue the store's merchandise with glamour, romance, and, therefore consumer appeal."[40] The stores were in the business of enchanting and seducing their customers. In these settings, consumers could live out many of their fantasies by either purchasing goods or merely imagining what it would be like to own them. In other words, the early French department stores strove mightily to be enchanted worlds.

Although Williams has done relatively little with the rationalized, and therefore disenchanted, characteristics of the early French department stores, that issue gets much more attention in Michael Miller's study of Bon Marché.[41] The early Bon Marché was a fusion of the emerging rationalized world with more traditional elements of French bourgeois culture; over the years it moved increasingly in the direction of becoming a rationalized, bureaucratized structure. That is, it encountered "an incessant push towards greater efficiency."[42] Among the rationalized elements of the store were its division into departments; its partitioning of Paris for the purposes of making deliveries; its files and statistics, records and data; its telephone lines, sliding chutes, conveyor belts, and escalators; and its "*blanc*," or great white sale, "the most organized week of the store."[43]

Taken together, the work of Williams and Miller indicate that the early French department store, like contemporary cathedrals of consumption, was both enchanted and disenchanted. Perhaps the most general conclusion to be drawn from this discussion is that enchantment and disenchantment are not easily distinguished from one another; one does not necessarily preclude the other. There is a reciprocal relationship. Fantasies draw people into the new means of consumption, and those fantasies can be rationalized in order to further draw people in and to reinforce the cage. The cage quality of the new means of consumption can itself be a fantasy—the fantasy of being locked into one of those cages with ready access to all of its goods and services. In fact, Campbell concluded his work with just such an image: "Modern individuals inhabit not just an 'iron cage' of economic necessity, but a castle of romantic dreams, striving through their conduct to turn the one into the other."[44]

Marxian theory leads us to see the new means of consumption as oriented to, and based on, the control (and exploitation) of the consumer. Weberian theory points us toward some of the problems involved in being able to control consumers. Enchanted settings would seem to be well-suited to controlling consumers by luring them into a dream-like state so that it is easier to part them from their money. However, in the long run, in order to service and control large numbers of consumers, the cathedrals of consumption are forced to rationalize, and rationalization leads to disenchantment and the decline in the capacity to continue luring consumers or to create the dream-like states needed for hyperconsumption. The cathedrals of consumption, therefore, are faced with a seemingly unresolvable dilemma. However, a third, very contemporary resource—postmodern social theory—suggests a way out of this dilemma.

POSTMODERN SOCIAL THEORY AND REENCHANTMENT

Postmodern social theory is a recent development in the social sciences. It is almost impossible to summarize postmodern social theory in a brief section of a book devoted to other matters, but I can offer a brief introduction to the theory as well as its role in this analysis.[45] Postmodern social theory is premised on the idea that in various ways we have moved beyond the modern world into a new, postmodern world that is very different socially and culturally from its predecessor.

New, postmodern theories and ideas are required in order to analyze this new world.

Both modern social theory and modernity itself were closely tied to the idea of rationality. Theorists (including Marx and Weber) were urged to think rationally about that world, and when they did, they discovered that it was a world that was best characterized as being rational. Although acknowledging the advantages of rationality, they were also highly critical of it on various grounds.

Postmodern social theory rejects the idea of rationality and is associated more with the ideas of nonrationality or even irrationality. This means that postmodern social theorists reject the careful, reasoned style of modern academic discourse. The author's objective is often more to shock and startle readers than to win them over with logical, reasoned argument. Postmodern social theory also tends to be more literary than academic in style. In fact, thinkers associated with this perspective reject not only the idea of drawing a clear line between academic scholarship and literature, but also, as part of a modern way of thinking, most or all efforts to draw boundaries.

Postmodern theory is of obvious relevance to this work because of its association with consumption and the idea that the postmodern world is defined by consumption (rather than production).[46] As Eva Illouz put it, we are dealing with a world "in which economy has been transmuted into culture and culture into the transient and disposable world of goods."[47] One of the leading postmodern thinkers is Baudrillard, whose contribution to our conceptualization of the means of consumption we have already encountered.[48]

More important, postmodern thinkers also reject the idea that society is highly rational. Although postmodern society may have some rational elements, it is even more likely to be characterized by "emotions, feelings, intuition, reflection, speculation, personal experience, custom, violence, metaphysics, tradition, cosmology, magic, myth, religious sentiment, and mystical experience."[49] Rather than discuss this in general terms, I will focus on an idea, "symbolic exchange," associated with the work of Baudrillard.

To Baudrillard, symbolic exchange involves "taking and returning, giving and receiving . . . [the] cycle of gifts and countergifts."[50] Baudrillard developed his notion of nonrational symbolic exchange as a contrast, and alternative, to the highly rational economic exchange that characterizes modern capitalist society.[51] For example, although economic exchange produces such things as goods and services, as well as profit, symbolic exchange is nonproductive. Economic exchanges tend to be limited to a specific exchange of, for example, goods and services for money, and symbolic exchanges occur continually and without limitation. In societies characterized by symbolic exchange, economic exchanges (considered of preeminent importance in modern societies) tend to be only a small portion of all exchanges.[52] Baudrillard prefers nonrational symbolic exchange and associates it with primitive societies. He uses the idea of nonrational symbolic exchange to criticize modern societies, which are dominated by rational economic exchange. Baudrillard argued that contemporary society was on the verge, or in the midst, of the transition to the postmodern. However, this newly emerging society to him offers powerful barriers to symbolic exchange. Although he develops a postmodern theory, Baudrillard ends up being a critic of both modern and postmodern society.

Two of Baudrillard's specific ideas—implosion and simulations—will play a prominent role in this book, as will other ideas closely associated with postmodern social theory such as spectacles, time, and space. Later, I will define and deal with these concepts. However, we must not forget that the greatest significance of postmodern social theory is its emphasis on enchantment, the lack thereof in the modern world, and the continuing need for it. For Baudrillard, the enchanted world of symbolic exchange continually haunts, and poses a threat to, the modern disenchanted world of economic exchange. There is no possibility of returning to the primitive society dominated by symbolic exchange, but there is the possibility of such exchange reasserting itself. In other words, postmodernists hold out the possibility of the *reenchantment* of the world.

Zygmunt Bauman accords great centrality to this process of reenchantment:

> Postmodernity . . . brings "re-enchantment" of the world after the protracted and earnest, though in the end inconclusive, modern struggle to dis-enchant it (or, more exactly, the resistance to dis-enchantment, hardly ever put to sleep, was all along the "postmodern thorn" in the body of modernity). The mistrust of human spontaneity, of drives, impulses, and inclinations resistant to prediction and rational justification, has been all but replaced by the mistrust of unemotional, calculating reason. Dignity has been returned to emotions; legitimacy to the "inexplicable," nay *irrational*. . . .[53] The postmodern world is one in which *mystery* is no more a barely tolerated alien awaiting a deportation order. . . . We learn to live with events and acts that are not only not-yet-explained, but (for all we know about what we will ever know) inexplicable. We learn again to respect ambiguity, to feel regard for human emotions, to appreciate actions without purpose and calculable rewards.[54]

To take a specific example, Baudrillard argued that "seduction" offers the possibility of reenchanting our lives. Rather than the complete clarity and visibility associated with modernity, seduction offers "the play and power of illusion."[55]

The introduction of the concept of reenchantment allows us to create an expanded model of Weber's theory. Weber offers a theory of the relationship among enchantment, rationalization, and disenchantment. We have seen that some neo-Weberians (Campbell, especially) allow for the possibility of enchantment in the contemporary world, but the postmodernists offer a stronger thesis. Postmodern thinkers such as Baudrillard tend to think of reenchantment as either a possibility within modern society or the basis of a future alternative to modern society and its numbing disenchantment. However, in this work, reenchantment will be viewed as an ongoing and very real development within the contemporary cathedrals of consumption. It constitutes the way out of the dilemma posed by the disenchantment of the world in general and of the means of consumption in particular. In order to continue to attract, control, and exploit consumers, the cathedrals of consumption undergo a continual process of reenchantment. Of course, those efforts at reenchantment may, themselves, be rationalized from the beginning. Even if they are not, with reenchantment the stage is set for the entire process to recur.

Postmodern theory offers us three other perspectives that are crucial to this analysis. First, postmodern theorists tend to see the contemporary world as both exhilarating and threatening. Most of the processes associated with the reenchantment of the cathedrals of consumption can easily be seen as quite exhilarating in reviving and reinvigorating those cathedrals. And many of those same processes are also quite threatening, even to the very existence of those cathedrals.

Second, postmodern theory offers a useful corrective on the idea that the means of consumption control and exploit consumers. Although there is control and exploitation in the sense that people are led to buy and to spend too much, the fact is that people are not, in the main, being coerced into doing so, but are quite eager to behave in these ways. As we have seen, this is not only true of American consumers; much of the rest of the world seems intent on consuming like Americans. Most consumers do not see themselves as being controlled and exploited and would vehemently reject the idea that this is what is taking place. Whatever the objective realities (if one can even speak of such realities in a postmodern world) of prices paid and quantities purchased, most consumers seem willing to pay the prices and would, if anything, consume even more if they could.

There is an even stronger point to be made about postmodern consumers. Rather than having their consumption orchestrated by people like advertising executives and directors of cathedrals of consumption, it may be that it is consumers who are in control. It is the consumers who demand reenchanted cathedrals of consumption and those demands must be met if their business is to be retained. However, once one setting has been reenchanted, competitors must follow suit or risk the permanent loss of business. The means of consumption are in constant competition with one another to see which one can be most responsive to the demands of consumers for (re-)enchanted settings in which to consume. In fact, it could be argued that consumers are forcing the means of consumption into a reckless and poten-tially destructive war to see which one can offer the most (re-)en-chanted setting. This is nowhere clearer than in Las Vegas today where old hotels are being torn down and enormously expensive new ones are being constructed with ever more enchanted themes and settings.

Third, modern social theory tends to focus on agents and their intentions. Postmodern social theory, however, seeks to decenter the analysis by abandoning such a focus. This is one of the reasons why this book does not focus on consumers as agents, but rather the settings in which consumption occurs. In addition, this postmodern perspec-tive leads us to the view that the processes involved in the reenchant-ment of the means of consumption are only in part a result of the intentions of the agents operating on behalf of the cathedrals of consumption (see Chapters 5 and 6).

CONCLUSION

In the end, this is not a work in postmodern theory, or any other theory for that matter. The goal is to gain a greater understanding of the new means of consumption and to that end theoretical tools that work will be employed, whatever their origin.[56] In order to create the theoretical framework for this book, I have borrowed the ideas of exploitation, control, rationalization, and disenchantment from mod-ern social theory and the notion of reenchantment from postmod-ern social theory. This book offers what the postmodernists call a "pastiche" (a mixture of sometimes seemingly contradictory ideas) of modern and postmodern ideas in order to analyze the cathedrals of consumption. The latter, of course, are themselves combinations of modern, postmodern, and even premodern elements. Both the subject matter and the theoretical perspective of this book stand with one foot in some of social theory's oldest ideas and the other in some of its most contemporary thinking.

4

RATIONALIZATION, ENCHANTMENT, AND DISENCHANTMENT

This chapter expands on the Weberian and neo-Weberian theories outlined in the preceding chapter and applies ideas derived from them to the cathedrals of consumption. The discussion is divided into three sections. First, I will examine the several dimensions of the rationalization of the new means of consumption. Second, I will link rationalization to the disenchantment of these settings. Third, I will deal with the degree to which rationalized systems can, themselves, be enchanting. Overarching all of this is the problem of continuing to attract, control, and exploit customers. Rationalization is needed to accomplish these objectives on a large scale, but the resultant disenchantment can have the opposite effect. It is this that leads to the necessity for reenchantment that is the subject of Chapters 5 and 6. Though always at risk of new disenchantment, reenchanted settings, especially in concert with rationalized procedures, can continue to attract, control, and exploit consumers.

THE RATIONALIZATION OF THE NEW MEANS OF CONSUMPTION

Rationalization has five basic elements: efficiency, predictability, calculability, control through the replacement of human by nonhuman technology, and the irrationality of rationality. I examine each in turn in this section using illustrations from a variety of the new means of consumption.

Efficiency

Efficiency involves the choice of the optimal means to an end. It is important to distinguish between efficiency for the sake of the customer and efficiency for the sake of the organization, which sometimes overlap and at other times stand in opposition to one another.

For the Customer

The mall has been described as "an extremely efficient and effective selling machine."[1] This, in turn, makes it a highly efficient "buying machine" from the customer's perspective. Consumption is obviously made far more efficient for the consumer by having virtually all shops in one location that also has a large adjacent parking lot. Similar efficiencies are provided by superstores for customers in search of a specific type of product.

Catalogs have grown in number and popularity because they represent a highly efficient means of consumption: "Lifestyles have changed dramatically and people are busier than ever. . . . Both parents often work and people don't have time to go shopping. Catalog people realized they were serving a purpose for consumers . . . "[2] Basically, the efficiency of catalog shopping stems from the fact that the customer does not have to leave home to shop. The same, of course, is true of shopping through home shopping networks and cybermalls; all the steps involved in getting to, through, and home from the shopping mall are eliminated.

The huge Las Vegas casino–hotels bring with them many fairly obvious efficiencies, most notably that a person can stay in a hotel room that is only an elevator ride away from the gaming tables and slot machines. Cruise ships have many similarities with Vegas hotels, not the least of which is that as many as 3,000 people can quickly and easily consume a large number of goods and services, including gambling in the ship's casino.

For the Organization

The mall creates many efficiencies for shop owners, including collective security and cleaning services, a large and steadily available pool of customers, the synergy provided by the existence of many shops, and so on. And, of course, these efficiencies (for both customers and merchants) are that much greater in the case of the mega-malls. (Many of these efficiencies do not exist in the case of the superstore, but there are various other kinds of efficiencies involved in selling only one type of product.)

Slot machines are the most profitable of undertakings from the point of view of the casino operators, and the machines are efficient in that they do not require employees to operate them—an example of putting the customer to work at no pay; the gambler both produces and consumes each play on the machine.

As an Internet provider of books, Amazon.com presents an interesting case of efficiency through putting the consumer to work. The most obvious point is that the customer does all the work involved in placing an order. Less obvious is the fact that customers are invited to submit thoughts on, and reviews of, books; these reviews are then posted on the Net. Customers, therefore, not only do the work of ordering, but also serve as unpaid book reviewers. Many other sites on the Net invite comments from people (e.g., cruise lines), and those who write the largely positive reactions are serving as unpaid public relations people.

At Wal-Mart, the emphasis is on efficient internal operations. "In its quest for finding more efficient ways to meet consumer needs, Wal-Mart significantly altered for years to come the ways in which Americans would shop."[3] For example, rather than having suppliers ship goods to each individual store, Wal-Mart created its own distribution centers. Suppliers deliver to these centers, and Wal-Mart then uses its own trucks to make deliveries to individual outlets. This efficiency allows suppliers to ship in bulk and therefore to charge Wal-Mart less for goods. Such distribution centers also permit the development of centralized procedures for receiving and processing goods, which is far more efficient than leaving it to each and every Wal-Mart to develop its own procedures.

Another efficiency at Wal-Mart involves distribution centers where the goods are not stored but simply transferred from incoming trucks and railroad cars to outbound company trucks (the procedure is known as "cross-docking"). Wal-Mart also employs its own fleet of trucks. More often than not, those trucks are used not only to deliver goods to stores but also to pick up products from manufacturers and wholesalers on their way back to the distribution centers.

Sam's Club increased efficiency still further. For example, the limited variety of merchandise sold at these warehouse stores permits truckloads of items to be delivered directly to them. Mechanical means of moving merchandise are employed throughout the process with forklift trucks even being used inside the clubs. Merchandise is often sold prewrapped and preticketed in, for example, three- or six-packs.

Catalog operations, home shopping networks, and cybermalls are even more efficient than Wal-Mart or Sam's Club in that they do not need retail outlets and can operate directly out of distribution centers.

Disney World is efficient in many ways, especially in processing the large numbers of people that would easily overwhelm a less rationalized theme park. The basic issue at Disney World is how to keep so many people moving through the park, or at least to give them the illusion that they are moving. Even though people often find themselves in long lines, they usually feel as if they are moving and that they are getting closer to the attractions. Once in an attraction, conveyances of one kind or another—cars, boats, submarines, planes, rockets, moving walkways—often keep people moving through them far more efficiently than they would were they on foot; no dawdling is permitted. The same efficiency is true of trash removal. Were this not the case, Disney World would quickly be swamped with debris. Crews are employed to sweep, collect, and empty trash. There is also an elaborate underground tube system into which trash is emptied and whisked away at sixty miles per hour to a central trash disposal plant far from the view of visitors. The trash seems to disappear magically; Disney World is surrealistically clean, especially when one considers how many people use the park each day.

The leader in the funeral business, Service Corporation International, has made the preparation and consumption of a funeral far more efficient. Take, for example, the preparation of corpses for burial:

> It [the corpse] will be sprayed with disinfectant, and his throat and anus will be packed with gauze to prevent fluids from leaking. His mouth will be closed with glue or sewn shut by a thread run through his septum and lower gum. His eyes will be closed with plastic eyecaps or glue. Then an incision will be made in his throat, upper arm, or pelvis, and embalming fluid . . . will be pumped into his body, forcing all the blood out. . . . Upon completion another worker will dab a bit of makeup on his face and hands . . . [4]

It is impossible to resist noting that one would be hard-pressed to find a better illustration of the disenchantment associated with rationalization than this description of routine procedures for handling human corpses in an assembly-line fashion.

Calculability

The second dimension of rationalization is *calculability*. Rationalization involves an emphasis on things that can be calculated, counted, quantified. It often results in an emphasis on quantity rather than quality. This leads to a sense that quality is equal to certain, usually (but not always) large, quantities of things.

McDonald's emphasis on quantity—as reflected, for example, in the "Big Mac"—is mirrored by the other fast food restaurants. The most notable is Burger King, which stresses the quantity of the meat in its hamburger called the "Whopper" and of the fish in its sandwich called the "Whaler" (renamed, a few years ago, not surprisingly, "Big Fish"). At Wendy's, we are offered a variety of "Biggies." Jack-in-the-Box® has its "Colossus," and Kentucky Fried Chicken offers us a "Mega" meal. Not to be outdone, Pizza Hut has its "Bigfoot" pizza, Domino's touts its "Dominator," and Little Caesar® pushes its "Big! Big!" The announcement of even bigger "Big! Big!" pizzas with no increase in price was pronounced "a stroke of genius" by an industry consultant.[5] Similarly, 7-Eleven® offers its customers a hot dog called the "Big Bite," a large soft drink called the "Big Gulp," and, now, the even larger, "Super Big Gulp." In fact, in recent years the tendency has been for fast food restaurants to push ever-larger servings. For example, McDonald's now offers "Super-Size" meals and invites customers to "super size it." Then there is the advent of the "Double Quarter Pounder" and the "Triple Cheeseburger."[6] Other recent additions to this list are Hardee's "Monster Burger" and the "Monster Omelet Biscuit." For those of you who want all the gory details, the Monster Burger includes *two* quarter-pound hamburgers, *three* slices of cheese and no less that *eight* (!) slices of bacon on a seeded bun with mayonnaise.

What is particularly interesting about all this emphasis on quantity is the seeming absence of interest in communicating anything about quality. The result is a growing concern about the decline of quality, not only in the fast food business but in society as a whole. Were fast food restaurants interested in emphasizing quality, they might give their products such names as the "Delicious Mac," or the "Prime McBeef," or the "All Beef McFrank." But typical McDonald's customers, or more generally those who patronize rationalized systems, know they are *not* getting the highest quality products in general, and food in particular (it isn't called "junk food" for nothing!).

Las Vegas hotels compete to see which one can offer the most hotel rooms, the largest casino, the "loosest slots,"[7] the biggest entertainment attraction. A similar competition takes place among the largest cruise lines, which boast about how many people their ships can carry, how long and wide the ships are, how many tons they weigh, how many different kinds of attractions they offer, and so on. In discount department stores, including Wal-Mart, customers are led to believe they can rely on three quantifiable things—low prices, large number, and a wide variety of goods. The same belief prevails about discount malls, although it often turns out to be illusory. The set prices for a daily or weekly pass at Disney World, as well as the abundant signs indicating how long a wait one can expect at a given attraction, illustrate similar calculability in the means of consuming tourism.[8]

The book superstores compete with one another and with small, local bookstores on the basis of how many books they stock. They must also compete with Internet booksellers such as Amazon.com. The book superstores emphasize quantity rather than quality by devoting a disproportionate share of their marketing budget and shelf space to what they perceive to be potential blockbusters. Publishers must print hundreds of thousands of copies of a book in order for it to be taken seriously by the superstores. Books that do not achieve best-seller status are often quickly returned to the publishers who reimburse the bookstores for unsold books. Independent booksellers sell about 80 percent of the books they order; superstores less than 70 percent; and discount chains such as Sam's Club about 60 percent. Books are increasingly like movies; the emphasis is on blockbusters that open big.[9] Not surprisingly, Disney is in the book publishing business (under the Hyperion imprint) and recently announced that, in order to be taken seriously by the superstores, it would print

300,000 copies of a book by a first-time novelist and spend $750,000 promoting it.

Indeed, being a "blockbuster" is what animates not only the super bookstores, but all of the new means of consumption. The chain of video stores, Blockbuster, is only the most blatant about it. The goal is to be big; no, huge—to straddle the nation—no, the world. The goal is defined quantitatively rather than qualitatively.

One of the major chains of discount department stores is Kmart. In a major advance, in 1997 it changed the names of some its revamped stores to Big Kmart and by the end of 1998 about half its stores will be similarly restructured and renamed. Kmart has been calling is superstores Super Kmarts for some time.[10]

Perhaps the best example of the emphasis on large quantity is found in warehouse stores such as Price Club. Everything about them is big. The stores are cavernous; goods are piled high; enormous sizes of individual products are offered for sale (a gallon of pickles that is unlikely ever to be finished; 200 ounces of laundry detergent that one can barely lift); other products are offered in multiple packages. The following case for the attractiveness of bigness at Price Club also applies to many other new means of consumption:

> Big has intrinsic value, especially to Americans. Price Club is the kind of big that's just right for difficult times. All the stresses of modern life . . . have stolen away the big things that used to make us happy. No more big cars. Who can heat a big house? The big vacation's out of reach. Big families are what we see in the movies.
>
> Of course, we still love big. . . . But these days, we take our big in smaller bites . . . if Price Club entertains us by tucking the mammoth-sized jars of Tabasco sauce down one of its shadowy aisles, we will say thank you and bring home the big game.[11]

Las Vegas casinos offer an interesting example of calculability. Free perks used to be doled out to gamblers largely on the whim of casino officials, but now it is all reduced to numbers. On average, regular gamblers are likely to receive about $1 worth of "comped" rooms, meals, or other perks for every $3 they can be expected to lose. One high roller was told that in exchange for a free $650 a night suite and other perks, he had to play blackjack for four hours at roughly $150 per hand. In order to gamble for the required number of hours, this visitor slept for only an hour and played blackjack in the wee hours of the morning. He commented, "If you went out and just paid for your room and your food, you'd probably be better off."[12] Whether or not this is true, the fact is that the modern casino has reduced comping to a highly calculable phenomenon.

In spite of all of this emphasis on quantity, there are examples of new means of consumption that do emphasize quality. Starbucks® is the best-known of these. In the realm of what is called the "home-meal replacement" business, Trader Joe's® and Eatzi's® specialize in gourmet-quality food.[13] Another example is the pizza chain, Papa John's®, which seems to be growing dramatically (the number of stores grew from 878 in 1995 to 1,160 in 1996) on the basis of the contention that its pizzas taste better than the others; its slogan is "better ingredients, better pizza."[14] Among other things, Papa John's claims to use vine-ripened tomatoes rather than sauce from concentrate, premium mozzarella, purified water in its dough, and so on. Competitors that focus on quantitative factors such as speed are working to come up with campaigns that emphasize quality. However, in order to maintain quality, Papa John's has had to rationalize its procedures by offering a stripped down menu in order to "ensure that even the newest employee can make a top-notch pizza. A 'keep it simple, stupid' approach pervades operations, from a goof-proof kitchen layout to dough mix that comes to regional commissaries pre-blended."[15] In other words, not only the food, but the jobs at Papa John's have been rationalized; they are McJobs.[16]

Predictability

Rationalization involves the increasing effort to ensure predictability from one time or place to another. In a rational society consumers want to know what to expect in all settings and at all times. They neither want nor expect surprises. They want to know that the

"Big Mac" they order today is going to be identical to the one they ate yesterday and to the one they will eat tomorrow.

The fast food industry perfected things such as replicated settings, scripted interactions with customers, predictable employee behavior, and predictable products. As Robin Leidner put it, "The heart of McDonald's success is its uniformity and predictability . . . [its] relentless standardization."[17] Such predictability is evident in more upscale chains such as Hard Rock Cafe:

> It is not as if the Hard Rock Cafe gained its fame from its food or even its association with any one place. Like McDonald's, its menu is identical all over the world, the Caesar salad tastes the same in Las Vegas as it does in Osaka, and the same Eric Clapton guitars grace the walls of the Berlin and San Francisco restaurants.[18]

Nor is it much different in various types of chain stores such as Pottery Barn®, Crate and Barrel®, the Gap, and J. Crew®, which "have raised standardization to a high art." These chains have brought high design to the mass market, but "the cost of this achievement is that while everything may be better, it is also increasingly the same. The khakis and sweat-shirts the Gap sells in Dallas shopping malls are the same as the ones it purveys along Columbus Avenue in Manhattan—in nearly identical stores."[19] Ironically, although these chains offer uniformity and predictability, they tout themselves as offering individuality.

There are many advantages to the homogenization of products and their display—even high-style, high-quality products—but there are liabilities associated with all of this. Some of these liabilities can be linked to the influence of McDonald's:

> But there's a downside, connected to the global homogenization of products and culture and shared with McDonald's, USA Today and Starbucks: the stuff may be good but it ain't special. . . . Everything seems more and more the same, wherever you are. Eccentric and idiosyncratic things fill the shelves of these mass stores, but they have been devalued by their very accessibility. The truly special and inventive is harder and

harder to find, unless you are very, very rich or have lots of time to look . . . we pay the price in a gradual but very real loss of individual variation: our houses and our wardrobes, like our entertainment, become part of mass culture, wherein we all increasingly consume and display the same thing. . . . That's the sad thing: that as uniformity becomes more and more what stores are selling—uniformity of presentation as well as uniformity of merchandise—a kind of high-level blandness begins to take over. . . . You begin to yearn for some off-note, something wrong, something even a bit vulgar, just to show individual sensibility.[20]

This passage reflects a feeling shared by many and one that is at the heart of this chapter and this book: Although not without enchanting qualities, the homogeneity of rationalized settings and their products seems to diminish our lives and leaves us craving some form of enchantment.

Control through the Substitution of Nonhuman for Human Technology

Because they are so closely linked, I combine the discussion of two elements of rationalization—increased control and the replacement of human by nonhuman technology. Replacement of human by nonhuman technology is often oriented toward greater control. The principal source of uncertainty and unpredictability in any rationalizing system is people—both the people who work within those systems and those who are served by them. McDonald's seeks to exert increasing control over both its employees and its customers. It is most likely to do this by steadily replacing people with nonhuman technologies. After all, technologies such as robots and computers are far easier to control. In addition to eliminating some people by replacing them, these nonhuman technologies also exert increasing control over the remaining human laborers and the people served by the system.

Wal-Mart's central distribution centers (there were forty-one of them in 1997) are fully automated. For example, there are enormous conveyor belts that move goods at 200 feet per second and allocate them to the proper location. Such technology removes control from the hands of human workers.[21]

Wal-Mart dove deeply into computer technology very early. Electronic cash registers were employed, and they generated point of sale data that could be used as the basis for automated decisions on replenishing store supplies. The computer system "logged every item sold at checkout counters, automatically kept warehouses informed of merchandise to be ordered, and directed the flow of goods not only to the stores but also even to the proper shelves."[22] When people were involved, it was most often to carry out the dictates of the technologies.

Wal-Mart also was an early user of bar codes and the Uniform Product Code (UPC) that, having been developed for supermarkets, was quickly seen as greatly relevant to Wal-Mart's business. By the end of the 1980s, UPC scanners were used throughout the Wal-Mart system, including its distribution centers. Scanners took the need to read certain information away from human beings and built it into the technology. The UPC also increased the efficiency with which customers could be processed through checkout lines and products reordered.

Laser scanners are used in the distribution centers, in the automated receiving in the stores themselves, as well as by stocking crews who use hand-held lasers to get the goods to the sales floor more quickly and efficiently. Similarly, employees use portable computers to automatically record relevant information on each product (e.g., inventory levels) and as an aid in the reordering process. Suppliers are able to respond quickly and accurately because they are directly supplied with relevant information as well as documents such as purchase orders and invoices. The company also has its own satellite system that facilitates communication within the Wal-Mart empire.

Borders Books employs a sophisticated computer inventory system and artificial intelligence technology to keep track of inventory. These technologies constantly adjust inventory on the basis of sales, eliminating certain titles and increasing the supply of others. There is, again, no longer any need for humans to make these decisions; the technologies do it for them.

The shopping mall can be seen as a technologically controlled kingdom with a variety of advanced technologies that control all aspects of its operation. Tight control is exercised over temperature, lighting, events, and merchandise. Time and space are controlled by making the malls windowless; there are few doors to beckon one outside; the uniformity of malls means they could be anywhere; in many cases there are no clocks; the maintenance and periodic remodeling make it seem as if the malls do not age; there is overall an unreal perfection about the malls.

Control is also exercised over customers. In this context, Kowinski discusses what he calls the "Zombie Effect," floating for hours in malls without an awareness of the passing of time. By inducing this state, malls make it likely that consumers will encounter many shops, see more goods and services, and purchase more of them. Malls control what we purchase not only by deciding what is included and excluded, but also by employing the principle of "adjacent attraction."[23] Through the latter, for example, mundane objects are made to seem more desirable by being surrounded with different and more exotic objects. Malls also manage the emotions of consumers by offering bright, cheery, and upbeat environments. "Controlling the emotions of customers is another natural aspect of the mall's basic control apparatus, which treats the consumer as an object to be lulled and manipulated."[24] Children are singled out for special attention on this count and are described as "growing up controlled."[25] Overall, Kowinski concluded, "Big Brother is managing you."[26] Even greater control is exerted over employees, who are described as "prisoners of the mall."[27]

The surveillance of consumers in the new means of consumption is integrally related to the ability to exercise control over them.[28] These settings are awash with surveillance cameras (and, increasingly, audio devices) and personnel on the alert for shoplifting and other crimes. However, all customers are watched; not just those deemed to be "suspicious." The people and machines that observe us are generally unseen and anonymous. Many settings are structured to maximize surveillance over our activities. The existence of electronic tags on many items allows us to be electronically "frisked" every time we leave a consumption site. Most of our dealings with these settings involve computers that yield data on us that can be used in various ways, especially to sell us other things. Transactions are frequently accomplished with credit (or debit) cards, leaving other sorts of information about us that can viewed and used by many others.

Luxury gated communities are also interesting from the point of view of surveillance and control over people.[29] Such structures have many of the trappings not only of a Weberian iron cage but also of total institutions such as prisons and asylums. Among the similarities are the rules and regulations governing individual behavior,[30] walls surrounding the communities, the guards at the gates around the clock, guard patrols, surveillance cameras, intruder alarms, and limitations on ingress and egress. Visitors are sometimes videotaped on arrival at the gates. The goal is to create "a nearly crime free bubble."[31] Although the barriers are there to prevent unwanted outsiders from gaining entry, they do place constraints on the "inmates" as well, the consumers of this way of life, who often find themselves on the video screen or the object of the gaze of security personnel.

In a sense, not only the gated community, but many of the new means of consumption, can be seen as elegant minimum security, albeit voluntary, prisons. Las Vegas casinos are heavily policed, and security cameras give personnel the ability to closely observe the activities of visitors to the casinos and guests in the hotels. The latter often must show their room keys to guards at the elevators in order to get to their rooms. Malls and mega-malls have similar means of observing and controlling consumers. Theme parks such as Disney World are notorious not only for their security efforts but also for their attempts to control both employees and visitors. Controls over employees tend to be blatant, but controls over visitors, though more subtle, are present nonetheless. For example, the parks and the attractions are structured to lead people to do certain kinds of things and not to do others. The paths are set up in such a way that people think they are making free choices when in fact they are generally moving in directions preordained by the designers. Another device to control visitors is the use of what Walt Disney called "wienies" to lead visitors in certain directions. Wienies are highly visible attractions (mountains, castles, and the like) to which virtually all visitors will find themselves drawn.

Disney parks, like the malls, are "preplanned, enclosed, protected, and controlled." Disney World is a triumph of nonhuman over human technology. The following description of the way most theme parks operate fits Disney World especially well:

> Thought and decisions are rarely necessary, because visitors are essentially batched through the various attractions. Each attraction is designed much like an assembly line, with long, regimented waiting lines leading to fixed cars or boats, which carry guests on an undeviating path through the event in a set period of time. Guests go in one end and out the other, having engaged in exactly the same sensual program as thousands or millions of other people.[32]

Nonhuman technology dominates not only the visitors, but also the human employees whose performances (through lip-synching, for example) and work (following scripts) are similarly controlled.

A major theoretical resource for those interested in surveillance and constraint on consumers (and many others) is the work of Michel Foucault. One of his well-known foci is the Panopticon, a structure that allows the complete observation of individuals. The most obvious example is a tower in the center of a circular prison from which guards can see into cells, but are themselves invisible to inmates. The Panopticon is a tremendous source of power because it gives prison officials the possibility of total surveillance. In such cases, officials need not always be present; the mere existence of the structure (and the possibility that officials might be there) constrains criminals. More important, its power is enhanced because prisoners come to control themselves; they stop themselves from doing various things because they fear that they *might* be seen by the guards. Foucault's ideas can be extended to the new means of consumption with his argument that the Panopticon becomes the base of "a whole type of society," the disciplinary society.[33] Although there may be no Panopticons per se in any of the new means of consumption, there are certainly many points (the video security room of a casino, the closed-circuit video surveillance at shopping malls[34]) at which both employees and customers may be observed, and that possibility of observation makes for control over both.

We can think of the new means of consumption as part of the "carceral archipelago" that has come to encompass the "entire social body."[35] Taken collectively and individually, the sites of these new means possess the ability to exert control over people throughout society. Although Foucault recognizes that there are forces operating against the carceral system (e.g., international processes that are beyond the control of any agency), his work leaves us with a sense that the carceral system has some of the characteristics of a Weberian iron cage.[36] Foucault focuses more on what he calls a micropolitics of power, which leads to a view that is more like an enormous number of mini cages in which our lives are more controlled and even more insufferable than they would be in a Weberian, society-wide iron cage.

At the most extreme end of the continuum of constraint is what Erving Goffman calls a "total institution"—that is, one that exerts near complete control over the people in it. Although Goffman has prisons and mental asylums in mind, his definition of a total institution could be applied to several new means of consumption, especially the cruise ship. A total institution is "a place of residence and work where a large number of like-situated individuals, cut off from the wider society for an appreciable period of time, together lead an enclosed, formally administered round of life."[37] Although sailors have already been examined from this perspective,[38] it also is possible to look at passengers in this way. Passengers are not nearly as constrained as members of the crew, to say nothing of inmates of prisons or mental institutions, but there is nonetheless significant constraint on them. They cannot leave the ship while at sea, they can only do what is available to them on board, and they can only consume when and what the ship offers.

Nonhuman technology not only controls people, in many cases it serves to eliminate them. Typically, this occurs as employees are rendered redundant by technological innovations that do their jobs more quickly and cheaply. For example, one of the home shopping networks uses a voice-response android to screen and process incoming calls; its studio cameras are electronically controlled and require no human personnel.[39] Technological change may also eliminate the physical presence of consumers. Peapod® is a service that allows customers to do their supermarket shopping on line. They can cruise virtual aisles comparing per unit costs, assessing the nutritional value of various foods, and using virtual coupons. Once an order is placed, Peapod's personal shoppers pick out the food. If goods are not in stock, or up to quality standards (e.g., the bananas are too ripe), the personal shoppers confer by telephone with the customers.[40]

Irrationality of Rationality

We can conceive of the irrationality of rationality in several ways. At the most general level, it is simply the overarching label for all of the negative aspects and effects of rationalization. More specifically, it can be seen as the paradoxical outcome of efforts to be completely rational. That is, rationalization can be viewed as leading to inefficiency, unpredictability, incalculability, and loss of control. The irrationality of rationality also means that rational systems are *unreasonable* systems.[41] That is, they serve to deny the basic humanity, the human reason, of the people who work within or are served by them. In other words, they are dehumanizing. This dehumanizing effect is related to another aspect of the irrationality of rationality, and the one of most concern in this context—the disenchantment of rational systems and, more generally, the society they come to dominate.

There are a number of ways in which the health and perhaps the lives of people have been threatened by progressive rationalization. One example is the high calorie, fat, cholesterol, salt, and sugar content of the food served in fast food restaurants. Such meals are the last things the vast majority of Americans (and Western Europeans) need. Many Americans already suffer from obesity, high cholesterol levels, high blood pressure, and diabetes. The kinds of meals typically offered at fast food restaurants only serve to worsen these problems. Even more worrisome, they help to create eating habits in children that contribute to the development of these, and other, health problems later in life. It can be argued that fast food restaurants are turning children into lifelong devotees of fast food, "addicted" to diets high in salt, sugar, and fat.

The fast food industry generates an enormous amount of trash, some of which is nonbiodegradable. Many people have been critical of the public eyesore created by litter from innumerable fast food meals strewn across the countryside. Even greater criticism has been leveled at the widespread production by the fast food industry of debris that piles up into mountainous landfills.

Rationalized institutions have a negative effect not only on our health and on the environment, but also on some of our most cherished institutions, most notably the family. For example, a key technology in the destruction of the family meal is the microwave oven and the vast array of microwavable foods it helped generate.

Another irrationality associated with rationalization is the possibility that we could lose control over the system so that it comes to control us. Already, many aspects of our lives are controlled by these rational systems, but at least it appears as though these systems are ultimately controlled by people. However, these rational systems can spin beyond the control of even the people at the top. Or these interlocking rational systems could fall into the hands of a small number of leaders who through them could exercise enormous control over all of society. There are authoritarian and totalitarian possibilities associated with the process of rationalization.

Virtually all of the means of consumption discussed in this book contribute to hyperconsumption. (For example, our supermarkets and supercenters are crammed with all sorts of foods that have disastrous effects on the health of many. Similarly, the stands throughout

Disney World purvey a wide range of junk food, Las Vegas casinos offer all-you-can eat buffets, and cruise ships compete to see which one can offer vacationers the most food.) In terms of family life, the best that can be said about the new means of consumption is that they give family members a chance to consume together.

There is no lack of irrationalities of rationality at Disney World. For example, in spite of its Herculean efforts, there are long lines and long waits; costs (for food, for countless Disney souvenirs hawked both in and out of the parks) mount up and often make what is supposed to be an inexpensive vacation highly costly. Most important, what is supposed to be a human vacation, turns at least for some into a nonhuman or even a dehumanizing experience as visitors are forced to deal with employees who relate to them by mindlessly reciting prearranged scripts.

An example of the irrationality of rationality at Wal-Mart is the ill-fated development of hypermarkets. Because bigger and bigger was working so well, Sam Walton concluded that this process was virtually limitless. Why not build hypermarkets that are infinitely larger than the typical supermarket? However, it turned out that there were limits. The stores were just too big. It took too much time to get around them; too much space had to be covered. According to one analyst, "In a hypermarket, by the time you've bought some aspirin, some Kleenex, and a bottle of milk, you could easily walk a mile."[42] Designed to increase efficiency, the hypermarkets actually made shopping less efficient for many consumers. This was especially true for the consumer who only needed a few items.

A good example of dehumanization in another of the new means of consumption is found in the new and increasingly popular "virtual universities." Here is a paradoxical statement from one student in such a program:

> I worried that a professor would be just this faceless entity out there I couldn't relate to. . . . But in the online class I have now, I feel like I know him, even though we haven't met. He could walk right by me on the street.[43]

LINKING RATIONALIZATION
TO DISENCHANTMENT

As we saw in the preceding chapter, the process of rationalization leads, by definition, to the disenchantment of the settings in which it occurs. The term clearly implies the loss of a quality—enchantment— that was at one time very important to people. Although we undoubt-edly have gained much from the rationalization of society in general, and the means of consumption in particular, we also have lost some-thing of great, if hard to define, value.

Efficient systems have no room for anything smacking of enchant-ment and systematically seek to root it out of all aspects of their operation. Anything that is magical, mysterious, fantastic, dreamy, and so on is apt to be inefficient. Enchanted systems typically involve highly convoluted means to whatever end is involved. Furthermore, enchanted worlds may well exist without any obvious goals at all. Efficient systems, also by definition, do not permit such meanderings, and designers and implementers will do whatever is necessary to eliminate them. The elimination of meanderings and aimlessness is one of the reasons that rationalized systems were, for Weber, disen-chanted systems.

As we saw earlier, one major aspect of efficiency is using the customer as an unpaid worker. It is worth noting that all of the mystery associated with an operation is removed when consumers perform it themselves; after all, they know exactly what they did. Mystery is far more likely when others perform such tasks, and consumers are unable to see precisely what they do. What transpires in the closed kitchen of a gourmet restaurant is far more mysterious than the "cooking" that takes place in the open kitchen of a fast food restaurant, to say nothing of the tasks consumers perform in such settings.

The same point applies to employees of rationalized systems. Their work is broken down into a series of steps, the best way to perform each step is discovered, and then all workers are taught to perform each step in that way. There is no mystery in any of this for the employee, who more or less unthinkingly follows the dictates of the organization. There is little or no room for any creative problem solving on the job, much less any sense of enchantment.

Compare the efficient and mechanical preparation and consumption of food in the fast food restaurant to the way food was cooked and eaten in the novel (and later movie), *Like Water for Chocolate*. Food was prepared lovingly over a long period of time:

> On Mama Elena's ranch, sausage making was a real ritual. The day before, they started peeling the garlic, cleaning the chiles, and grinding spices. All the women in the family had to participate. . . . They gathered around the dining-room table in the afternoon, and between the talking and the joking the time flew by until it started to get dark."[44]

And the eating of the food had a magical effect on those who participated in the meal:

> The moment they took their first bite of cake, everyone was flooded with a great wave of longing. Even Pedro, usually so proper, was having trouble holding back his tears. Mama Elena, who hadn't shed a single tear over her husband's death, was sobbing silently. But the weeping was just the first symptom of a strange intoxication—an acute attack of pain and frustration—that seized the guests . . . [45]

Or,

> tasting these chiles in walnut sauce, they all experienced a sensation. . . . Gertrudis . . . immediately recognized the heat in her limbs, the tickling sensation in the center of her body, the naughty thoughts. . . . Then she left. . . . All the other guests quickly made their excuses, coming up with one pretext or another, throwing heated looks at each other. . . . The newlyweds were secretly delighted since this left them free to grab their suitcases and get away as soon as possible. They needed to get to the hotel . . .
>   . . . Everyone else, including the ranch hands, was making mad passionate love, wherever they happened to end up.[46]

With regard to *calculability*, in the main, enchantment has far more to do with quality than quantity.[47] Magic, fantasies, dreams, and the like relate more to the inherent nature of an experience and the qualitative aspects of that experience, than, for example, to the number of such experiences one has. An emphasis on producing and participating in a large number of experiences tends to diminish the magical quality of each of them. Put another way, it is difficult to imagine the mass production of magic, fantasy, and dreams. Such mass production may be common in the movies, but magic is more difficult, if not impossible, to produce in settings designed to deliver large numbers of goods and services frequently and over great geographic spaces. The mass production of such things is virtually guaranteed to undermine their enchanted qualities. This is a fundamental dilemma facing the new means of consumption.

Take, for example, the shows that are put on over and over by the various new means of consumption—the "Beauty and the Beast" show at Disney World, the sea battle in front of the Treasure Island casino–hotel in Las Vegas, or the night club shows on cruise ships. The fact that they must be performed over and over tends to turn them into highly mechanical performances in which whatever "magic" they produce stems from the size of the spectacle and the technologies associated with them rather than the quality of the performers and their performances.

In any case, it could be argued that by its very nature fantasy has more to do with the consumer than with the means of consumption. Huxtable, for example, has defined fantasy as a "freeing of the mind and the spirit to explore unknown places," which she distinguishes from, for example, "a handshake from some unconvincingly costumed actors in a totally predictable and humdrum context."[48] There are inherent limitations on the ability of rationalized settings to create fantasy for people.

No characteristic of rationalization is more inimical to enchantment than *predictability*. Magical, fantastic, or dream-like experiences are almost by definition unpredictable. Nothing would destroy an enchanted experience more easily than having it become predictable.

The Disney theme parks sought to eliminate the unpredictability of the midway at an old-fashioned amusement park such as Coney Island with its milling crowds, disorder, and debris. Instead, Disney World built a setting defined by cleanliness, orderliness, predictability, and—some would say—sterility. Disney has successfully destroyed the old form of enchantment and in its place created a new, highly predictable form of entertainment. As the many fans of Disney World will attest, there is enchantment there, but it is a very different, mass-produced, assembly-line form, consciously fabricated and routinely produced over and over rather than emerging spontaneously from the interaction among visitors, employees, and the park itself.

A similar point could be made about the "new" Las Vegas. In the "bad old days" when it was run by the "mob," it was a much less predictable place and therefore, arguably, a far more enchanted one than it is today under the control of large corporations and their bureaucratic employees. What is true about Disney World and Las Vegas also can be said about fast food restaurants, cruises, and so on.

Both *control* and the *nonhuman technologies* that produce it tend to be inimical to enchantment. As a general rule, fantasy, magic, and dreams cannot be subjected to external controls; indeed, autonomy is much of what gives them their enchanted quality. Fantastic experiences can go anywhere; anything can happen. Such unpredictability clearly is not possible in a tightly controlled environment. It is possible that tight and total control can be a fantasy, but for many it would be more a nightmare than a dream. Much the same can be said of nonhuman technologies. Such cold, mechanical systems are usually the antitheses of the dream worlds associated with enchantment. Again, it is true that there are fantasies associated with nonhuman technologies, but they too tend to be more nightmarish than dream-like.

An interesting example of the replacement of human with non-human technology is currently taking place in Las Vegas. Shows in the old casino–hotels used to feature major stars such as Frank Sinatra and Elvis Presley. One could argue that such stars had charisma; they had an enchanted relationship with their fans. Now the emphasis has shifted to huge, tightly choreographed (i.e., predictable) extravaganzas without individual stars. For example, the Rio Hotel and Casino features "ballet dancers who bounce, toes pointed, from bungee cords, hooked to the casino ceiling . . . [and] a mechanical dolphin that dives from aloft with a rider playing Lady Godiva."[49] The focus is on the nonhuman technology (which controls the performers) and not on the individuals performing the acts. The performers in such extravaganzas are easily replaceable; they are interchangeable parts.

The point of this section has been to argue that increasing rationalization is related to, if not inextricably intertwined with, disenchantment. However, as we shall see, there are aspects of rationalization that actually heighten enchantment.

RATIONALIZATION AS ENCHANTMENT

There is no question that although rationalized systems lead in various ways to disenchantment, they paradoxically and simultaneously serve to create their own kinds of enchantment. We should bear in mind that this enchantment varies in terms of time and place. Because these settings are now commonplace to most of the readers of this book, few of them (especially fast food restaurants) are likely to be thought of as enchanting. However, it should be remembered that they still enchant children, as they did us for some time (and, in many cases, may still); it is certainly the case that they enchanted our parents and grandparents; and they are found enchanting in other societies to which they are newly exported. It is also worth remembering that there are degrees of enchantment; Disney World and Las Vegas are undoubtedly seen by most as more enchanting than Wal-Mart and the Sears catalog.

Reflect for a moment on the highly rationalized, and therefore presumably disenchanted, setting of Sam's Club and other warehouse stores. What could be more disenchanting than stores built to look like warehouses—comparatively cold, spare, and inelegant? Compare them to the "dream worlds" of early department stores like Bon

Marché. Great effort was made to make the latter warm, well-appointed, and elegant settings that helped enflame the consumer's fantasies—in a word, enchanting. Sam's Club has gone to great lengths in the opposite direction; it seems to have sought to create as rationalized and disenchanted a setting as possible. It comes strikingly close, in the realm of retailing, to Weber's image of the rational cage.

Yet this disenchanted structure produces another kind of fantasy —that of finding oneself set loose in a warehouse piled to the ceiling with goods that, if they are not free, are made out to be great bargains. It is a cold, utilitarian fantasy, but a fantasy nonetheless. As a general rule, disenchanted structures have not eliminated fantasies, but rather replaced older fantasies with more contemporary ones. The new, rationalized fantasies involve getting a lot of things at low prices rather than the fantasies associated with the older department stores that might involve imagining what it would be like to wear elegant clothing or to surround one's self with luxurious home furnishings.

People often marvel at the *efficiency* of rationalized systems; their ability to manage things so effectively can seem quite magical. For example, the ability of Disney World to process so many of us through the park, or to dispose of all the trash we produce, is a source of amazement to many people.

As we saw in the example of Sam's Club, rationalized systems also often amaze on the basis of the large *quantity* of things they can deliver at what appears to be such a low cost. The cruise is another good example of this, especially the food that is available in great abundance and with great frequency and the bundling of lots of entertainment into one package: casino, spa, nightclub, visits to islands, and so on. Similarly, the continual expansion of Disney World makes it seem increasingly like a world that offers unlimited possibilities for entertainment.

The *predictability* of the new means of consumption can be astounding. This can range anywhere from amazement that the "Big Mac" we ate today in New York is identical to the one we ate last week in London and will eat next week in Tokyo to being struck by the fact that today's sea battle at Treasure Island casino is identical to the one we saw on our last trip to Las Vegas.

Perhaps the ultimate in the capacity of the rationalization of the new means of consumption to enchant us comes from their advanced *technologies*. Although at one time enchantment stemmed from human wizards or magicians, it now stems from the wizardry of modern robotic and computerized technology. Ultimately, it is the technology of the modern cruise line, the Las Vegas casino, and Disney World that astounds us, not the humans who happen to work in these settings or the things they do.[50] Our amazement can stem from the technologies themselves or from what they produce. We can, for example, marvel over how McDonald's french fries always look and taste the same. Or we can be impressed by the fact that Wal-Mart's shelves are always so well-stocked.

It is interesting that EPCOT Center in Disney World has run into difficulties in recent years, at least in part because its futuristic technologies have grown increasingly dated. It became more difficult for visitors to fantasize about the future in such obviously dated settings. As a result, EPCOT is undergoing a transformation and moving in the direction of becoming more like a conventional theme park.

Are the contemporary fantasies associated with rational systems as satisfying as those conjured up in the past? This is a complex and highly controversial issue. Clearly, the huge number of people who flock to the new means of consumption find them quite magical. However, it is fair to wonder whether rationally produced enchantment is truly enchanting or whether it is as enchanting as the less rational, more human, forms of enchantment that it tends to squeeze out. We might ask whether one of the *irrational* consequences of all of this is that these contemporary fantasies come closer to nightmares than did their predecessors. After all, it is far harder to think of a nightmare associated with an elegant department store than with a warehouse. In any case, it is clear that rationally produced enchantment is deemed insufficient as reflected in the many efforts at reenchantment that are the subject of the next two chapters.

CONCLUSION

This chapter has made three related points: First, the cathedrals of consumption can be described as being highly rationalized; second, rationalization leads to disenchantment; third, rational means of consumption can themselves have enchanting qualities inherent in their rationalized natures. In spite of the latter, the central problems confronting the cathedrals of consumption remain rationalization and the disenchantment engendered by it.

5

REENCHANTMENT: CREATING SPECTACLE THROUGH EXTRAVAGANZAS AND SIMULATIONS

The cathedrals of consumption must be reenchanted if they are to maintain their ability to attract a sufficient number of consumers. Without large numbers of consumers, the mechanisms oriented to control and exploitation will not yield the desired profits. In this chapter and the next I examine some of the ways in which reenchantment occurs. Spectacle, which I define as a dramatic public display, is key. Spectacles may be created intentionally (these will be called *extravaganzas),* or, as we will see, they may be partially or wholly unintentional.

The basic premise behind this chapter and the next is that it is not enough to simply open a shop, a mall, a theme park, or a casino and wait for the customers to arrive.[1] As a representative of one chain put it: "You've got to romance the product . . . You can't pile it high and watch it fly. You've got to give something extra."[2]

SPECTACLE

The reenchantment of the cathedrals of consumption depends on their growing increasingly spectacular.[3] Spectacle itself is not new; it has been used throughout history to accomplish all sorts of objectives. Fairs, expositions, and the like are early examples of the use of spectacles to sell commodities. In fact, spectacle lay at the base of the success of one of the most important and immediate precursors of the new means of consumption: the department store. For example, of the French department store Bon Marché of the mid-1800s, Miller said, "Spectacle and entertainment, on the one hand, the world of consumption, on the other, were now truly indistinguishable."[4] The early American department stores used color, glass, light, art, shop windows, elegant interiors, seasonal displays, and even Christmas parades in order to create a spectacle.[5] Similarly, at the turn of the twentieth century Coney Island relied heavily on the creation of spectacle to attract visitors. Over the years, the bar has been raised progressively, with the result that the display needs to be bigger and bigger in order to work. Furthermore, spectacles are no longer isolated events, spatially and temporally, but are increasingly ubiquitous.

The concept of the spectacle lies at the core of thinking of the French social thinker, Guy Debord and his influential work, *The Society of the Spectacle.*[6] Debord said "the spectacle is the *chief product* of present-day society."[7] Central to the argument of his book, Debord argues that one of the functions of the spectacle is to obscure and conceal "the rationality of the system."[8] I contend that the spectacle is used to overcome the liabilities, especially the disenchantment, associated with highly rationalized systems. Debord has argued that the spectacle associated with commodities is a kind of opiate that obscures the true operation of society (including its rationality). It also serves to conceal the fact that the goods and services purchased are ultimately dissatisfying.

The spectacle is closely linked in Debord's eyes to consumerism and commodities: "THE WORLD THE SPECTACLE holds up to view is . . . the world of commodity ruling over all lived experience."[9] Commodities and the spectacles that surround them have come to dominate not only the economy, but also the entire society. As a result, to Marx's alienated production it is necessary to add alienated consumption as a necessity imposed on the masses. That is, consumption is imposed from without and people are unable to express themselves in the process of consumption, or in the goods and services they obtain through it. Ultimately, Debord sees the emergence of a "society of the spectacle, where commodity contemplates itself in a world of its own making."[10] People, as spectators, are not part of these contemporary spectacles; indeed they are alienated from them. People watch them because they are alluring, but the spectacles are put on *for* them; people are not an integral part *of* them.

David Chaney has done much to clarify the meaning of the spectacle by differentiating between two related but very different cultural orders: the early modern "spectacular society" and today's "society of the spectacle."[11]

In the past, spectacle tended to be an integral part of, and emerged from, everyday life (e.g., a county fair). In contrast, in the contemporary society of the spectacle, drama is not an inherent part of everyday life. Rather, we travel to a Disney World where, far from our homes, we participate in various attractions in ways that are largely predetermined by the park's designers and not at all connected to our lives.

In addition, in the spectacular society, there were possibilities of excess and at least limited transgression (the "carnivalesque"[12]). An example might be illicit sexual relations in public. In the society of the spectacle, transgressions are likely to be systematically prevented from occurring by the control over, and close surveillance of, the spectators. Many of the spectacles that will concern us have been systematically sanitized by those who create and control them.

Although these differences are important, we must not take them too far. It is impossible to draw absolute distinctions between past and present spectacles,[13] to say nothing of the cathedrals of consumption in which they occur. Although Mardi Gras (and Carnaval in Rio de Janiero) have ancient roots, they continue today and they retain elements of transgression (for example, women showing their bare breasts in response to chants from the crowd). And transgression continues to occur in contemporary cathedrals of consumption, ranging from the mundane such as brawls in the stands of modern athletic stadia to the extraordinary periodic massacres that plague fast food restaurants.

We should bear in mind that the new means of consumption create spectacles[14] not as ends in themselves but in order to bring in large numbers of people to buy more goods and services.[15] A mall, a casino, or a theme park that is empty, or only half full, not only has a smaller population to sell to but also does not generate the same excitement as a full house. Sparsely populated cathedrals of consumption generate less word of mouth appeal and are apt to fail as a result. People seem to be animated by the presence of large numbers of other people and that animation could translate into increased sales of goods and services.[16]

EXTRAVAGANZAS

There are obviously many different ways of producing a spectacle, but the most obvious is simply intentionally to put on a show, an extravaganza. This is nowhere clearer than in Las Vegas and in its casino–hotels. There are the shows themselves at the big casino–hotels, which seek to distinguish themselves by being more spectacular than the ones next door. A variety of devices are used to create a spectacular show—legendary stars (more common in the past), huge casts, large orchestras, elaborate production numbers, live animals, blinding light shows, booming sound, ostentatious sets, breathtaking technology, incredible costumes and daring nudity, and so on. Notable in Las Vegas at the end of 1998 were Cirque du Soleil's "Mystère" (an avant-garde circus) at Treasure Island and Siegfried and Roy and their white tigers at the Mirage.

The exteriors of the casino–hotels are incredible shows in their own right. The Luxor sports the largest pyramid in the world, as well as a monolith and a replica of the sphinx. Excalibur is designed to look like an enormous medieval castle. New York, New York offers an image of the New York skyline with a roller coaster, complete with screaming riders, weaving around the skyscrapers and even the casino itself. In addition, there is a 150-foot replica of the Statue of Liberty. The soon-to-be completed Paris casino–hotel will include a fifty-story Eiffel Tower built to half the scale of the original and a copy of the Arc de Triomphe at the front of the property. Stratosphere is the highest tower in town, in fact the highest west of the Mississippi. A volcano erupts periodically at the Mirage. A pitched sea battle, complete with the sinking of a British ship by a pirate ship, occurs several times a day outside Treasure Island. Of course, the entire Las Vegas strip, with its enormous neon signs and displays, is a spectacular show. The downtown Fremont Street casinos were in danger of being overwhelmed by the strip and its spectacular shows in the mid-1990s. To resolve this problem, several blocks of Fremont Street were covered over by a 100-foot high electric canopy that created an enclosed pedestrian mall and spectacular light and sound shows (the Fremont Street Experience) that play themselves out on the canopy for seven minutes on the hour.

The Las Vegas strip can be seen as the world's largest and most spectacular carnival midway. Owners of each casino–hotel must decide how they are going to get visitors to enter their attraction rather than some other. The answer, of course, is that they have to build increasingly spectacular exteriors and put on more and more incredible shows out front. As one well-known Las Vegas entrepreneur puts it, "You've got to get people wondering if what's inside is as wacky as the outside."[17] (Virtually all of the external shows last only a few minutes so that those who take the time to see them will still have plenty of time to gamble before the next show.)

In fact, the entire casino industry in Las Vegas is driven by the need to be collectively spectacular enough to continue to attract visitors to the city. Legal gambling is spreading throughout the country —Atlantic City; Tunica County; Mississippi riverboats; the New Orleans river front; an increasing number of Indian reservations—and gamblers need a powerful reason to travel all the way to Las Vegas. Also posing a threat to Las Vegas is the growth of on-line gambling. To continue to attract large crowds, "the most over-the-top city in America has been forced to become more sensational."[18] And this need can do nothing but accelerate in the coming years, producing even more spectacular extravaganzas both inside and outside the casino–hotels.

Not to be outdone, the interior structures of the casino–hotels are incredible shows, almost as spectacular as the exteriors. For example, the interior of the Luxor pyramid is a vast open space surrounded on all sides by corridors that lead to guest rooms. Each floor grows smaller with fewer and fewer rooms as one ascends (in glass-enclosed "inclinators") toward the peak of the pyramid. Inside the Mirage one encounters a fifty-foot aquarium (with sharks and exotic fish) behind the registration desk, a 1.5 million gallon dolphin habitat, and the "Secret Garden"—a zoo with rare and exotic animals, including white tigers. "Masquerade Village," which is part of the Rio Hotel and Casino, has a twelve-minute show featuring five Mardi Gras floats (with live performers) suspended from the ceiling.

The scenes in the casinos, on the strip, and on Fremont Street are themselves incredible shows. The large number of people wagering huge sums of money in the casinos is one type of spectacle. The wide range of people in the hotels and in the various shows, bars, and restaurants is another. Yet another is the swarm of people parading up and down the Strip or appearing on Fremont Street to view the light shows.

Las Vegas and its casino–hotels represent the ultimate extravaganza, but other means of consumption have sought to learn from Las Vegas (one could speak of the "Las Vegasizing of America," the process by which "American culture is being transformed into one long and uninterrupted show business act"[19]), in developing their own spectacles to attract and keep customers.

As mentioned previously, the most obvious example is Dave and Buster's, one of whose cofounders was a former Las Vegas blackjack dealer. The attractions at a Dave and Buster's arcade include "Dactyl Nightmare," a virtual reality game involving the zapping of flying dinosaurs, a virtual driving range for golfers, an Alpine skiing video game, gunfights against laser-activated desperados, and the "Million Dollar Midway" that includes computerized casino games.[20]

Sega World® has sought to compress the theme park into a single building and to duplicate it in various locales. The Sega World in Sydney, Australia, for example, offers more than 200 games, nine rides, a food court, live entertainment, and a retail store. There are three themed "worlds." The Past includes a subterranean roller coaster on which riders are able to put out a fire with an infrared water cannon. The Present features the "Visionarium" with 360-degree images provided by nine screens. The Future has, among other things, rides that take the visitor underwater and into the belly of a shark, a futuristic "dodgem" car ride, and a virtual reality spaceship ride.

Theme restaurant chains are obviously in the business of putting on extravaganzas for their customers. One can imagine one's self in the rock world in the Hard Rock Cafe and in the Hollywood scene in Planet Hollywood. If you want to imagine yourself in a tropical rainforest, Rainforest Cafe features "cascading waterfalls, tropical rain showers, simulated thunder and lighting, and live tropical birds . . . animated talking trees, butterflies, and crocodiles."[21] Not to mention the retail area selling products with animal themes and sporting the Rainforest Cafe logo.

As for more mundane new means of consumption, we can look to fast food restaurants. Though hardly spectacular now to jaded American consumers, they are all about extravaganza with vibrant colors, playgrounds, and so forth:

> The competition among fast-food giants has always been as much about appearances as reality—a lot, in fact, like a three-ring circus, with ever new, ever more flashy show stoppers needed to keep the crowds coming into the tent. Toy giveaways, movie tie-ins, glitzy ad campaigns and new food products have all done the job.[22]

In the retail business the increasing need to put on an extravaganza is known as "retailtainment" or "entertainment retailing," which involves the "use of ambience, emotion, sound and activity to get customers interested in the merchandise and in a mood to buy."[23] For example, take the "show" at the superstore Niketown® in New York City:

> Niketown's facade is a takeoff on an old New York high-school building. You enter through turnstiles, in the manner of a sports arena, to find yourself in a sleek, futuristic, five-story atrium into which, at 30-minute intervals, a three-story-high screen descends and a video softly plugging Nike products is played along with a crescendo of recorded music. There are displays of sports memorabilia and a chance to hit a punching bag . . . the merchandise is secondary to the experience of being in this store, an experience that bears more than a passing resemblance to a visit to a theme park. Niketown is a fantasy environment, one part nostalgia to two parts high tech, and it exists to bedazzle the consumer, to give its merchandise sex appeal and establish Nike as the essence not just of athletic wear but also of our culture and way of life.[24]

Bass® Pro Shops Outdoor World stores include such things as indoor waterfalls, archery ranges, shooting ranges, and outdoor decks where fly fishermen can try out their casts. Then there is the flagship store of Recreational Equipment (REI)® in Seattle with its "nearly 100,000-square-foot, warehouselike structure that contains a sixty-five-foot-high freestanding artificial rock for climbing, a glass-enclosed wet stall for testing rain gear, a vented area for testing camp stoves and an outdoor trail for mountain-biking."[25] These elaborate new settings seem to work. The new 31,000-square-foot Sneaker Stadium® in Paramus, New Jersey, takes in 3.5 times the revenue per square foot of an average mall sneaker outlet.[26]

What about book superstores? Surely these are places for serious people to do serious browsing and purchasing. Unless, of course, they are one of the modern super bookstores such as Borders. Such a superstore has become much more than simply a place to purchase books:

> It's a place to meet, eat, drink, romance, discuss, *dream* [italics added], read, write or just hang out. A safe, smoke-free gathering place for kids, teenagers, singles, couples, moms, dads, grandparents and rebels with laptops. There are book groups, discussion groups, support groups. There are speakers, writers, storytellers, musicians and chefs. Breakfast, lunch, dinner. Coffee, juice and milk.[27]

Although obviously sold in large numbers, the books themselves seem little more than the backdrop for this new center of fun. "It's almost like a library. . . . But at a library you can't talk, can't eat, can't drink, you can't laugh and carry on and have fun."[28] For some it is just another spectacular place to while away the hours, merely an alternative to an adult game center such as Dave and Buster's. Those who tire of the electronic games and the alcohol at the latter can amble on over to Borders for quieter, more linear variety of fun. It's yet another alternative setting for people to go, "hang out," and have a good time. Unlike many of the others, there is no entry charge and very little pressure to actually buy anything. But though many do just go to hang, many others buy enough to sustain the book superstores and their enormous expansion. One customer who belongs to several book clubs at Borders spends about $3,000 a year on books. Why? "It's entertainment."[29]

One observer sees this phenomenon of putting on a spectacular show as increasingly true for many kinds of stores:

> Retailers are working to make stores provide something that catalogues, the Internet and home shopping cannot—the thrill of an event. Make it

spectacular enough and they will come. In a culture that is starved for public experiences and that increasingly consumes entertainment in private, stores are functioning more and more as an escape from the personal space of computers and VCRs. Stores entice us into their versions of a public realm, offering a Faustian bargain: step into our commercial world and we will give you the kind of communal excitement that it's hard to find this side of Disneyland. . . . What happened? Put simply, retailers came back by figuring out how to compete with other forms of selling. Instead of convenience, they had to give shoppers the one experience that technology could not replace—indeed, the experience that technology almost eliminated in our time. That is, to give the pleasure of physically being somewhere, of going to a place that was bigger, grander and in every way more exhilarating and more energizing than anything the customer could experience at home.[30]

The spectacular new means of consumption are, in turn, forcing other attractions to become more of an extravaganza. There is a move afoot to make skyscrapers more spectacular. The Empire State Building and the panoramic view available on its observation deck are no longer spectacular enough in themselves. The "New York Skyride" (sponsored by JVC) was added, "a theme-park-style simulated space shuttle flight . . . visitors watch from movie-theater seats that jolt and shake as the shuttle zooms over the Brooklyn Bridge, around the Statue of Liberty and along the hair-raising track of Coney Island's roller coaster."[31] At this point in the book it probably goes without saying that there is a gift shop adjacent to "New York Skyride."

CREATING SPECTACLES WITH SIMULATIONS

Implicit in the preceding section is the use of simulations to create spectacular fantasy worlds. However, the idea of simulations is so pivotal to understanding the enchanting aspects of the cathedrals of consumption that it must be discussed separately. In fact, if I had to choose only one term to catch the essence of the new means of consumption, as well as their capacity to create enchanting spectacles, it would be *simulations*.

The Age of Simulation

Baudrillard has argued that we live in "the age of simulation."[32] This implies that we have left behind a more genuine, more authentic social world. Examples of simulation proffered by Baudrillard include

- ◆ the primitive people the Tasaday, found in the Philippines. At least as it exists today, the Tasaday is a simulation because the tribe has been "frozen, cryogenized, sterilized, protected *to death*."[33] It may at one time have been a "real" primitive group, but today what exists is nothing more than an approximation of what it once was.
- ◆ the caves of Lescaux in France. The actual caves have been closed, but an exact replica, a simulation, is now open to the public.
- ◆ Disneyland. Baudrillard sees it as "a perfect model of all the entangled orders of simulation,"[34] One of Disney's classic attractions,[35] the simulated submarine ride to which people flocked in order to see simulated undersea life, is a good example. Many more went there than to the more "genuine" aquarium just down the road (itself, however, a simulation of the not-too-distant sea).

The widespread existence of such simulations, in the world of consumption and elsewhere, contributes enormously to the erosion of the distinction between the real and the imaginary; between the true and the false. Every contemporary structure and event is at best a combination of the real and the imaginary. In fact, to Baudrillard, the true and the real have disappeared in an avalanche of simulations.

Las Vegas casino–hotels have a field day with the line between reality and unreality. The Bellagio, which opened in late 1998, is a simulation of the Italian region of the same name, but it also houses $260 million in original fine art by such masters as Renoir, Cézanne, and Picasso. At about the same time, the Rio casino–hotel began hosting a six-month exhibit of treasures from Russia's Romanov Dynasty. It includes Peter the Great's throne and a Fabergé pen used by Czar Nicholas to abdicate in 1917. These authentic artifacts are housed in a replica of the Russian royal galleries including "a reproduction neogothic ceiling from high density foam." King Tut's tomb in the Luxor hotel is called a "museum" even though everything in it is a reproduction. However, its gift shop sells "genuine ancient coins, 18th century Egyptian engravings, oil lamps and other artifacts." Said an art critic, "The museum had all fakes, and the gift shop had the real thing. It just summed up Las Vegas for me."[36]

Huxtable, following Umberto Eco (and Baudrillard), argues that the "unreal has become the reality. . . . The real now imitates the imitation."[37] For example, the clearly simulated and unreal Disney World has become the model not only for Disney's town of Celebration, but many other communities throughout the United States. Seaside, Florida, and Kentlands, Maryland, are two examples of popular communities that have tried to emulate the ersatz small-town America that is championed by Disney World. Specifically, Huxtable has emphasized the growing importance of fake, synthetic, artificial, simulated architecture: "Real architecture has little place in the unreal America."[38]

Our environment has come to be dominated by entertainment and to emulate the theme park. Huxtable's architectural model of this is the casino, New York, New York, and more generally Las Vegas: "the real fake reaches it apogee in places like Las Vegas. . . . The outrageously fake fake has developed its own indigenous style and life style to become a real place . . . this is the real, real fake at the highest, loudest and most authentically inauthentic level of illusion and invention."[39] Huxtable has argued that visitors seem to find things such as the artificial rainforests, volcanos, and rock formations in Las Vegas far more impressive than the real thing. In fact, a spokesperson for the industry goes so far as to make the case *against* reality: "You get a very artificial appearance with real rock."[40]

All of our environments are becoming increasingly spurious; Las Vegas is simply the extreme that defines the entire genre of simulated environments, especially those characterized by "unreal" architecture. This is of great relevance because many of the new means of consumption are architectural spaces. In fact, Huxtable has examined several of the new means of consumption from this perspective. Among other settings scrutinized by Huxtable are Colonial Williamsburg (created in the 1920s, a forerunner and another model for

Disney World and other settings), Disneyland as faux Americana ("expertly engineered, standardized mediocrity, endlessly, shamelessly consumerized, a giant shill operation with a Mickey Mouse facade"[41]), Edmonton Mall with among other things its replica of Columbus's *Santa Maria* ("fantasy run amok"[42]), and so on.

Simulated People

Not only are the new means of consumption simulations, but often so are the people who work in them and the interactions that take place between employees and visitors. The most blatant examples of simulated "people" are the employees who dress up in a variety of costumes. McDonald's Ronald McDonald is obviously a simulated clown. The same is true of the characters—Mickey Mouse, Pluto, Snow White—that one encounters wandering the grounds of Disney World. Then there are the sports mascots such as the San Diego Chicken and the Baltimore Orioles' Bird.

Far more important, however, is the fact that most of the people we encounter in the new means of consumption are simulations, even if they are not wearing costumes. The entertainment director of the cruise ship, the blackjack dealer at a Las Vegas casino, the ticket taker at Disney World, the host on HSN, the counterperson at McDonald's, and the cashier at Wal-Mart are all playing well-defined roles. Their employing organizations have developed a series of guidelines about how they are supposed to look, speak, behave, and so forth. The result is that these positions can be filled by a wide range of individuals. There is little or no room for creativity or individuality. It could be argued that the blackjack dealer and the counterperson are simulations—they are fakes.

As a result of the same dynamic, the interaction that takes place between visitor and employee in a new means of consumption has a simulated character. For example, instead of "real" human interaction with servers in fast food restaurants, with clerks in shopping malls and superstores, with telemarketers, and so on, we can think of these as simulated interactions. Employees follow scripts,[43] and customers counter with recipe responses (that is, those routine responses they have developed over time to deal with such scripted behavior),[44] with the result that authentic interaction rarely, if ever, takes place. In fact, so many of our interactions in these settings (and out) are simulated, and we become so accustomed to them, that we lose a sense of "real" interaction. In the end, all we have are the simulated interactions. In fact, the entire distinction between the simulated and the real is lost; simulated interaction *is* the reality.

Nowhere is this type of simulated interaction more obvious, or more inevitable, than in our dealings with hosts of home shopping television programs. A typical "interaction" on the part of one of those hosts: "Thank you so, so, so much for calling in today. . . . We took a risk and brought some new items. You responded with an outpouring of support—and we love you for it."[45] Did they really take a risk? Do they really love every member of their audience? All of this taking place in the medium that best exemplifies simulation: television!

Simulations and the New Means of Consumption

Clearly, the new means of consumption contain a variety of simulations. There is little that is "real" about them. Even when real elements remain, there is an almost irresistible compulsion to alter them so that they, too, become simulations. There are undoubtedly many reasons why there is a drive to replace reality with simulations as quickly and completely as possible. It is far easier, for example, to control simulated than real environments. Take Baudrillard's example of the simulated caves at Lescaux. It is much easier to restructure the simulated cave (in the case of danger to visitors) than it is the original cave, which one would feel constrained to alter as little as possible. It also is easier to repair the simulation than the original that, in a sense, is not repairable. In fact, once one begins altering the caves, one has begun turning them into simulations. This is a very important point: Most "real" settings have been so altered to accommodate visitors that they already are simulations (see, for example, the Disneyesque re-invention of Times Square in New York discussed previously and the later discussion of underwater reefs). This buttresses Baudrillard's point that there is no more reality; all is simulation.

Perhaps the most important reason for creating simulations, or transforming "real" phenomena into simulations, is that they can be made more spectacular than their authentic counterparts and, therefore, a greater lure to consumers. Take the example of Las Vegas again: Where else can you find New York City, Monte Carlo, Bellagio, Venice, and Paris within a few minutes walk of one another? Even if you went to one of those "real" cities, you would be able to experience only it and not the others. In any case, the tourist areas of those cities have themselves become simulations.

Why do so many of us increasingly find simulated settings to be more spectacular than what remains of the real world? For example, although Las Vegas draws throngs of visitors, the natural spectacle of Death Valley a few hundred miles away attracts only a fraction of that number; few who go to Las Vegas bother to take the drive to Death Valley. The stillness, the parched earth, and the great sweep of nothingness simply cannot compete with the noise, the glitter, and the vast expanse of neon that is Las Vegas. For a society raised on the movies, television, video games, and computer imagery, Death Valley can seem dull and uninteresting. The glitter of Las Vegas fits better with the desires and interests of this generation. If some Vegas entrepreneur were to erect a new themed casino named "Death Valley," it might well be a great success.

Simulations lie at the heart of the fast food industry. The foods— the hamburgers, the pizza, the tacos—may be very good simulations of others of their genre, but they are poor copies of their ancestors, bearing only the faintest resemblance to homemade hamburgers, pizzeria pizzas, and roadside-stand tacos. In fact, such "real" food, if it ever existed, has largely disappeared under an avalanche of simulations. Today, to most Americans under the age of thirty or forty, the McDonald's burger is the "real" burger. One who wants to unmask these simulations for what they are runs the risk of discovering that there are no "real" hamburgers, there is no "true" hamburger (or anything else real or true, for that matter).

There are even completely invented foods. Each of the millions, perhaps billions, of virtually identical (and simulated) Chicken McNuggets, for example, fits perfectly Baudrillard's idea of a simulation as an identical copy for which no original ever existed. The original, the "real" chicken, had the temerity to be created with bones, skin, gristle, and so on. But then chickens themselves, given modern factory farming, are nothing more than simulations that bear little resemblance to the dwindling number of their free-ranging brethren.

Then there is the structure and decor of the fast food restaurant. The Roy Rogers'® chain is modeled, I suppose, after the late movie cowboy's ranch house, a ranch house that never existed except perhaps in the movies where it already was a simulation. The whole western atmosphere created by the chain and its commercials has much more to do with the movies (simulations) than it does with the "real" old west (whatever that was).[46] A similar point could be made about the fictional Long John Silver® (known best to the public, of course, from the movie [i.e., simulated] version of *Treasure Island* rather than the original book, which itself could have been a simulation of some real events) chain of seafood restaurants, as well as many other simulated purveyors of simulacra. These examples reflect the importance that the media (movies, television) play in the contemporary world. In these instances, they are affecting us indirectly, but they also have a more direct impact that has been the concern of many postmodern social theorists.[47]

The fact that fast food restaurants are hard-pressed to distinguish themselves on the basis of their food, settings, and service leads them to rely on various types of simulations in order to attract customers within the budgetary limits of such outlets. For example, there are the simulated playgrounds that are grafted on to the entrances of many.

The creation of spectacular, simulated interiors has been brought to new heights in recent years by the chains of theme restaurants. The very basis of their appeal, given the widely acknowledged inadequacies in their food, has to be these simulated interiors. If you ever fantasized about eating lunch or dinner in a simulated submarine, then the place for you is the theme restaurant DIVE!®:

> The exterior of DIVE! Las Vegas is anchored at one end by the yellow and purple nose of a life-size submarine, crashing through a 30-foot water wall. The water wall cascades into an oversized pool which randomly "explodes" with six synchronized depth charges. The nose is complete with other details to enhance the "water effects" including six blast blow holes that emit water and twelve fog misters at the "scupper" drains; and it is topped with an "up-periscope" and radar light resembling a giant olive on a toothpick. . . . At the other end, a 35-foot lighthouse welcomes guests with a working beacon. Between the nose and lighthouse, the body of the restaurant is painted gunmetal gray and accented by nine porthole-shaped "bubble-windows" and neon accents.
>
> The body of the two-story, 16,000-square-foot restaurant replicates the hull of a submarine with vaulted cylindrical ceilings and bowed exterior walls, braced by "ribs." DIVE!'s interior shell is constructed of a variety of metal materials, painted in accent colors and treated to create the feeling of an authentic sub. Overall, a network of technical sub-apparatus details the entire restaurant including: exposed conduits (that actually burst with steam), pressure gauges, throttles, control panels, sonar screens and a bathysphere that hangs from the ceiling . . .[48]

The presumption is that not enough people would come to restaurants like DIVE! and Rainforest Cafe and pay the relatively high prices for food were it not for the spectacular simulations. The assumption is that people will find lunch or dinner in a simulated submarine a spectacular and enchanting experience.

We are beginning to see malls that simulate other kinds of settings. One example is the 1.5 million square foot "Park Meadows Retail Resort" in suburban Denver, which opened in August 1996.[49] It is described as a resort in order to distinguish it from a mall, and that label is reflective of the fact that for many Americans shopping is a vacation. The structure is a simulation of the rustic Timberline Lodge[50] on Mount Hood in Oregon: "On the inside, Park Meadows is full of rustic Colorado overtones with stone fireplaces and wood and copper interiors . . . the experience is less like shopping and more like going for lunch at the ski lodge."[51] Other examples of this trend toward shopping malls as simulations include Newbury Street in Boston, which evokes New England charm, and the small-town feel of Bellevue Square in Seattle.

None of the new means of consumption is more spectacularly simulated than Las Vegas and its casino–hotels. And none has proven better at luring consumers. Las Vegas is built in the most inhospitable of settings—the desert. As a result, virtually nothing natural, or real, is able to survive on its own in the city. The grass, the trees, the shrubs, the flowers—all have been unnaturally imposed on the environment. Furthermore, in order for all of it to survive, it must be artificially maintained and sustained. Although most true of Las Vegas, these kinds of things take a simulated form in virtually all of the new means of consumption (even inside the Mirage). Even in quite hospitable climates, the grass, the trees, and so on are brought in from outside and imposed artificially on the environment. This is true of Disneyland in Southern California and Disney World in Florida, even though the climate is much more appropriate to this vegetation than the Las Vegas desert. Similar things are artificially transplanted in luxury gated communities, most notably in Florida, Arizona, and Southern California—and, needless to say in simulated towns such as Disney's Celebration.

In terms of the hotel–casinos, Las Vegas has drifted more and more in the direction of simulated environments. The earliest post-1947 Las Vegas hotels such as the Flamingo did not try to simulate other environments. Later hotels, such as the Sands®, The Dunes®, The Sahara®, and the Aladdin®—had an Arabian fantasy motif, but they did not try hard to simulate Arabia.[52] They were spectacular, but they did not attempt to copy another reality to the extent that has become common in Las Vegas in recent years. Perhaps the beginning of this change can be traced to the opening of Circus, Circus® in 1968, which featured a gambling casino surrounded by a simulated circus. It was followed by Caesar's Palace® and its effort to simulate ancient Rome. In addition to the spectacularly simulated casino–hotels discussed previously, others include

- ♦ *Main Street Station.* Its Victorian design seeks to evoke an earlier era in American history.

- ♦ *Monte Carlo.* Built to resemble Place du Casino in Monte Carlo, Monaco, its hotel hallways resemble European streets with faux cobblestone and fake building facades.

- ♦ *Orleans.* It simulates New Orleans down to the iron balconies and greenery that characterize that city.

- ♦ *Project Paradise.* Scheduled to open in the Fall of 1998, it will have a South Seas theme with snorkeling reef and surfing "beach."

The much discussed New York, New York is a beautiful example of a spectacular simulation and, as result, one that has been enormously successful at attracting gamblers (and their families):

Inside this very condensed version of Manhattan, separate banks of elevators—in the Empire State, Century, New Yorker and Chrysler towers (all respectable imitations of those in their 1930s prototypes)—deliver guests near to their rooms. On the outside, the lower-level stage set includes simplified models of the Immigration Hall at Ellis Island, the New York Public Library (minus the lions), the Soldiers' and Sailors' Monument on Riverside Drive and about a dozen other New York (or New Yorkish) facades, jammed eclectically together. At the corner stands a half-size Statue of Liberty, sprayed by jets from two New York fireboats in a semicircular pool. Downriver on the Strip side rises a superfluous, a miniature Brooklyn Bridge. Through and around all this coils the red track of an awesome roller coaster, intended to honor Coney Island's. Inside the building . . . a stone footbridge meant to evoke Central Park . . . a copy of the pedimented front of the New York Stock Exchange . . . a tribute to Rockefeller Center, with a sleek waterfall and a copy of Lee Lawrie's Atlas statue. . . . The cleverest features of the casino floor are the rambling, asphalt-paved alleyways of the "Villages" (part SoHo, part Little Italy, part Greenwich Village), in which a number of genuine food stalls and shops . . . are surrounded by and enclosed in make-believe shops, townhouses and apartments, their lower floors full-size, the upper floors in Disneyland reduction. The fire escapes, mailboxes, trash cans, newsstands, manhole covers, subway entrances and street signs all look reasonably authentic, as do the neatly sprayed-on graffiti, the air conditioners and glowing TV sets that mark upstairs apartments. . . . Of course, this isn't a "real" New York, or anything like it. If you look closely, almost everything dissolves.[53]

A reexamination of this description would yield an extraordinarily lengthy list of simulations. As was the case with DIVE!, New York, New York can be seen as a simulation, but one that itself encompasses a number of other smaller, but no less spurious, simulations.

In the newly remodeled Tomorrowland at Disney World there are long lines everywhere, especially at the simulated astro orbiters and rocket rides. The exception is the "real" display sponsored by the Jet Propulsion Laboratory and NASA, which includes a "diorama of that plucky little rover that trundled over the bumpy surface of Mars."[54] The new Animal Kingdom is rife with examples of the preference for the "fake" over the "real":

'We have the roseate spoonbill here in Florida, but of course they didn't want to use a Florida bird' . . . 'Look, there's fake mist! It's coming out of a spigot. It's fake mist! Unbelievable!'

The triumph of the faux is one aspect of Disney . . . 'They think they can improve on nature' . . . 'At some level, that's creepy.'

He walks past a fake bamboo fence and some fake boulders and checks out a display that is supposed to include an anteater. But the anteater is hiding in the bushes, so a Disney employee is showing the tourists a photograph of the beast. . . .

'She's passing out pictures of the anteater because the anteater has enough sense to hide' . . . 'Oh, that's perfect! It's a great country!'[55]

Worthy of special note from the point of view of simulations are virtual theme parks such as United Artists' Starport entertainment centers. One of several now open, the Denver location has, among other things, a virtual reality center that includes "Showscan's 'The Edge' (a hydraulically controlled motion simulation theater), The Amazing Space (a new concept in family entertainment created from a kid's point of view), Virtual Gliders (hang-gliding without the risk) and Virtuality (head-mounted virtual reality with 360-degree interaction)."[56]

Virtual reality is by definition a simulation. It may be distinguished from most of the simulations being discussed by its even greater distance from anything resembling "reality." As a result, it possesses possibilities for enchantment that exceed those offered by other simulations. The coming of virtual reality will mean a vast increase in the scope of simulations. There is already, for example, a virtual tour for use at home of the tomb of the Egyptian queen Nefertari.[57] Why bother to leave home, when all one is going to see is simulations? Better to stay at home and view the virtual version, which in some senses is even more spectacular than the simulated version one would have to travel to see.

At least some people are coming to prefer virtual simulations to reality. For example, the MCI center, home stadium of professional basketball's Washington Wizards and professional hockey's Washington Capitals, offers a miniature basketball court with a massive video image of a Washington Wizards's star who "interacts" with the player. Said one eleven-year-old participant, "I like watching basketball . . . but this is better." A father and his two sons are seen playing virtual hockey twenty minutes after the "real" game starts. Says the wife and mother, "This is not athleticism . . . This is entertainment."[58]

Virtual reality offers the possibility of simulations of simulations. For example, the Sega theme park in Sydney offers a simulated (via virtual reality) ride on a spaceship that has already been simulated in many world fairs, amusement parks, and theme parks. In fact, the simulation of simulations may be the coming trend in the cathedrals of consumption. For example, Disney is simulating some aspects of its already simulated theme park experiences in its new chain of mall locations, the Disney Club. The new fast food satellite locations (mini-McDonald's, for example) can be seen as simulations of the larger fast food restaurants.

Theming

Theming, or the effort to carry a particular motif throughout all aspects of a cathedral of consumption, is a natural extension of the idea of simulations discussed in the preceding section. Through theming,[59] many Las Vegas hotels seek to follow through on their simulated image. Many of the employees dress in costumes consistent with the casino–hotel's theme. Internal decor is designed to be in tune with the overall theme. Restaurants often are structured in such a way that they too fit the theme, as does the nature of the food that they serve (for example, the Orleans Hotel has the French Market Buffet serving Louisiana specialties). The shows put on in the major theaters also are often designed to carry through on the theme. The first show in residence at New York, New York was "Madhattan," in which an array of New York street performers were brought together to represent the New York style of entertainment. Similarly, the extravagant fantasy world that is created at the Mirage is supported by the illusions of Siegfried and Roy's long-running show.

Of course, much the same can be said about the spectacularly simulated and themed nature of the Magic Kingdom at Disney World. Each of the worlds has a theme, and the rides, restaurants, dress, talk, and so forth are designed to support that theme. Theming is so important at Disney World that employees in the costume of one land are not permitted to enter other lands out of a fear that they will compromise the theme and surely destroy the fantasy. There is an elaborate system of tunnel-like corridors beneath Disney World that allow employees to get to the appropriate locale without intruding into others. (The corridors also serve to conceal similarly intrusive deliveries.) One of the spectacular aspects of Disney World derives from the fact that visitors spend time completely enveloped by one land (and one set of simulated themed elements) and then suddenly cross a threshold and find themselves in a completely different land with an entirely different simulated theme.

Perhaps the ultimate illustration of a simulated theme park (as well as of the fact that virtually *anything* can be turned into such a site) is the planned "Ossi Park"[60] in what was East Germany (the German Democratic Republic):

One-day visitors will be *required* to leave by midnight, as they were in the GDR; *guards* will patrol the border; attempts to escape will lead to hour(s)-long *imprisonment*. All visitors will be *required* to exchange a minimum of hard currency for eastern marks . . . [The whole park will be surrounded by *barbed wire* and a *wall* and will] include badly stocked stores, snooping state *secret police* . . . and scratchy toilet paper known as 'Stalin's Revenge,' whose texture, according to an old GDR joke, ensured that 'every last ass is red.'[61]

Clearly, being in such a simulated environment would be quite spectacular. Even more fantasy-like would be the knowledge that one could leave anytime one wanted to.

"Authentic Simulations"

Although the creation of entirely new simulations is an extreme case, most "authentic" tourist destinations have been turned into simulations, at least in part. Examples include the colonial town of Williamsburg in Virginia and Windsor Castle in England, among many others. The motivation behind these transformations is that the "real" sites are no longer spectacular enough to attract tourists and their money. Visitor centers, movies introducing the attraction, people in costume, actors putting on shows, and themed restaurants and gift shops are required to draw adequate numbers of people. Of course, adding things such as these to the attraction transforms it into a simulation; it is no longer the original setting. But the increasing demand for a spectacle necessitates greater use of simulations.

Take, for example, the fact that the sea itself, at least in one setting, has been altered (simulated) to accommodate the tourist:

For the snorkeling enthusiast, the place to head is Folkestone National Marine Reserve, Park and Marine Museum at Holetown [Barbados]. . . . The government has built an area where the novice can swim and follow a series of underwater markers that picture what fish are likely to be seen.[62]

Relatedly, a number of tropical islands are now owned and completely controlled by the cruise lines.[63] Only passengers of the cruise line are allowed on shore. The islands are described as "reassuringly Disneyesque."[64] There are already a number of such islands, with more sure to come. In fact, Disney itself acquired Gorda Cay in the Caribbean and renamed it Castaway Cay for its cruise line, which began operations in mid-1998. Castaway Cay features "Cookie's Bar-B-Que," "Teen Beach," and "Marge's Barges and Sea Charters." On such islands, the tourist finds no hawkers, no overbuilding, nothing (except perhaps the uncooperative storm) to mar the "perfect vacation." No cash is needed; everything can be charged to one's ship bill. "Real" Caribbean islands pale in comparison. According to one tourist, "St. Maarten wasn't a very attractive island. . . . It was dirty. The shops were kind of junky." Said another, "Jamaica was pretty run down to us."[65]

On simulated islands the bathrooms are squeaky clean. Food and drink are brought on shore from the ship. The service is provided by the ship's crew. There is even an ersatz market; natives (presumably carefully selected and trained so that little or no trace of their real culture remains) of a nearby island sail over to staff it. On one of the islands, "a *replica* of a 16th century ship [was purposely] sunk in the harbor to give snorkelers a thrill."[66] More recently, a plane was submerged. Some kill-joy academic (an anthropologist) described a visit to such an island as a "virtual experience" and complained that tourists "don't want to see any of the consequences of colonialism—the poverty, the sex trade."[67]

Certainly, there are those tourists, and consumers more generally, who continue to search out authentic settings and they can, at least to some degree, still find them. However, visits to authentic sites tend to be more expensive than to inauthentic locales. More important, it is likely to grow increasingly difficult to find the authentic. Authentic tourist sites are likely to go the way of the caves at Lescaux. Or they are likely to be so altered by the demands of catering to large numbers of tourists that they are apt to become simulated versions of the originals.

Even museums are being forced to offer simulations in order to compete with the more obvious forms of simulated entertainment:

The art, science and culture museum of the University of California at Berkeley . . . augmented its 1991 show of New Guinea artifacts with a "science theatre," where an experience called Nature's Fury produced a rocking earthquake simulation from a minivolcano; going a step further for "lifelike" relevance appropriate to the community, a suggested survivor's kit was displayed in the trunk of a BMW . . . With nothing to recommend them except their often shabby authenticity, the real objects simply have less appeal than snappy simulations.[68]

Simulated Communities

Moving out of the realm of tourism, new luxury gated communities are inherently simulated (artificial community, imported trees and shrubs). Some also seek to give themselves a particular theme or look. Shady Canyon in California, with an ersatz country look, has narrow roads with no sidewalks, limited street lighting, and a layout that conforms to the local topography. Coto de Caza has horse trails, even though few residents have horses. According to the community's vice president for marketing and sales: "Most residents don't own horses, but they like the idea of living in an area with an equestrian-oriented feel."[69] The community was built to accommodate existing trees and, where that was not possible, trees were transplanted. In this "New Ruralism" the objective is to create new communities that look like, that simulate, old-time communities. The rural look might include houses with front porches, a community square, and shops that are within walking distance of one's home.

Simulation defines Disney's town of Celebration.[70] A whole new level of spectacle is reached when an entire simulated community is created. Journeying to a single simulated setting may be impressive, but it pales in comparison to the spectacle of living one's life in a wholly simulated community. "The town's entrance is straight out of a Disney movie, with white picket fences, wrought-iron street lamps, lush landscaping and an old-timey wood-slat water tower luring visitors with a vision of a simpler time."[71] The simulated character of the town is nowhere more obvious than in the fact that there will be a town hall in Celebration, but there will not be a real town government.

The town's sales brochure makes it clear what is being simulated at Celebration:

> There once was a place where neighbors greeted neighbors in the quiet of summer twilight. . . . Where children chased fireflies. And porch swings provided easy refuge from the cares of the day. The movie house showed cartoons on Saturday. The grocery store delivered. And there was one teacher who always knew you had that special something. Remember that place?"[72]

Being promised is a resurrection of pre–World War II, small-town America. This is clear, as well, in the town seal (copyrighted by Disney), which is "a cameo of a little girl with a ponytail riding a bicycle past a picket fence under a spreading oak tree as her little dog chases along behind."[73]

As in Disney theme parks, those who show prospective home-owners around are "cast members." Before touring the grounds, prospective home owners are shown a film with the following script:

> Our memories of childhood. . . . There is a place that takes you back to that time of innocence. . . . A place where the biggest decision is whether to play kick the can or king of the hill. A place of caramel apples and cotton candy, secret forts and hopscotch on the streets. That place is here again, in a new town called Celebration.
>
> Celebration. . . . A new American town of block parties and Fourth of July parades. Of spaghetti dinners and school bake sales, lollipops and fireflies in a jar. And while we can't return to those times, we can arrive at a place that embraces all of those things. Someday 20,000 people will live in Celebration. And for each and every one of them, it will be home.[74]

Celebration's glorification of tradition does not stop with its architecture, its sales brochure, or its introductory video. There is a Celebration Foundation in charge of the culture of the town. It will create such organizations as Rotary Clubs and the Boy Scouts, as well as the town's newspaper (to be controlled by the Disney corporation).

Celebration's houses have many simulated elements. For example, in one model the panel doors in each room are made of imitation wood. The exterior clapboard is made of a synthetic concrete. With its similarly simulated exterior (e.g., the rustic porches), these houses are described as "outwardly rustic, inwardly corporate."

The town has been described in terms that all but label it a simulation:

> The entire awkward struggle to manufacture a tradition for the town revealed . . . a hollowness at its core, the absence of a bona fide purpose such as inspired the creation of most towns. Of course, "bona fide," like "authenticity" and "rigor," is a complicated concept in Celebration. What do such terms mean in a town whose history is retroactive, whose tradition is that of the entertainment company that founded it, whose lake is dammed and whose creek is pumped, whose creators say "lifestyle" for "life" and insert the phrase "a sense of" before every vital principle? Celebration is billed as being in the great American tradition of town building, but it is a town whose mission isn't the pursuit of commercial advantage, or religious or political freedom, or any idea more compelling than a sense of comfortable community. Its ambition is, in the end, no greater than to be like a town.[75]

CONCLUSION

The chapter has documented the fact that the new means of consumption have become ever more spectacular by increasing the number and size of the extravaganzas and simulations (and even simulations of simulations) they offer. Such spectacles serve to reenchant the cathedrals of consumption so that they will be a continuing attraction to increasingly jaded consumers. Extravaganzas and simulations are generally created by those who control the cathedrals of consumption with the intention of reenchanting the settings in which they occur. I turn in the next chapter to other processes that, less intentionally or even unintentionally, also serve to reenchant the cathedrals of consumption.

6

REENCHANTMENT: CREATING SPECTACLE THROUGH IMPLOSION, TIME, AND SPACE

In this chapter I look at the way implosions of various types serve to create spectacles. I will also examine the spectacular use of time and space in the new means of consumption. The implosion of temporal and spatial boundaries is an important source of spectacles. As we will see, there is more to time and especially space as they relate to the new means of consumption than can be discussed under the heading of implosion. For example, there are the seeming abilities to defy the constraints of time and to create a sense of infinite space. Spectacles involving implosions and the extraordinary use of time and space serve to reenchant the cathedrals of consumption. Some of the reenchantment comes about quite unintentionally, but intentional or not, the processes to be discussed do serve to reenchant the means of consumption and thereby to attract consumers.

IMPLOSION

The term *implosion* refers to the disintegration or disappearance of boundaries so that formerly differentiated entities collapse in on each other. The explosive growth in the new means of consumption has led to a series of such implosions.[1] There has been a kind of chain reaction: The collapse of one set of boundaries leads to the breakdown of a number of other frontiers. Boundaries between the cathedrals of consumption have eroded and, in some cases, all but disappeared. Borders between the means of consumption and other aspects of the social world similarly have been breached. In this way, we have witnessed the disappearance of many distinctions to which people had grown accustomed. The result is a reenchanted world of consumption seemingly without borders or limits.

These imploded worlds represent a kind of spectacle that draws consumers into them and leads them to consume. For example, only a few decades ago people had to trek from one locale to another for various goods and services; now they can find that variety in a single mall. And it was not that many years ago that if one wanted to gamble, one went to Las Vegas, but if one wanted to visit a theme park one went to Orlando or Anaheim. Now one can go to the MGM Grand or Circus Circus in Las Vegas, for example, and find both a casino and a theme park on the hotel's grounds. The local Wal-Mart, or corner service station, might well encompass a satellite fast food restaurant. REI in Seattle not only offers mountain climbing shoes but even a "mountain" to practice on.

It is often the case that the conscious motivation behind implosion has not been to create a spectacle. Entrepreneurs may be motivated by a variety of reasons such as economies resulting from having two or more means of consumption within one setting, the desire to offer consumers the conveniences associated with such imploded locales, and so on. Whether or not the motivation behind implosion is the creation of spectacle, the fact is that spectacle often results.

As with many other ideas in the previous chapter and this one, the idea of implosion, at least as it is used in this context, is derived from postmodern social theory, most notably the work of Jean Baudrillard. Baudrillard defines implosion as the contraction of one phenomenon into another; the collapse of traditional poles into one another.[2] To Baudrillard, all things are capable of dissolving not only into each other, but also into a single huge undifferentiated mass (a sort of "black hole"). As an example outside of the cathedrals of consumption, contemporary television talk shows are dissolving into life and life is dissolving into talk shows. Consider the well-known case of a Jenny Jones talk show in which a gay admirer, Scott Amedure, expressed a homosexual interest in, and hugged, a straight male, Jonathan Schmitz, on the air. Schmitz (who expected to encounter a female admirer on the show) later killed Amedure (and was sentenced to twenty-five to fifty years in prison for it) in a case in which reality and television culture clearly imploded into one another.

We can get at this phenomenon in another way by distinguishing between differentiation and dedifferentiation. The modern world can be said to have been characterized by *differentiation*—that is, the creation of more new and different things. Throughout the industrial revolution more and more things were invented, created, produced, and distributed widely. This wide variety of products led to a parallel differentiation in the settings in which they could be consumed.

Modernity, then, was characterized by highly differentiated and rigidly separated means of consumption: the butcher shop sold meat, the baker bread, the greengrocer fruits and vegetables, and so on.

Although such differentiation has not completely disappeared, postmodernists argue that today's world is increasingly characterized by dedifferentiation:[3] a growing inability to differentiate among things and among places. They all are coming to interpenetrate, all imploding into one another. This is nowhere clearer than in the contemporary world of consumption in general and in the relationship among and between the new means of consumption in particular. The separate shops of the butcher, baker, and greengrocer have all but disappeared into the supermarket that has imploded into the supercenter into which a discount department store has also imploded. This dedifferentiation is spectacular and serves to draw consumers to these dedifferentiated entities.

Implosion in the Means of Consumption

The means of consumption are in the process of blending into one another.

Shopping and Fun

The distinction between shopping malls and amusement parks[4] has always been somewhat illusory, and in recent years it has grown ever more so. Both have always been means to sell stuff as well as to sell entertainment, but in the past, malls were mostly in the business of selling goods, whereas parks focused on entertainment. That difference is no longer so clear. Malls also offer fun to both adults and children—especially the new mall outlets housing Dave and Buster's, Gameworks, Jeepers®, Club Disney, and so on.

Mega-malls such as Mall of America and the Edmonton Mall encompass entire amusement parks, as well. Then there are the increasingly large multiplex theaters offering twenty or more screens that are increasingly important to many malls. Some of the stores in the malls use things like children's play areas to entice people into the stores. The trend in many malls is away from selling goods and toward selling services, especially entertainment.[5] The Edmonton Mall, which at one time was divided 80 percent to 20 percent between retail sales and entertainment, is now moving closer to a 60 percent to 40 percent split. Friedberg has described a shopping mall as "a consumer theme park."[6]

Ontario Mills (outside Los Angeles) is specifically pinning its hopes on "fun and games."[7] There are no large department stores to anchor the mall; it is a combination of discounted, outlet-like shops, theme restaurants, and entertainment settings such as iWerks® theater and Dave and Buster's. There is also a zoo! Ontario Mills has an enormous food court that can seat more than 1,000 people. Attendance thus far has been huge and the developer has claimed it is on track ultimately to attract more people than Disneyland. One reason for this shift toward entertainment is that malls need to induce people away from shopping at home. They are becoming destinations in their own right. The chair and chief executive of the company that developed Ontario Mills said, "Shoppers want an experience."[8]

Likewise, amusement parks are marketing more and more goods. An extreme form of this is Santa Claus Village in Rovaniemi, Finland, which offers woefully little entertainment and is almost entirely devoted to the consumption of souvenirs and food.[9] Less extreme is Disney World, which certainly offers entertainment, but is also liberally studded with souvenir shops, food stands, and restaurants. Main Street and Marketplace areas focus on selling Disney products of one kind or another. Disney uses its amusement parks to advertise its shops in malls (and vice versa). These shops, of course, are primarily interested in selling Disney merchandise. The vast majority of Disney stores are in the malls. The line between the mall and the amusement park has almost been obliterated.

Also imploding is the distinction between entertainment and the cybermalls on the Internet. Even though they are the wave of the future, the Internet in general and cybermalls in particular need to be entertaining. According to the president of an on-line advertising and shopping service: "People using on-line shopping want the entertainment experience. They want it to be pleasant. They want access to the cool stuff."[10]

More generally, the distinction between shopping and fun has completely imploded. The fun of shopping for goods and services is no longer enough, but must be supplemented by other amusements. Even shopping itself has to be more fun as reflected in the growth of discount malls and the idea of discovering (supposed) bargains.

For competitive reasons, both fast food and (to a lesser degree) upscale restaurant (e.g., Morton's) chains are increasingly in the business of fun. The food seems to be secondary, or of little significance at all. Said one diner, "I would rather eat mediocre food in a fabulous room than sit somewhere dull and boring and eat fabulous food. . . . I'm looking for decor, scale, *theatrics*, a lot going on."[11]

Gambling and Shopping

Also eroding is the boundary between gambling and shopping. Time was that people went to Las Vegas to gamble and had little interest in shopping while there. In fact, there were relatively few shopping areas available because the objective was to keep people in the casinos and at the roulette wheels and slot machines. Now, however, shopping is increasingly integral to the Las Vegas experience. Under construction is the Venetian that, in addition to a huge casino, 6,000 suites, and a convention center, will include a shopping mall.[12] There is already a large mall on the Strip. An elegant mall, the Forum, is adjacent to and contiguous with Caesar's Palace. The $94 million Showcase Mall adjacent to the MGM Grand opened in the spring of 1997, giving that casino–hotel an amusement park *and* a mall.

Space in casino–hotels is being increasingly devoted to shops of all types. This has come about as a result of the shift in focus in Las Vegas from individual gamblers to families. Malls and shops give some family members ways to spend money while other members gamble. Furthermore, the malls stand ready to take the money of those few who emerge from the casinos as winners. Malls and gambling operations work in tandem to be sure that visitors leave Las Vegas with little, if any, money.

As the barriers to gambling come down around the country, we can expect to see more gambling in shopping malls. Already there is the Palace Casino in the Edmonton Mall. Race tracks are having a hard time surviving amid the rapid growth of all these new forms of gambling. Other types of gambling have imploded into race tracks (slot machines, poker rooms, and so on). And lottery tickets are for sale in a wide range of shops in many states.

Touring and Consuming

The changes in Las Vegas are related to a more general implosion of the boundaries between touring and consuming. Of course, touring always involved the consumption of tourist activities and sites. Along the way, tourists generally were interested in purchasing everything from trinkets to trophies. Now, however, there are more and more instances in which the main objective of touring *is* the consumption of goods.[13] For one thing, malls have become tourist destinations. According to a travel consultant, the lure of a mall vacation is that "the malls have everything. . . . They have a water park. They have an amusement park. They have a roller coaster. Mom and dad can get what they want."[14] This combination is spectacular and a powerful lure to the traveler. Airlines offer day trips to Mall of America; bus lines offer package trips that might involve visits of several days to the mall. Mall of America attracted 12 million tourists in 1995— "more than Walt Disney World, the Grand Canyon and Graceland combined."[15] In Canada, the largest tourist attraction is *not* Niagara Falls but rather the Edmonton Mall. Potomac Mills outside Washington, D.C., had 4.5 million visitors in 1995. By comparison, 4 million visited Arlington National Cemetery, 2.5 million journeyed to Colonial Williamsburg, and 1 million visited Mount Vernon. Franklin Mills, outside Philadelphia, drew 6 million visitors in 1995, four times as many as visited the Liberty Bell.[16] NikeTown is Chicago's largest tourist attraction.[17] Many tourist destinations are surrounded by outlet or discount malls that are the fastest growing segment of not only the mall business but also of the travel industry. People are almost as apt to journey to such locales for the malls as they are for the sea or the air. Indeed, it often seems as if almost as many people are at the malls as are on the beach.

Also worth noting in this context are the cruise ships that have malls on board and that turn the islands on their itinerary into little more than indigenous malls. There are "even shopping cruises, outfitted with shops, catalogues and stops in strategic ports."[18]

Fast Food Restaurants, Convenience Stores, and Superstores

Fast food restaurants are imploding into virtually every other new means of consumption. As discussed previously, they are now found within Las Vegas casino–hotels and Disney World. They are finding their way onto college campuses and into the nation's hotels and hotel chains.[19] In fact, some hotels are installing mini versions of the food courts we find in shopping malls, airports, and on the nation's highways. Smaller satellite fast food restaurants are found in places such as 7-Eleven, Wal-Mart, and the like.

Convenience stores (as well as gasoline stations) are currently experiencing the implosion of many other means of consumption into them: ATMs, dry cleaners, theater ticket sales, gasoline stations, coffee shops, and many others.[20]

A good example of implosion in superstores is that taking place in book superstores: "These days, a bookstore is a bookstore, food court, music shop and newsstand rolled into one."[21] In fact, so many things have imploded into the superstore that it can now be viewed as a kind of minimall (one that is destined to drive some of the weaker full-fledged malls out of existence):

> The category killer has indeed become a distinct breed of retailer. . . . It's a place to shop, yes, but a place to linger, too, to take a family on a Saturday afternoon, to meet a friend for breakfast, to steal a few minutes for yourself on the way home from work, to daydream, perhaps, over

a magazine and a cup of coffee that's infinitely more aromatic than anything at the local coffee shop. . . . Sure, a superstore is a stationery shop or hardware store writ huge. But far more to the point, it's also a mall writ small.[22]

Malls

Malls are turning up in more and more places, accelerating the process of implosion. For example, modern airports are coming to look more and more like shopping malls. As one observer put it, "What could be a truer gateway to the U.S. than a shopping mall?"[23] (The predecessors to this were the duty-free shops and shopping plazas at international airports such as the one in Shannon, Ireland, and at Schiphol airport in Amsterdam.) The pioneer in the malling of airports, Pittsburgh International Airport, has 100,000 square feet of shops at its "Airmall." The new terminal at Ronald Reagan (formerly National) Airport in Washington, D.C., has been described "as much a mall as it is an airport," or "an airport-cum mall."[24] It has thirty-eight retail shops and twenty-four restaurants occupying 65,000 square feet. Among its shops are national chains that are found at other airports (Gap, Disney Store), as well as some that are appearing in an airport for the first time (Gymboree® and Victoria's Secret). Among the twenty-four restaurants are outlets of Legal Sea Foods®, Cheesecake Factory® (2 kiosks), Cinnabon®, TGI Friday's®, and McDonald's. There also are local restaurants such as former Washington Redskin Charles Mann's All-Pro Grill.

Airport malls exist to lure passengers into making purchases they otherwise might not have made. And they seem to work. Retail sales at Pittsburgh's airport have grown from an average of $2.40 per departing passenger in 1992 to $7.60 in 1998.[25] The existence of such malls also seems to lure people to use one airport rather than another. In one survey, 11 percent of passengers said that one of the reasons they chose to change planes in Pittsburgh was its mall.[26]

Major train stations such as Union Station in Washington, D.C. (with 100 shops) have followed the lead of airports, and others (e.g.,

Grand Central Station in New York) are in the process of refashioning themselves as malls.

Athletic Stadiums

New athletic stadiums include far more than simply a playing field, stands, and concessions. Among the things found at newer stadiums are private pools with adjacent hot tubs, virtual reality games, hair salons, cigar bars, and mini-shopping malls. One observer described this as the "amusement-park school of stadium construction."[27] Tropicana Field, the new home of major league baseball's Tampa Bay Devil Rays, has a three-level mall that includes places where "fans can get a trim at the barber shop, do their banking and then grab a cold one at the Budweiser brew pub, whose copper kettles rise to three stories. There is even a climbing wall for kids and showroom space for car dealerships."[28] Computers at some upholstered seats allow fans to access video replays and order hot dogs. The MCI Center in Washington, D.C., involves the implosion of several new means of consumption:

> Walk through the main entrance to the stadium, a three-story glass atrium. . . . Anchoring one end of the floor is the Discovery Channel store, selling nature and science under a 42-foot-tall Tyrannosaurus Rex. At the other end, a two-level "sports gallery," where fans wind through a maze of "museum" displays . . . and empty into a buzzing, beeping arcade of electronic games. With no clocks, no windows and dim lights, it has all the ambiance of a casino.[29]

The public relations people associated with the Atlanta Braves new stadium, Turner Field, describe it as "not just a ball park. It's more like a baseball theme park."[30] In addition to the usual components, Turner Field includes a plaza that has been described as "a virtual Disney World of Baseball."[31] There is the Braves Museum and Hall of Fame, a souvenir shop, and a children's area. Over the team store is a bank of television sets that offer live broadcasts of other major league baseball games. There is a videoboard that allows fans to interview players. There are electronic kiosks that permit access to scouting reports and the Braves Internet home page. For food, there is a chop house and a beer joint, Taste of the Major Leagues. There is also a "kid's zone" that includes interactive games and souvenir shops. Scouts Alley tests fans' hitting and pitching skills. Fans can learn more about scouting by studying the scouting reports of famous Braves players. Then there is Coca Cola's rooftop park in Turner Field, which is a minitheme park designed to sell the Braves, Coke, and paraphernalia associated with each. To help fans pay for all of this there are seven ATMs. A representative of one of the firms involved in planning Turner Field said, "If we are going to hook people on baseball, we don't do it by making them sit through nine innings. If we can make the experience more pleasurable, we should."[32] Said the Braves's president: "I like spending. . . . So let's design this (Turner Field) space with something for them to do when they come early. And while we're at it, let's give them a reason for staying late. They will like it more, and we should make more money."[33]

The Braves new spring training facility, Disney Wide World of Sports Baseball Stadium, is located on the grounds of the Disney complex in Florida. Said the general manager of the new park, "I have never seen a (spring) facility like this. . . . This is classic Disney."[34]

Educational Settings

The student unions at some universities are taking on an increasingly mall-like quality:

> They stood eye to eye and nose to nose for almost 40 minutes, exchanging heavy talk, soulful looks, and angry glares outside Mrs. Field's Cookies at the food court entrance. . . . It was the kind of minor mall world melodrama that plays out all the time whenever kids gather over their Whoppers, Pizza Hut personal pan pizzas, and Freshen's Premium Yogurt —everywhere from Tyson's Corner Center in suburban Washington to the Galleria in Dallas and Phipps Plaza in Atlanta. The only difference was that this was no shopping center, it was the student union at Boston University.[35]

In addition, educational institutions are growing more and more like theme parks, as well as like other new means of consumption.[36]

For their part, shopping malls are increasingly likely to encompass university satellite schools (and medical facilities) of various kinds. For example, National College has recently begun offering seventeen courses in the Mall of America.[37]

Then there is the "shopping mall high school," a high school that offers the student–consumer a variety of choices about which classes to take.[38] There are a number of similarities between such schools and the shopping mall:

♦ Both are highly oriented to the desires of their consumers; students shop for courses and other services "conveniently assembled in one place with ample parking."[39]

♦ As in the malls, some students make choices, others browse, others just "hang out," and still others never come in. Both need to be fun to attract "consumers."

♦ "The mall and the school are places to meet friends, pass the time, get out of the rain, or watch the promenade. Shopping malls or their high school equivalents can be *entertaining* places to onlookers with no intention of buying anything."[40]

♦ "Many contemporary high schools even look like shopping malls. One is a complex of attached single-story buildings whose classrooms open to the outdoors rather than to locker-lined corridors. Between periods students go outside to find their next destination, entering and leaving classrooms as if they were adjacent stores."[41]

♦ Like shopping malls, high schools must also compete with a variety of other settings for students' time and attention.

♦ Like shopping malls, "the shopping mall high school is committed to luring and holding the largest possible crowd."[42]

Corporate Hospitality Centers

What were once known as corporate hospitality centers (or corporate tours) are growing more like museums and increasingly important tourist attractions. Examples include the Goodyear World of Rubber museum, Hormel Foods' Spamtown USA, World of Coca-

Cola, and Hershey's Chocolate World. Kellogg's Cereal City USA, which in addition to having the characteristics of a museum, also resembles an amusement park (the director spent a quarter of a century with Six Flags® Theme Parks, Inc.) with "a musical review staged amid oversized spoons and bowls, personalized boxes of corn-flakes, and a 'Digestive Fun House,' with tunnels resembling the gastrointestinal tract."[43] Of such company-sponsored museum–amusement parks, the author of a book on them says that they are "cheaper than going to Disney."[44] And less demanding than the Metropolitan Museum of Art.

Mausoleums

Perhaps the most astounding example of implosion is the collapse of the distinction between the mausoleum and the theme park. Under construction in Vancouver, British Columbia, is a nine-story mausoleum designed to inter the remains of 90,000 people. Its developer said, "It will be the tallest, biggest, most diversified mausoleum in North America."

> Atop the 110-foot-high edifice, mourners will be able to watch loved ones being cremated on a pyre overlooking the city. Below will be theme floors: one for Catholics, with a nativity scene; a floor for Buddhists, with statues and incense burners; one for Canadian military veterans, with medals and weaponry; and a simulated tropical island, with palm trees and piped-in ukulele music, for late members of Vancouver's substantial Fijian community.[45]

Cities and Small Towns

Another kind of implosion is the erosion of the distinction between shopping in rural or small towns and in the big cities. New York City is currently grappling with the entry of the superstores and the threat they pose to small indigenous shops and businesses. While superstores boomed throughout the rest of the nation, New York and other major cities were largely bypassed. Once the center of innovations in retailing—Macy's, Bloomingdales, the discount pioneer

Korvette's—New York is in the early stages of having its retail landscape transformed into something shockingly, at least to New Yorkers, similar to small-town and rural America.[46]

Similarly, the reinvention of Times Square, spearheaded by Disney's renovated New Amsterdam Theater, a Disney Store, and a new Virgin Megastore, has a virtual game center, XS®, and giant multiplexes with as many as forty screens are on the way, as are a Warner Brothers store and, as if to parallel the opening of New York, New York in Las Vegas, a "Las Vegas-style theme restaurant called Vegas."[47] As one journalist put it, "The once-greasy, beating heart of New York is being homogenized, sanitized and packaged as a theme park for out-of-town tourists."[48]

Real and Fake

So far I have been discussing the postmodern idea of implosion as it relates to the dwindling distinctions between various means of consumption. However, the postmodernists in general, and Baudrillard in particular, also use the idea of implosion in a more general sense of an implosion in the distinction between the real and the unreal; that is, we find it increasingly difficult to differentiate the real from the fake. Indeed, we come to stop trying and to live with the fake at least as easily, and perhaps more easily, as we live with the real. In this sense, implosion is very close to the idea of the increasingly simulated character of our society discussed in the preceding chapter.

The difficulty involved in differentiating between the real and the fake is well illustrated by the new Animal Kingdom at Disney World. The center of the park is the "Tree of Life," which looks real from a distance but up close is a fake with hand-carved animals growing out of it. Africa has "real" live animals; Dinoland has extinct dinosaurs; and the soon-to-be built Beastly Kingdom will include imaginary dragons. Even the real animals live in artificial environments that eventually may change them in various ways, turning them into simulations. An excursion through an artificial savannah takes the visitor to the Conservation Station, which is the "real" headquarters for the care of wildlife in Animal Kingdom. In other words, there are degrees of the fake at Animal Kingdom and it is not always easy to distinguish the very fake from the not-so-fake.

TIME AND SPACE

The issues of time and space have received a great deal of attention from both modernist and postmodernist social theorists.[49] Among the modernists, best-known for his work on these issues is Anthony Giddens; his entire theory concerns the analysis of institutions across time and space.[50] To Giddens, the primordial human condition involves face-to-face interaction, in which others are present at the same time and in the same place. However, in the contemporary world, social relations and social systems extend in time and space, so we increasingly relate to others who are physically absent and more and more distant. Such distancing in time and space is facilitated by new forms of communication and transportation.

Such distancing has certainly taken place in several of the new means of consumption, especially the dematerialized ones based on the telephone, television, and the computer. In such cases, there is no face-to-face interaction, and those who communicate with the consumer can be quite distant physically. In fact, the consumer rarely has any idea, or cares, where such people are. In some cases they may be distant in time as well. Information on a cybermall Web site may have been loaded long before the consumer visits, and infomercials may have been taped for later broadcast. Giddens has argued that because of such distancing, place becomes increasingly "phantasmagoric." This is in line with the new means of consumption as being dreamlike, fantastic, and spectacular.

Also relevant is David Harvey's work on time–space compression. Harvey believes that the compression of time and space characteristic of modernity has accelerated in the postmodern era, leading to "an intense phase of time–space compression."[51] While Harvey tends to have a negative view of this process as "disorienting" and "disruptive," the point being made is simply that the new means of consumption have tended to compress time and space. Indeed, it is their ability to do so that has helped make them so phantasmagoric, so spectacular. That ability, that spectacle, has enhanced their capacity to sell goods and services. If consumers stopped to think about it, they would be stunned by the fact that goods once available half a world away (say, French brie or Russian vodka) can now be purchased in local shops. They would be astounded by the fact that products that once took days or weeks to obtain can now be procured overnight, in hours, or in some cases even almost instantaneously (e.g., by downloading over the Internet).

The notion of the compression of time and space has much in common with the idea of implosion, at least as it applies to time and space. In order to compress time and space, the barriers between various dimensions of time and space must be eroded. Indeed, another way of saying that time and space have been compressed is to say the differences within each have imploded. There is more to implosion than simply time and space compression, but the latter have certainly experienced implosion.

It is worth noting that space is not nearly as amenable to implosion as time. Time creates no barriers to those who seek to use it differently. As we will see, differences between day and night, one season or another, or even the past, present, and future (including past, present, and future incomes) can be overcome in efforts to sell more things to more people. Space, by definition, presents obstinate physical hurdles to those who want to use it in new and different ways. Most of these obstacles are not insurmountable, but they do tend to impede the revolutionary use of space more than they do that of time. In spite of the barriers, there have been enormous changes in the spatial characteristics associated with consumption. The spatial boundaries in and around consumption are imploding at an accelerating rate. In so doing, they create spectacles that, although not always intentionally manufactured by those in charge of the means of consumption, do serve to heighten consumption.

Space: Implosion into the Home

Throughout the vast majority of history, people produced and consumed most, and sometimes all, of what they needed inside, or within hunting and gathering distance of, the home. For most people this remained true up to and even through the Industrial Revolution. However, a clear distinction eventually emerged between where one lived and where one obtained goods and services. In general, one had to leave one's home and go to some other place (the market, the bazaar, the arcade, the Exposition, the fair, the country store, Main Street, downtown, the supermarket, the mall) to obtain what was needed for consumption. There have long been simultaneous efforts to eliminate the need to leave home, to turn the home into a place to obtain commodities (for example, the Yellow Pages campaign, "Let Your Fingers Do the Walking"). The Sears Catalog was an early effort. Milk products used to be delivered, and scissor grinders went door to door. Then there were traveling salespeople who might have shown up on one's doorstep (and sometimes still do) in the hopes of using one's house to sell brushes, a vacuum cleaner, or aluminum siding. Another early example were the home "parties"[52] run by organizations such as Tupperware® and Avon® in which the objective was to turn the home into a site for consumption.[53] Although these kinds of efforts have long existed, the home was, in the main, separate from settings in which one purchased goods and services. That barrier, however, has imploded: *The home has become a, perhaps the, major site for obtaining goods and services.*

There are several longstanding ways to breach the front door. One can personally visit the home much like the brush and vacuum salespeople of past decades. This continues to occur, but it is a rather primitive and expensive method. It also requires face-to-face contact and interpersonal skills that people today may be less inclined or able to practice. Furthermore, with many more women in the labor force, there is a greater likelihood that no one will be home when a salesperson calls.

The mail is another traditional invader of the home, now used much more aggressively. The number and variety of mail order catalogs have escalated dramatically in recent years. Also reaching us by mail are circulars and letters of all types and shapes designed to sell all sorts of goods and services. The credit card companies have been extremely active in using the mail to interest people in acquiring more and more cards. We are swamped by letters offering us, for example, low interest rates or preapproved credit cards. Mail is a relatively inexpensive method of getting inside the home (newspaper, magazine, radio, television, and cyber ads are others), but a very large number of things sent through the mail find their way unopened into the trash.

Another traditional way of gaining entree to the home has been the telephone, and it too is now being used more actively and aggressively than ever before. An executive of a firm in the business says that telemarketing "has become the junk mail of the '90s."[54] Few of us can get through the dinner hour without an overture or two from telemarketers. (Because federal guidelines forbid calls after 9 p.m., most calls are made between 6 p.m. and 9 p.m.) Beyond the sheer volume of calls, contemporary telemarketers have revolutionized this process in various ways. For example, they purchase specialized and targeted lists that allow them to focus on the types of people who have some probability of buying their product. They use technologies such as speed dialing and computers that allow them to come on the line when someone picks up the telephone rather than wasting time holding on calls that end up not being answered. There are even completely computerized calls, which are "dialed" by computer and make the sales pitch with computerized voices.

We can think of the personal visit, the mail, and the telephone call as traditional, but limited, efforts to breach the home. The idea is to get a person, a piece of mail, or a voice into the home so that it becomes a site for consumption. These are primitive techniques, but they are obviously effective, especially given the relatively low cost associated with most of them.

The most dramatic changes, especially in the coming years, are associated with newer technologies, particularly the television set and the computer. Television has always used advertising; commercial television programming would be impossible without it. In the main, however, these advertisements have been aimed at motivating us to leave our home at some future point to buy a car or a refrigerator at a retailer. We were not asked to buy those things *in* or from our homes. There were a few exceptions such as the 1-800 ads for things such as the $9.99 slicer-dicer or the "Greatest Hits of Rock n'Roll," but these ordinarily were low-priced or shady operations that did not play a major role in transforming the home into a house of consumption.

Then came infomercials, shows that fall somewhere between normal television programs and commercials. Without the notice that we are viewing a paid advertisement, we might mistake these for educational or entertainment programs. In fact, those who produce such shows count on the fact that large numbers of people will fail to realize, or forget, that they are watching an infomercial. We are likely to be given a 1-800 telephone number to call to order the product and charge it to our credit card account (or we can pay the bill COD).

Falling into the same category are advertisements and infomercials for spoken services such as the "psychic hotline" and telephone sex. In these cases, the viewer automatically purchases and receives the service by calling the appropriate number. Billed later at a substantial cost per minute, some people have found themselves in deep economic trouble through the purchase of such calls and the "services" they offer.

Of course, advertisements and infomercials pale in comparison to home shopping television and the television channels and entire networks (Home Shopping Network) devoted to it. Here our homes are invaded around the clock by slick-talking salespeople, often joined by celebrities hawking their own products or those from whose sale they stand to profit. There is no need to leave home to purchase: Just telephone and charge.

Much the same could be said about cybermalls and other forms of cybershopping. Increasing numbers of people have computers in their homes, and many of them both work and play on their computers. We may turn on our computers to escape the lure of television's

Home Shopping Network only to find the equally seductive lure of our favorite cybermalls. Computer-based consumption is even easier than consumption via the home shopping networks. In the case of HSN, we have to turn our attention away from the television set to make a telephone call. With cybermalls, we already are on-line, so that a visit to the mall and a purchase can be accomplished simultaneously. Innumerable other goods and services—including stocks, psychic advice, sex, and gambling—are being sold on-line, thereby greatly increasing the amount of consumption that can done through our home computers.[55]

Traditional and new means of consumption have been battering so hard and so often at our doors that many of us simply have given up and welcomed them all in. Why not? Spread before our eyes and ears is a cornucopia of goods and services. All that is required is a telephone call, a keystroke, and a credit card number. In this way our homes have become means of consumption. It is one thing to be trapped at the mall, but quite another thing to be trapped at home. No matter how trapped one is at the mall, one must eventually leave. However, most people do not have the option of leaving a home that has become commercialized. In any case, large numbers of people are quite happy with their commercialized homes and that contentment is likely to increase in the future as the possibility of purchasing more and more goods and services is brought into the home:

> The marriage of technology and commerce will make consuming ever more convenient: Our homes can become retail outlets, we can visit virtual shopping malls from our couches, shop for new homes on CD-ROM. We will, in other words, never have to leave home to fill the needs that marketing creates.[56]

There is spectacle in all of this; for some nothing could be more spectacular than to be able to acquire the fruits of our commercial world without ever having to leave the comforts of our home.

It is worth noting that the home is not only increasingly becoming a means of consumption, but also a means of production. For example, the same computer that is allowing us to shop at home is permitting us to work there. The home, the center of production and consumption before the Industrial Revolution, is once again becoming such a center in our postindustrial society. (And the home is also now becoming, again, an important means of consuming education, through televised and on-line courses and degrees.) Although production and consumption are again frequently occurring in the home, they are not the same kinds of production and consumption and they are not occurring in the same way.

Time: The Implosion of Times Available for Consumption

The ultimate objective in a capitalist economy (and today that is about the only economy that exists in most of the world), at least as far as time is concerned, is to allow people to consume around the clock, every day of the year. In other words, the objective is the implosion of all differences in time as far as consumption (and production) is concerned. Historically, there have been a number of impediments to reaching this objective. Before the advent of electric light, nightfall was a powerful barrier to consumption.[57] Means of consumption were often great distances away, and transportation was slow. As a result, trips to market were infrequent. Large numbers of people lacked the economic resources they needed to do much, if any, consumption beyond that which they collected or produced for themselves. Religion, especially in its promotion of asceticism and a day of rest, also served to impede consumption. The polity was responsible for laws that restricted consumption in a wide variety of ways (for example, Sunday "blue laws" that restrict alcohol sale). Long hours of work on the farm, in the factory, or in the household greatly restricted the amount of time and energy people could devote to consumption. Children and adolescents lacked the resources. People tended to work late into life leaving few, if any, "golden years" devoted to consumption.

In the last few decades most, if not all, of these barriers have imploded, or at least eroded, in the United States and in many other parts of the world. Electricity and other technological innovations have largely eliminated nightfall as a significant obstacle to consumption. Means of consumption seem much closer as automobiles, trains, busses, and even airplanes make it possible for people to get to them more quickly and whenever they want. The increasing wealth of the society has given more and more people the wherewithal to be active players in the malls of America as well as in all the other cathedrals of consumption. Even those without cash in hand or in the bank can play the consumer game, thanks to the ubiquitous credit card. In our increasingly secular society, religion has come to exert little influence over consumption (except, perhaps, as a spur to the commodification of religion and religious products). Most legal restrictions on consumption have been wiped from the books. Although there is some debate over this, work hours are more limited,[58] and work itself is less arduous, allowing people more time *and* energy to consume. Young people now have lots of resources at their disposal. People are living longer with the result that large numbers of retirees find themselves with many years to devote primarily to consumption.

As with many things related to the new means of consumption, the United States is the innovator and the world leader in the use of time. Said a student of time as an economic resource, "Compared to Europe, the U.S. is miles ahead in mining the economic value of time."[59] Factors inhibiting the greater use of time in Europe include legal restrictions on the hours businesses can be open and high social welfare costs that work against hiring extra people to handle night shifts. European culture and traditions are another factor. For example, "Much of the small business in Italy is family-owned and operated. Extending hours means going outside the family for labor, which is not the norm. America, on the other hand, is synonymous with new ideas, entrepreneurship and business competition."[60]

Even in the United States, it was not that long ago that there was little or no possibility of purchasing goods and services from dark to early morning. Over the years, hours were stretched and in some cases people became able to shop until 10 p.m. In a few cases, such as with the advent of the supermarket open 24-hours a day and the coming of convenience store chains such as 7-Eleven and Wawa® that never close, shopping could be done around the clock. However, there are a limited number of people who are interested in trekking to the market in the middle of the night. Furthermore, with the perception that crime and violence is increasing, a not insignificant number of people are reluctant to venture out of their homes late at night, especially in urban areas.

To truly make all time available for consumption the means of consumption had to implode into the home. The new means of consumption—especially HSN, cybermalls, catalogs[61]— have served to literally eliminate time as a barrier to consumption.

Time has imploded in other ways. In the past, it might have taken a week or more for a mail order to get to Sears, to pass through its shipping department, and to be delivered to the consumer. Now orders can be placed almost instantaneously by telephone, fax, or computer. Processing has been expedited greatly, and the time it takes to move an order out the door reduced enormously. Shipping has been revolutionized with the advent of the express parcel delivery services. The result is that an order–delivery cycle is now often completed in a day or two. Of course, because the new goods are in hand more quickly, one is likely to tire of them more rapidly as well.[62] This means that one may feel the need to plunge more quickly back into the consumer game.

Do any time barriers to consumption remain? Most adults must work many hours a week in order to earn the income needed for consumption, not to mention savings, and to have the credit base to qualify for credit cards[63] and other forms of credit. Presumably, time on the job is time that cannot be devoted to consumption. But various changes are making it easier for people to work and to consume at the same time. For example, the cybermalls and other types of cyber shopping, especially as they will evolve in the future, make it easy for workers to switch from work-related tasks to a quick visit to a "store" within a favored cybermall, a favorite cyber-casino, or to trade a stock electronically. Even time on the job will be less and less a barrier to consumption.

Not only is any time of the day, the night, the week, or the year increasingly defined as a "good" time for consumption, but any stage of a lifetime is now a good stage to consume. Infants, at least through their parents, grandparents, and so on, have been drawn into the world of consumption by, for example, the growth of baby superstores devoted solely to them. The toy superstores are oriented toward children, or at least to those who purchase things for them. Teenagers have become a huge market, and many of the new means of consumption (music, video, and electronics superstores, for example) could not exist without their business. The retired and the aged are no longer excused from consumption, either. Among other things, they are expected to consume the homes and lifestyles associated with retirement communities and to become morning mall walkers who might just stay around to sample the mall's offerings later in the day. Even the dying are expected to purchase the services of nursing homes and hospices and the dead (or their heirs) are consumers as far as chains of funeral homes and cemeteries are concerned.

Although I am emphasizing the ability of people to consume at all times, we must not forget the spectacular and enchanted (reenchanted) character of all of this, at least from the point of view of the consumer. Suppose the ghost of a nineteenth-century farmer found itself in the contemporary world of consumption. Many things would be amazing and seem magical (especially the appearance of the ghost), but one of those would certainly be the ability to consume at every minute, of every week or every year, virtually from birth to death. Although entrepreneurs have been instrumental in increasing the time available for consumption, they have not always been conscious of the fact that a spectacle would be created that would help sell goods and services.

Time: Implosion of Past, Present, and Future Earnings

The consumer possesses three basic types of resources of interest to merchants: money currently being earned and in hand; money that has been earned in the past, not spent, and saved or invested; and money that is likely to be earned in the future. Significant differences among the three types of resources have eroded in recent years; there has been an implosion of monies earned in the past, present, or future. As far as the contemporary merchant is concerned, there is no significant difference among them: Money is money whenever it is earned, and in any form it can be transformed into goods and services. A supermarket is more likely to get at cash in hand (although people are increasingly charging their groceries), a new car dealer is more likely to get at longer-term savings (past earnings) in the form of a down payment (plus continuing payments), and a home mortgage company will probably get at mostly future earnings via future principal and interest payments. However, the supermarket, the car dealer, and the mortgage company really do not care which "pot" the money comes from as long as they get their share of it. In this sense, the different pots of money implode into one another, leaving merchants with one huge cauldron from which profits can be ladled.

Merchants have few problems inducing people to spend present income. Past income, in the form of savings and investments, is harder to tap. Still, the capitalist economy has a wealth of experience with various techniques designed to induce people to spend this kind of money in the present. For example, the advertising industry devotes a lot of attention to creating seductive advertisements for luring people into parting with their savings. In the banking industry, the advent of checks made it easier for people to spend past earnings. A more recent innovation is the ATM, which allows people easy access to their money in situations in which cash rather than a check is required.

What is really new and of enormous importance is the incredible expansion of the implosion of future income into the present. It is certainly the case that techniques have long existed to get at future earnings (installment buying, for example), but there has been a tremendous expansion in traditional techniques (home and car loans, for example) and, more important, in the development of new methods and technologies (for example, the growth in the leasing of automobiles), especially the credit card (as well as credit instruments such as home equity loans). Although merchants care little whether sales are in cash or on credit,[64] credit card companies have a strong preference for customers to spend future income. The reason is that, if money that has not yet been earned is spent, consumers will be unable to pay their credit card bills in full immediately. Such consumers must go into debt to the credit card companies and pay the usurious interest rates associated with their cards.

The use of credit, especially via the credit card, and the spending of future income is an increasingly ubiquitous part of all of the new means of consumption. The most extreme are infomercials, the home television shopping networks, and the cybermalls and other forms of cyber-shopping that simply could not operate without credit card purchases. Las Vegas and Disney World would not exist, at least at their present scale, without credit cards. Cruise lines would be less affected, because they require lump sum payments that easily could be handled by check. However, even they are moving more into business done on credit. For example, Princess Cruises recently instituted a program whereby passengers can finance their cruises.[65] More important, cruise lines earn a lot of money from extra expenditures while on board (in the shops, at the spa, in the casino), and much of that is done on a credit card basis.

The economy is increasingly dependent on the expenditure of future income, the implosion of future earnings into the present. That is, it is not enough for us to spend all of our cash in hand or in the bank. We also must spend an increasing portion of money we have not yet earned in order to keep the economy humming at the level it expects and to which it has become accustomed.

Indeed, were large numbers of us to eliminate credit card debt, to begin living within our means, the effect on the economy would be disastrous. Among the thngs that would be dramatically altered were there no credit card debt is consumer spending. A decline in such spending would reverberate throughout the economy. The banking industry as we have come to know it would be badly shaken and dramatically altered. Many banks have come to rely on credit card loans as one of, if not *the*, most profitable of their businesses. In fact, some "monoline" banks rely exclusively on credit card business. Such banks would disappear, and many others would be forced to downsize and reorient their remaining business in order to survive. Some retailers would disappear altogether, and others would shrink dramatically. Particularly affected would be businesses that rely on sales via the telephone and computer. Most of that business would dry up without the credit card. Obviously, a contraction in banking and retailing would lead to a slowdown and scaling back in goods production and service provision. There would be many other reverberations throughout the economy, but overall we would likely face recession or depression.

The main spectacle in this context as far as the consumer is concerned is the seemingly unbelievable ability to buy goods and services without any cash in hand or in the bank. And this spectacle serves to draw the consumer into the cathedrals of consumption where it can be played out.

Time as Spectacle

The implosion of time barriers is a spectacle in itself, but there are other types of spectacles associated with time and the new means of consumption.

Speed

In fast food restaurants the spectacle is the speed with which one can obtain and a devour a meal. Although limited in terms of what it can do with space, at least within the confines of the restaurant (and even more so in a satellite location), the fast food restaurant obviously has been a highly revolutionary force in the realm of time. What once took hours at home, or many minutes in a traditional restaurant, now generally takes a matter of seconds in a fast food restaurant. We now take this for granted, but when first introduced it represented a spectacular reduction in the amount of time needed to produce and consume a meal. Furthermore, as the number of these restaurants proliferated, it took less and less time to get to one. It also is worth noting that the nature and spread of these restaurants also served to free time that could be used in other ways, especially consuming other goods and services in malls as well as many other new means of consumption.

All of the chains and franchises serve in one way or another to speed up the process of consumption. For example, if one wants a particular type of jeans, one can be pretty well assured that the Gap will have it; this cuts down on the time required to wander from shop to shop, or department store to department store (which are likely to have a much narrower selection of jeans). By the way, the reduction of time spent finding just the right pair of jeans does not necessarily mean that one will spend less time shopping. In fact, the likelihood is that with new jeans in hand, our consumer will wander off to other kinds of shops in the mall. After all, although fast food restaurants may want to get you in and out quickly, a mall wants to keep you in the mall, moving from shop to shop for as long as possible.

An interesting example of the speeding up of time in a realm in which one would not expect it is in "mass customization." It obviously takes a great deal of time to make and then receive clothing or shoes that are made to order for a specific individual. However, various businesses have dramatically reduced that time through mass customization.[66] For example, Custom Foot® is able to produce a customized shoe in about three weeks; Hallmark's® "Personalize It" allows people to create computer-generated greeting cards almost instantaneously; and Levi's® has developed a system to produce customized jeans far more quickly than it took in the past. We can expect to see more and more goods being produced and sold in this way in the future.

Spectacular Use of Time

Fast food restaurants and other chains reduce the time needed to consume, sometimes spectacularly, but this is not typical of the other new means of consumption. The spectacle in the vast majority of them is generally the feeling of a *loss* of a sense of time, a dream-like state in which time—unlike in the rest of one's life—seems not to matter. In many cases this works in conjunction with the spectacular size of these new means; getting lost in space also often means getting lost in time. And getting lost in time is often critical to the success of the new means of consumption. It is a key part of the dream they are marketing to customers.

Let us start with the idea that what is being marketed is an experience that offers the spectacle of seeming to be able to defy the constraints and inexorability of time. Las Vegas casinos, as well the city in general, are famous for this and they seek to accomplish it in various ways. First, they truly are 24-hour a day operations, so that one day rolls seamlessly into another. Second, efforts are made to eliminate any external signs (sunshine, darkness, and so on) of the time of day or night. Third, clocks are forbidden in casinos. Fourth, the vast, cavernous space operates in conjunction with the absence of indicators of time passing to create a dream-like world in which time is not a factor, or at least less important than it is elsewhere. Fifth, basically the same kinds of activities are taking place around the clock. Gambling tables are open, drinks are served, the distinctive noise of the casino continues unabated, and people sit in front of slot machines or at the gaming tables, pulling levers, taking cards, throwing dice, and so on. There is the sound of a few coins dropping and occasionally of large numbers of coins being won. The slot machines themselves make their odd whistles and screeches, and so on. The casinos are not completely successful in their efforts (fewer people gamble in the early morning than at night, and they are more likely to drink coffee than cocktails), but they come as close as any of the new means of consumption to altering or eliminating a sense of time passing. Representative of what takes place in casinos is the sky effect on the ceiling of the Forum Shops adjacent to Caesar's Palace. The projected sky image changes quickly and dramatically leaving the viewer with the impression of rapidly passing time. Although it has not eliminated the sense of time passing, the Forum's "sky" has greatly altered it, thereby symbolizing the continual effort to disorient the visitor to Las Vegas.

The sports books in the casinos offer betting on horse and dog races around the country from early morning to late at night. Given time zone differences (in fact, in the sports books time zones implode[67]), one can begin by gambling on East Coast tracks early in the morning and end up betting on races being run at night on the West Coast. Time is magically stretched so that the inveterate gambler can spend twelve hours or even more betting on horse races (compared to the normal four or five hours a day at a racetrack). Of course, this constitutes not only a spectacular expansion of time, but also of space, because a gambler can readily move from betting on races on both coasts as well as on those anywhere in between. One might go from betting on a horse race being run in the snow in Boston to one being run on a sun-drenched 85-degree day in southern Florida or California.

These examples communicate a sense of time passing that is radically different from what is experienced normally. But the spectacular elimination of a sense of time and its passage approaches its ultimate form in shopping in cyberspace. For example, the 24-Hour Mall offers about two dozen round-the-clock cyberstores.[68] The "surfer" can see and do exactly the same things at any time of the day or night. There are no indicators of night or day in cyberspace; one is adrift there. It is possible, even highly likely, that one is going to lose one's sense of time (and one's money!).

An interesting example in this realm is the on-line casino. Although Las Vegas casinos work hard to eliminate a sense of time, what they can do pales in comparison to the capabilities of on-line casinos. After all, in a cybercasino the gambler is given absolutely *no* sense of the time of day or of time passing (although some help might come from the time indicator at the bottom right of most computer screens). The on-line player has a similar absence of sense of place; casino operations can take place anywhere in the world. (Other examples of 24-hour consumption include selected Wal-Marts, fitness centers, bank by phone or computer operations, and so on.)

Another way in which many of the new means of consumption make spectacular use of time is to present attractions that are drawn from many points in humankind's past, present, and future, so that the past, present, and future implode into one another producing a pastiche. Las Vegas offers us the ancient past at the Luxor, the Middle Ages at Excalibur, the near-past in New York, New York,[69] and the future in the Stratosphere as well as "Star Trek: The Experience" at the Las Vegas Hilton. Malls increasingly juxtapose the ersatz artifacts of the Museum Store and the Natuie Store with futuristic gadgets available at Sharper Image. The best example is Disney, which cavalierly juxtaposes the past in the form of such exhibits as "Pirates of the Caribbean" and the future in the form, say, of "Space Mountain" with a number of timeless attractions traceable to Disney characters of one kind or another. The message seems to be not only that Disney can collapse time barriers, but also time itself does not matter (at least as long as one is within the Disney confines and spending a sufficient amount of money to keep the Disney empire operating at the level to which it has grown accustomed).

It is important to remember that the new means of consumption manipulate the customer's sense of time in order to earn greater profits. The assumption is that the spectacular manipulation of time is likely to lead to more customers and more expenditures. And the more time available for consumption, the great the number of goods and services that will be sold. Furthermore, consumers who are disoriented in terms of time are likely to be disoriented in other ways, including their thinking about money.

Extraordinary Spaces

Beyond the implosion of the distinction between home and the means of consumption, the most general objective in the spatial realm is to offer a sense of an expanse that is somehow different from that ordinarily encountered by the customer. An effort may be made to draw the customers' attention to or away from some spatial aspect of the setting to impress them. This is usually accomplished by creating the sense, often illusory, of a colossal, nearly boundless space.

Manipulating Spatial Constraints

A sense of infinite space is easiest to create in the very newest, dematerialized means of consumption. Cybermalls, as well as the other modes of selling commodities in cyberspace, could be anywhere; they could sell anything; and there appears to be no end to their potential number. Because they are at the outer limit in terms of the spatial dimension, cyberspace and its cybermalls offer the greatest potential for a spectacular sense, and use, of space. Increasing that potential is the fact that one may use cyberspace in innumerable ways to sell and to buy. Current examples include ordering airplane or cruise tickets, "playing" the stock market, purchasing (even reading) books and enrolling in and taking academic courses.

There are limitations on the cyberworld's capacity to create a spectacular sense of space. Consumers are likely to be sitting in their studies, offices, or dens and peering at tiny video screens. Those who control and manage cyberspace must create spectacular images in order to get viewers to abandon their sense of where they are physically and to lose themselves in the cyberworld. The analogy is a video game (especially those relying on virtual reality goggles) in which players are treated to an incomparable spectacle *if* they can suspend their sense of reality and distance themselves from their physical surroundings (e.g., the virtual reality goggles) and immerse themselves completely in the game world. Cyberspace and cybermalls offer the same possibility, at least theoretically. If users can, in principle, be led to completely lose themselves, and it remains to be seen whether enough of them can, they become ideal targets to those who control the cybermalls. Adrift in cyberspace, one has lost touch with reality (at least day-to-day reality) and is in a state that makes one vulnerable to buying things one does not need and cannot afford.

Similarly advantaged is television, especially the television shopping networks, which offer an analogous sense of infinite space. Their signals, like those in cyberspace, are adrift in the ether. The relationship between customer and seller is not restricted by the usual spatial constraints associated with malls or shops. Of course, the den, the television screen, and the telephone necessary to place orders do impose some restrictions. However, space constraints are reduced, if not eliminated, when customers can become as immersed in the goings-on of their home shopping network as they can in their video games or explorations of cyberspace. There are certainly cases of people whose major reality has become their relationship to the hosts of, and the products purveyed on, the home shopping network. Immersed in this ethereal world, they buy lots of things (often things they have no need for) and, as a consequence, many of them become deeply indebted to their credit card companies. The home shopping networks have succeeded, at least for some viewers, in creating the kind of boundless space that cybermalls are trying to create.

Credit cards facilitate this process, as they do much of what transpires in relationship to the new means of consumption. The ability to merely enter card numbers into the computer, or to repeat them to someone who is taking our order over the phone, helps to eliminate spatial barriers to consumption. Of course, although people can defy space while ordering and paying, most goods must still be delivered across physical distances. Exceptions to this are digital products, stock positions, and so on.

Seeming to Be Everywhere

Some new means of consumption create a spectacle by limiting or eliminating spatial constraints, but most are still limited by material realities that force them to find other ways to make a spectacle of space. One course of action is to be, or at least seem to be, everywhere in the world. The number of outlets of a fast food chain, combined with the fact it not only spans the nation but also the world, gives the diner a sense of participating in a massive phenomenon, of being an infinitesimal part of a globe-straddling operation. In eating burgers and fries, Americans may be merely feeding themselves in the most prosaic of ways, but at the same time they may feel themselves to be a players in a colossal national and international operation. The diners at a McDonald's in a remote Russian city are, in contrast, eating what is for them exotic food. At the same time, they may feel that they are participating in an enormous international experience that has its origins in the United States. For many outside the United States, dining in a fast food restaurant allows them to transcend spatial limitations and dine, in their fantasies anyway, in America—or at least allows them to dine like Americans.

For most people, getting to a theme park requires a major trip. To overcome this problem, the parks are in various ways moving closer to the consumer. One example is the Disney stores in many malls. We may not be able to enjoy the rides, but we can still get the souvenirs and have a "Disney experience." Another is the entertainment centers aimed at adults such as Dave and Buster's that are increasingly finding their way into our malls. As we mentioned, Disney is entering this market as well with Club Disney, which is oriented more to children and projected to grow to 100 or more outlets:

> Kids can play alongside such favorite characters as Goofy . . . enjoy shows in the Applaudeville Theater, create "mouseterpieces" in art classes or climb around a 30-foot-high jungle chamber. Or grownups and youngsters can work together in the Mouse Pad computer laboratory, where 16 computers feature multimedia software designed to combine education and entertainment. They also can visit Animation Alley, where cartoon and animatronic techniques are demonstrated, using popular Disney characters.[70]

Then there is the relatively new chain of indoor play centers for children, Jungle Jim's®, which has miniature amusement park-type rides (e.g., roller coaster, bumper cars, scrambler), games, and restaurants oriented to children's tastes. One parent called it a "nightmare cash machine."[71]

A potential blockbuster in this realm is Gameworks arcades and eatertainment centers. There are currently two Gameworks in operation, and 100 more are planned by 2002. Designed as a kind of three-ring circus, Gameworks is defined by the virtual reality game designed by Steven Spielberg: "Vertical Reality is a 24-foot-high attraction, designed to look like a four-story high-rise. A dozen customers—paying $4 apiece—race to rid the building of villains on video screens. The competitors are strapped into seats that rise as they succeed and fall as they fail."[72] This is an effort to adapt the theme park model (as well as the movies) and bring it into closer proximity to a large proportion of the population.

A Sense of Enormous Space

Another course taken by the new means of consumption to create a spectacle is to use enormous physical spaces (or to create the sense of a far larger space than is actually occupied). Most of the cathedrals of consumption are unable to come to us. They therefore must give us a very good reason to leave our homes (with our cybermalls, home shopping networks, catalogs, and home-delivery pizza). With their spectacular use of enormous spaces, shopping malls have long sought to draw us out of our homes. Take this description of the Westminster Mall in California provided by William Kowinski, author of *The Malling of America*:

> Westminster Mall was a classic California cathedral . . . it opened into a soaring central court. . . . The court covered an enormous area, both horizontally and vertically. High above was the orange ceiling dome, layered with white. From it hung a huge net sculpture. . . . Altogether this court combined intimate spaces with monumental scale and audacious effects. . . . I was awestruck.[73]

If a student of the malls is awestruck by the physical space and the way it is used in this mall (as well as its amenities), you can imagine the reactions of an ordinary, first-time visitor. Even more extreme are the responses of those from other cultures, especially those from developing nations.[74]

Other spatial developments set the stage for such capacious malls and our sense that they are spectacular. Most of us spend most of our lives in confined spaces such as classrooms, small apartments, tract houses, and office cubicles. This helps to make the use of huge spaces by shopping malls (and other new means of consumption) so stunning and attractive to us.[75]

Of course, the spectacle of the mall has led, inexorably, to the mega-mall where the objective is to create much larger settings, to make even more spectacular use of space. For example, as of mid-1997, Mall of America had more than 400 stores, employed almost 12,000 people, accommodated 35 million to 40 million visits a year, with the average visitor staying three hours. Thirty-forty percent of the visitors were tourists, many of whom were in the area for the express purpose of visiting the mall. They are *not* drawn there by the chains and franchises, because they are nearly indistinguishable from those available in their local mall. What draws them is the sheer size of the place and the fact that it encompasses so many things. People are drawn to what they think will be a colossal cornucopia of goods and services, a phantasmagoria.

The colossal size of the Mall of America permits it to house not only a shopping mall, but also a theme park (Knott's Camp Snoopy) within its confines. The enchantment lies in the fact that one of our fantastic means of consumption—the theme park—is simply a small part of an even more fantastic means—the mega-mall. Knott's Camp Snoopy covers seven acres and boasts twenty-five rides. It also includes entertainment, shopping, and eight places to eat.

In addition to the shopping mall and the theme park, Mall of America encompasses Underwater World. Visitors to it are transported by a moving walkway through an aquarium that takes them through several areas—Minnesota dawn, Minnesota cold water lakes, Mississippi River, Gulf of Mexico, and tropical Barrier Reefs off the coast of Belize. The trip takes an hour; as they progress through it, visitors are surrounded by 8,000 sharks, sting rays, and many other types of sea life.

Then there is the admission-free Lego Imagination Center that includes more than thirty Lego constructions, play areas for children and, need we say, a Lego shop. Catering to the adults is the fourth-floor entertainment district that includes, among other things, a four-teen-screen movie theater, Planet Hollywood, and Hooters®.

Mega-malls expect the visitor to be impressed not only by their sheer physical size, but also by all of the things that space permits under one roof. Impressing visitors in these ways, these malls expect that many other visitors will be drawn to the mall with a similar desire to be astounded. Of course, the ultimate goal is not merely to astound, but to lure the consumer to the mall and into spending.

Although they now may be inside mega-malls, amusement parks or theme parks preceded the malls in the use of great expanses of space to create a spectacle for park visitors. This was clear in Disney's parks, especially in its Orlando site where it was able to buy up huge tracts of land and create a park with seemingly limitless space. Each of the elements of Disney World is spectacular by itself. But, when taken together, they are designed to overwhelm the visitor with the size of the place and the ever-increasing range of entertainment that is offered. It seems like a self-contained universe that cannot possibly be explored fully on one, or even a few, visits. The addition of more and more attractions and hotels serves to continually buttress that sense, as well as the spectacular image that Disney World works so hard to create.

A similar development has occurred in the cruise business. There has been an ongoing effort to build bigger and bigger liners. The goal is to offer the vacationer a physical space that is mind boggling in size as well as in what it encompasses

Positioning cruise ships as floating resorts is a prime motivation for the many new plush spas and high-tech fitness centers, the Broadway-sized revues in Broadway-sized theaters, bigger and more attractive casinos, upscale shops and boutiques, miniature golf courses and, in 1999, an ice skating rink aboard a new Royal Caribbean ship.[76]

The largest cruise ship ever built, a mega-ship (following in the tradition of the mega-malls and reflecting the importance of large spaces to the cathedrals of consumption), is the Carnival Cruise Lines' Destiny. It is 101,000 tons (Disney Magic is a mere 85,000 tons). It is almost 900 feet long (Disney Magic is 964 feet long), more than 100 feet wide, and has twelve passenger decks with a passenger capacity of 3,400 (Disney Magic's capacity is a 1,000 fewer passengers). There are two 2-level dining rooms, one seating 1,114 people and the other 706. There also is a restaurant seating 1,252, a pizzeria open twenty-four hours, ethnic restaurants, and a grill. The spa is 15,000 square feet. The central atrium is nine stories high; it has four glass-walled elevators and a glass ceiling, further allowing the passenger to take in the enormous space encompassed by the ship and to give still broader vistas of the sky, day and night. Outdoors there are four swimming pools, a jogging track, a 214-foot-long water slide, and a bandstand. Among the entertainment centers are Millionaire's Club, a 9,000-square-foot casino with more than 300 slot machines and twenty-three gaming tables; Down Beat, a small jazz club; Point After, a disco with 525 television monitors; Criterion Lounge, featuring comedy and dance; All-Star Bar, a sports bar; and Palladium, a three-story, 1,500-seat show lounge featuring a Las Vegas-type show with fireworks and lasers. According to two analysts of the cruise industry, it is "a ship that has truly married the dazzling glitter and entertainment facilities of a large Las Vegas-style resort with a ship's hull."[77]

I have emphasized the spectacle of the size of the ship itself, but we should not ignore the fact that cruise ships also attract people by offering them the great vistas open to ships at sea. However, as was pointed out in the last chapter, it may well be that many people on cruises tend to be more impressed by the artificial vistas provided on the ship than by those provided by nature.

The modern hotel offers spectacular use of space as well. I will focus on the Peachtree Plaza in Atlanta, created by world-famous architect John Portman. Portman's capacious lobbies or atriums have been the paradigm for the use of this kind of space in many other new means of consumption[78] (including cruise ships). In fact, "the Portman name is synonymous with the soaring hotel atrium."[79] Open, glass-enclosed elevators take visitors from the lobby to the hotel floors. The elevators are designed to give guests an unbroken view of the expanse of the atrium. "The elevator is like a seat in a theater, but one in which your vantage point is moving continuously."[80] The elevator can be seen as providing "the same sort of thrill as a ride in an amusement park."[81] The balconies on each floor of the hotel also provide a perspective on the expanse of the atrium. Adding to the impact of the atrium is the inclusion of various types of indoor pools and a park-like setting with lots of vegetation.

It cannot be reiterated too often that all of this attention to things such as the hotel atrium is not an end in itself, but designed to further consumption. Portman's work is described as having the "merchandiser's instinct."[82] The lobbies include various places to eat, drink, and shop. These are all enormous producers of income for hotel owners.

The emphasis on great expanses of space also is certainly the case in the Las Vegas casino–hotels, many of which have been influenced by Portman's concepts. Luxor, at the moment the world's second largest hotel, was built at a cost of approximately $650 million. The heart of the hotel is a pyramid with thirteen acres of glass. It encloses the world's largest atrium (the Portman influence, again); one could fit nine Boeing 747 airplanes in it. The pyramid is topped by the most powerful beam of light in the world; at 315,000 watts it is forty times stronger than the most powerful commercial spotlights. Almost lost in all of this is the fact that the grounds of the Luxor also contain a ten-story Sphinx; taller than the original in Egypt. The Luxor casino covers 120,000 square feet. Also to be found in the hotel is a motion-based simulator, an IMAX theater, and a Sega Virtualand. There is a range of themed shops including Cairo Bazaar, Treasure Chamber, and Scarab Shop.

Not to be outdone by mega-malls, several Las Vegas casinos now have, as we have seen, roller coasters. If you think it is spectacular to ride a roller coaster in a mega-mall, how about riding one over and through the skyscrapers that make up part of the facade of the New York, New York casino–hotel? Or consider the 1,149-foot-high Stratosphere, the tallest structure in Las Vegas. In addition to the High Roller roller coaster, the Stratosphere features Big Shot, a thrill ride that shoots people 160 feet in the air more than 1,000 feet above the Strip, in the twelve-story pod that sits 100 stories atop this enormous tower. It is touted as the tallest freestanding observation tower in America and the tallest building west of the Mississippi.

Turning to more prosaic means of consumption, superstores offer huge spaces with overwhelming quantities of goods: "To enter a superstore is to know what the scale of Olympus or Eldorado must have looked like in the imaginations of mortals."[83] Here is a description of a Wal-Mart supercenter in those terms:

> The first impressions are obvious but overwhelming. The place, like the country, is big. The Supercenter spreads over 201,000 square feet, the size of four American football fields. Man (or, in this instance, a young woman) resorts to technology to conquer distance: she is employed to whizz around on roller skates, fetching and returning goods.[84]

CONCLUSION

Implosion has served to reenchant the cathedrals of consumption by bringing together two or more means of consumption in one setting. Implosion into the home has created seemingly magical new ways to consume such as television shopping networks and cybermalls. The implosion of times available for shopping has created an enchanted world in which one can shop around the clock for 365 days a year. The implosion of past, present, and future earnings, especially the easier access to future earnings, means that people can buy things they could never have bought in the past. Finally, the spectacular use of both time and space has also served to reenchant the cathedrals of consumption.

7

SOCIETAL IMPLICATIONS AND THE FUTURE OF THE NEW MEANS OF CONSUMPTION

In the United States, and increasingly in much of the rest of the world, the last half of the twentieth century witnessed the emergence and explosive growth of a wide range of new means of consumption. This is a part, as well as a reflection, of the shift away from a society dominated by production toward one dominated by consumption. In an earlier era, it was the means of production that were predominant, but today it is the means of consumption that have gained ascendancy. The shopping mall has replaced the factory as the defining structure of the age. Like it or not, our future lies mainly in consumption and the means that allow, encourage, and even coerce us to consume.

Most of the new means of consumption—shopping malls, megamalls, superstores, Disney World, cruise ships, casinos—are quite obvious. Others, such as the luxury-gated community, are not so apparent. Still others such as athletic stadiums, airports, high schools, universities, and museums surprisingly reflect the steady penetration of the new means of consumption into society as a whole. Nothing speaks more clearly of the expansion and invasion of the new means of consumption, their increasing ubiquity in all sectors of our lives, than the fact that even the home has joined their ranks.

The new means of consumption are revolutionary not only in themselves but also for the central role they play in the development and sustenance of contemporary hyperconsumption. However, the new means of consumption and their role in hyperconsumption have generally been ignored or subordinated to a concern with other economic issues.

This book has focused on an inherent dilemma confronting the cathedrals of consumption. In order to succeed and grow economically, as well as to serve the wants of their huge and growing clientele, the new means are forced to rationalize their operations. Rationalization may help the cathedrals to serve their clientele—and not incidentally increase the bottom lines of their balance sheets—but it brings with it disenchantment. Coldly efficient settings are not well-suited to succeed for very long in attracting and retaining the throngs of consumers required for economic success. It is true that rationalization tends, paradoxically, to bring with it a limited kind of magic. For example, the efficiency with which the new means of consumption dispense goods and services can seem quite magical to the consumer. But though the enchanting aspects of rationalized systems are important, they do not adequately support the profit demands of the new means of consumption.

A variety of developments have served to reenchant the cathedrals of consumption. Some of these have been developed quite intentionally, and others have come about more as byproducts of developments in a world on the cusp of the modern–postmodern divide. Indeed, the fact that the new means of consumption are *both* rationalized and disenchanted (modern) and enchanted and reenchanted (postmodern) is reflective of this divide. All of these reenchanting developments involve spectacles of one kind or another, which create reenchantment and tend to lure consumers into the means of consumption.

The most intentional spectacles involve efforts on the part of those who control the new means of consumption to put on extravaganzas for, and to offer simulations to, consumers. There are the often less purposeful and even unintentional spectacles associated with implosion, time, and space. Intentionally or not, the cathedrals of consumption have been reenchanted by their increasingly simulated nature, by their dedifferentiation, by the implosion of temporal and spatial distinctions, and by the extraordinary use of time and space.

This, however, brings us again to the inherent dilemma confronting the new means of consumption. However they have accomplished it, they have managed to become reenchanted and, as a result, grown infinitely more attractive to consumers and effective in luring them into consumption. The problem is that these efforts at reenchantment may be rationalized from their inception. Even if they are not, the new means of consumption are often so enormous in size or encompass so many settings that they are forced to rationalize that which reenchants consumers. However, in rationalizing these forms of reenchantment they are disenchanting them. Can rationalized forms of reenchantment remain enchanting and attractive to consumers? Can the cathedrals of consumption continually generate new, nonrationalized forms of reenchantment? Time will tell, but it is clear that there are inherent contradictions at the heart of the new means of consumption and it is possible that they could ultimately prove to be their undoing.

Spectacles tend to grow dated and boring quite quickly. The already spectacular new means of consumption are under constant pressure to create ever more spectacular settings. This is nowhere clearer than in Las Vegas where the most spectacular new casino (e.g., New York, New York) succeeds, and yesterday's spectacle (e.g., the Sands) falls to the wrecking ball. The success of spectacular new casinos leads to the creation of even newer and more spectacular ones. Great costs are involved in wrecking perfectly good casinos and in erecting ever more spectacular (and costly) new ones. Is there some upper limit to the creation of spectacles?

At one level, this book can be seen as constituting simply an examination, through the lens of a variety of theoretical perspectives, of a significant, but largely ignored trend, in contemporary consumption. At another level, it can be seen as a paean for the clearly spectacular cathedrals of consumption as well as their ability to deliver an unprecedented cornucopia of goods and services to large numbers of people. At yet another level, what is offered can be viewed as a critique of the new means of consumption and their central role in control, exploitation, and hyperconsumption.

While I have discussed the cathedrals of consumption in general terms, there is great range among them, extending from the humble satellite location of a fast food restaurant in the corner of a convenience store to the floating palaces of cruise lines and the stationary ones on the Las Vegas Strip. Whatever their differences, and they are enormous, all of the new means of consumption have progressively enhanced their ability to sell commodities. I have emphasized the inherent dilemmas facing the cathedrals of consumption, but I have perhaps not said enough about what the payoff is for them: the enhanced ability to sell goods and services.

The following description of Disney World illustrates that it is, above all else, a selling machine:

The huckstering is relentless. Behind every fake front, at every entrance and exit of every feature, something is inescapably for sale—refreshments, related merchandise, or concession goods—all of which goes like popcorn.

Things seem wildly overpriced. Just in case a shopping opportunity may have been missed, however, a giant store of all-Mickey merchandise offers a last chance before the final exit to part with real money or Disney dollars (purchased with real money at the gate, on the assumption that it will surely be parted with).[1]

Like Disney World, cruise ships purport to offer an all-inclusive price, but before one is done one is likely to spend much more than the price of the cruise. A cruise ship is a selling, or money, machine that offers the vacationer many other places to spend money such as the ship's photographer, bars, casinos, boutiques, shops, beauty salons, spas, art auctions, telephone calls, and shore excursions.

Of course, Las Vegas casinos do not promise all-inclusive vacations so there are no barriers to their efforts to maximize visitors' expenditures. Once content to rake in the enormous profits derived from gambling, casino–hotels have now found a variety of other revenue streams including hotel rooms, restaurants, shows, virtual reality game rooms, elegant boutiques and souvenir shops hawking all sorts of merchandise, especially t-shirts, sporting the appropriate logos.

It is easy to see Disney World, cruise ships, and casino–hotels as selling machines, but it might be a bit harder to see the more mundane new means of consumption in this light. Yet all of them, in their own ways, have become increasingly well-oiled selling machines. The fast food restaurant has greatly increased the ability to move people through, and to move food out of, its doors and drive-through windows. Superstores have focused their attention on refining their ability to sell a specific line of merchandise. In contrast, malls have concentrated on constructing a system that maximizes the sale, through "adjacent attraction" and other devices, of an extraordinarily wide range of goods and services. Television's home shopping network as well as various sites in cyberspace have progressively increased their ability to sell commodities and, in the process, to turn the home into a means of consumption.

The preceding is a summary of the main thrust of this book. The remainder of this concluding chapter has four additional missions. First, to briefly reconsider whether the new means of consumption are truly revolutionary. Second, to examine a range of issues suggested by the foregoing chapters. Third, to discuss the relationship between race, class, and gender and the cathedrals of consumption. Fourth, to offer some thoughts on the future of the cathedrals of consumption.

DETERMINING IF THE NEW MEANS OF CONSUMPTION ARE TRULY "NEW"

I have defined the new means of consumption as "new" because they came into existence, at least in their contemporary forms, after the end of World War II. But is there anything really new here? What clearly and unequivocally distinguishes the new means of consumption from their predecessors? The short answer is that there is little or nothing that is qualitatively new, but the quantitative increases associated with the new means of consumption add up to a revolutionary change in them and in consumption more generally.

Modern and Postmodern

The new means of consumption have many of the same characteristics as predecessors such as the fair, the Parisian arcade, the department store, and the world exhibition. Although the earliest forms were generally nonrational, there have long been efforts to rationalize the means of consumption. For example, there were a number of rational components of the Parisian department stores of the mid-1800s. As nonrational as it was in comparison to the Disney World of today, Coney Island's Steeplechase Park was an attempt to be more rationalized than the amusement parks that preceded it. From this perspective the new means of consumption are part of a gradual, long-term process of increasing rationalization, and there is no clear dividing line between those of concern in this book and their predecessors.

The same point can be made about the various processes that have served to reenchant the new means of consumption. The creation of spectacles through extravaganzas, simulations, implosion, and the extraordinary use of time and space are not peculiar to the new means of consumption. For example, customers of the early Parisian department stores found the implosion of many specialty shops into that single setting to be quite spectacular. A similar spectacular implosion lay at the base of the success of the early supermarkets. World exhibitions and fairs have long made use of extravaganzas and have been characterized by efforts to simulate many of the world's cultures. However, today's spectacles are of a far greater magnitude than those that characterized the predecessors of the new means of consumption.

Given the existence of these processes in earlier means of consumption, how can we label them as postmodern? The answer, following Jean-François Lyotard, is that the modern and the postmodern have always coexisted,[2] although today we are witnessing the ascendancy of the postmodern. Implosion, simulation, and so on are now more common and more developed, but they are not discontinuous with processes that existed a century or more ago.

Specific Continuities and Discontinuities

The case of the fast food restaurant, especially McDonald's, illustrates some of the specific continuities and discontinuities associated with the new means of consumption. People have always eaten fast food and there have been "take-away" shops of one kind or another for centuries. Even the franchised fast food restaurant can be traced back to the 1920s and the immediate predecessor of the McDonald's chain, Mac and Dick McDonald's hamburger stand. In a general sense, all that the McDonald's chain did was to combine a system for cooking and serving food developed by the McDonald brothers with the idea of franchised fast food, which had been in existence for several decades.

However, it was McDonald's (in conjunction with the other new means of consumption) that dramatically altered the way in which we consume. In this sense, there *is* something new about the new means of consumption; in fact, they have many new and distinctive characteristics. Some of these are quite specific and relate to a particular means of consumption, and others apply to many, perhaps even to all, of them.

In terms of specific factors, one of the reasons that many of McDonald's predecessors in the franchise business failed was that regional franchise systems were allowed to develop and they had the power to subvert the basic principles of the franchiser. In contrast, McDonald's franchise founder Ray Kroc did not permit regional franchises and granted franchises one at a time, rarely granting more than one to an individual. This served to give McDonald's centralized control over its franchises and helped ensure uniformity throughout the system. Another reason for the failure of early franchises was that they set high initial fees, but once central management had that money, it tended to lose interest in the franchises. Kroc set a low initial fee, but he demanded a higher continuing percentage of sales from the franchises. The result was that central management had a vested interest in how well each of the franchises was run and in how much profit it earned. These seemingly minor variations helped to make McDonald's different from its predecessors and a revolutionary force in the fast food industry and in the means of consumption more generally.

More General Factors

There are, of course, broader factors that make the new means of consumption different from their predecessors. First, as a result of the transition from a focus on production to consumption, the means of consumption play a far greater role in peoples' lives than they ever have in the past. New groups, including the very young and the very old, have been more integrated into the world of consumption. Furthermore, many Americans are more affluent than ever before, especially given the economic boom of the 1990s, and they are in the position to consume much more, to use the new means of consumption (and many other older ones) to an unprecedented extent. And there are simply a lot more consumers, with a lot more demands, creating the need for bigger and better means of consumption.

Second, enormous corporate structures have come to control many of the new means of consumption. A century or so ago, consumers were most likely to encounter small "mom and pop" operations when they found themselves in a consumption setting. Today almost all of the new means of consumption are but small components of huge corporate enterprises. This has dramatically altered the way they are run. Great size also demands increasing rationalization and provides the resources needed to create unprecedented spectacles.

Third, technology has wrought at least as great a change on the means of consumption as it has on the rest of society. Indeed, the new means of consumption, as discussed throughout this book, would be impossible without the innumerable technological advances of the last half century. Most notable, of course, is the computer. All of the new means of consumption rely on the computer for various aspects of their operation. Some, such as the cybermall, would literally not exist were it not for the computer. And the computer has made possible facilitating means, most notably the credit card, without which all of the new means of consumption would be at best hard-pressed to function.

In sum, there *is* enough new to draw a clear dividing line between the means of consumption as they existed before the close of World War II and those that came into existence afterward. In the cumulative effect of incremental changes there is a revolutionary change in the way Americans, and much of the rest of the world, consume.

OTHER ISSUES

The following sections will touch on a variety of other issues, many of which will cast further light on the uniqueness of the new means of consumption.

The Blurring of Once-Clear Distinctions

If in the modern world everything seemed pretty clear-cut, on the cusp of the postmodern world many things seem quite hazy. This is especially true in the realm of consumption. The implosion of the real and the unreal leaves us with an unclear sense of the distinction between them. Virtually every means of consumption is a simulated setting, or has simulated elements, or simulated people, or simulated products. Even those things that still seem real have an increasing number of unreal elements. As a result, it is no longer so clear what is real and what is unreal.

Furthermore, so much around us is unreal that we have grown far more comfortable with the unreal than the real. A tropical island owned by a cruise line and staffed by its employees seems more attractive than a "real" tropical island and its native inhabitants and their indigenous habits, foods, and products. Acclimated to the unreal, we are either oblivious to, unconcerned about, or may even revel in the increasing disappearance of reality. The world is increasingly being defined by its unreal elements.

Also being obscured is the distinction between the private and the public. Information that was once considered private has now become part of the public domain. All sorts of very personal information is being accumulated and bought and sold for profit. Another aspect of the blurring of the private–public distinction involves the invasion of the home by the new means of consumption. Once largely a sanctuary from the incursions of the commercial world, the home has now become an integral part of that world. We can no longer retreat to the sanctity of our homes in an effort to escape commercialization. And if we cannot escape into the home, there is no escape.

Distinctions relating to time have similarly been obscured. For example, the notion of biological time, that there are different times of life for different sorts of things, has eroded. Not too long ago, adulthood was defined as the prime time of life for consumption, but now childhood, adolescence, the retirement years, and even old age have also been defined as life stages in which one is expected to consume actively. Different kinds of cathedrals of consumption may be used, and different products may be consumed, but one is expected to consume, whatever the life stage.

Similarly, differences between times of the day, days of the week, weeks of the year, and so on have all collapsed with the result that every minute of every day is considered a good time to consume. Gone are the respites from consumption that used to be associated with nighttime hours, the sabbath, holidays, and so on. There is literally no rest for weary consumers.

The Black Hole of Consumption

A similar conclusion can be drawn from thinking about the new means of consumption, and consumption more generally, from the point view of view of Baudrillard's thinking on a postmodern black hole into which everything is imploding.[3] At one level, this implies that more and more of what we do relates to consumption. At another level, more specific to the concerns of this book, it suggests that many formerly "noncommercial" settings are becoming cathedrals of consumption. In other words, distinctions in the realm of consumption in general, and between the cathedrals of consumption and other types of settings, are growing increasingly blurred.

The emulation of the new means of consumption is accelerating and is likely to continue to do so. An increasing number of settings are taking on the trappings of the shopping mall (and other new means of consumption); in many cases they are becoming shopping malls. Falling into this category are high schools, universities, museums, athletic stadiums, airports, television, the Internet and, the home.

In Baudrillard's terms, we can say that these extensions of the new means of consumption are converging with the new means themselves to produce a world in which all settings are about consumption. It becomes harder and harder to go anywhere that is not emulating the shopping mall, that is not a cathedral of consumption, in one way or another. What of the concert hall? Or the opera? Surely, they are oases of culture free of this pressure? But the fact is that major concert halls are increasingly characterized by shops and kiosks selling food and souvenirs of various types.

Of course, the more general implication of this is that we are all, ourselves, sinking into a black hole of consumption. More of our actions, along with more of the settings in which we act, end up converging in a black hole of consumption. And still more actions and more settings are destined to descend into that black hole.

Homogenization

Many of the new means of consumption seek to replicate, more or less, the same setting from one geographic location to another and to offer in those locales essentially the same, or very similar, goods and services. The Gap in Chicago and the clothing being sold there are essentially the same as those in New York or San Francisco. The income tax services being offered by H&R Block® in those cities are also very similar. The design of shopping malls may (or may not) differ from one city to another, but there is inevitably great similarity from one to another in the chain stores housed in them and the goods and services being offered by them. The result is a growing homogenization of the American means of consumption and of the goods and services being purchased. That is not to say that there is not a great profusion and diversity of commodities available to Americans, but essentially the same profusion is increasingly available everywhere. American consumption is characterized simultaneously by diversity and homogeneity, or "homogeneous diversity."

There is great variation from one country to another, but it is clear that the owners of the American means of consumption are seeking to impart a similar kind of homogeneity to much of the rest of the developed world. Cultural differences will prevent those efforts from being anywhere near as successful as they have been, and will be, in the United States. Nonetheless, one can count on finding familiar settings and products in an increasing number of destinations around the world. And the owners of American means of consumption are not alone in these efforts. Chains based in Europe, such as Benetton and the Body Shop, are increasing global presences and bring with them the same kind of uniformity.

This is to be welcomed for many reasons. Many find it quite reassuring to know that such familiar settings and products will be available in the most unfamiliar of settings. And the cathedrals of consumption bring with them certain standards of quality. They may not be the highest (and in many instances they are quite mediocre), but they are standards and they may well be higher than those previously available in some locales.

There is a price to be paid for all of this, of course, the essence of which is caught well by Baudrillard in his thinking on "the hell of the same."[4] The fact is, however, that most people today find the national and international spread of the new means of consumption and their wares to be closer to nirvana than to hell. Most of us seem to revel in the increasing homogeneity rather than to be repelled by it.

Sanitization

Closely related to homogenization is the sanitization of the settings in which we obtain goods and services. Because they are all oriented to attracting the largest number of consumers, anything that might be construed as being offensive is ruthlessly eliminated. Contrast the purity of Disney World to one its predecessors, Steeplechase Park at Coney Island, which opened its gates in 1897.

The symbol of Steeplechase Park was the "grotesque, vaguely diabolical"[5] face of a "huge devilish jester with broad cheeks, hair parted in center and flying out in wings to either side, and sporting a massive grin."[6] The jester suggested fun but was tinged with more than a hint of deviance, lasciviousness, and disorder. Disney World's most visible symbol is Mickey Mouse. There is *nothing* devious, lascivious (it's almost impossible even to imagine sexual congress between Mickey and Minnie Mouse), or disorderly about this symbol.[7] The antithesis of the jester, Mickey is "hairless, sexless, and harmless."[8] The differences between these two symbols suggest a dramatic change not only in amusement parks, but also in the way we consume.

Although Steeplechase Park was part of a turn-of-the-century effort to offer "respectable" entertainment to the masses, and in spite of efforts to make it more respectable, Coney Island continued to be tarred by an appearance of deviance. In keeping with the symbol of the jester, Steeplechase Park never totally surrendered its slightly illicit appeal. For example, from its ocean-side entrance "visitors had to pass through the Barrel of Love, a ten-by-thirty-foot revolving, highly polished wooden drum that rolled unwary revelers off their feet and frequently into rather suggestive if careless contact with total strangers, hopefully of the opposite sex."[9] A similarly free and risque atmosphere was created by the "blowholes" in the flooring of the Barrel of Love that often sent skirts flying. But the topper was the "insanitarium" through which Barrel of Love riders had to exit:

> Here the unsuspecting but hesitant pair was eyed by a clown and a dwarf while snickers from a large audience could be heard. Suddenly a gust of wind whipped the young lady's skirt around her ears while the clown aimed a rod producing an electric shock between the legs of her beau. As he clutched his wounded parts and the lady tried to reassemble her attire, the crowd's howls increased the couple's humiliation. Their ordeal was far from over, as they still had to endure whacks with slapsticks, more blowholes, and a pile of barrels ominously tottering just above their heads. Stripped of any self-conscious dignity, they finally limped off-stage to join the audience and laugh at the next victims.[10]

Nothing like the insanitarium could be allowed to find its way into Disney World. This is exemplified by the following description of the philosophy behind the new Tomorrowland:

> We want to live in a Ralph Laurenized mega-cabin in the Bitterroot Mountains, wired with fiber optics and a fast modem. We want to go back to the land, as long as the land is devoid of the kind of hardscrabble mongrels who used to live in the West. We want to be cable-ready. We want good take-out. We want aromatherapeutic herb gardens and a nearby trout stream where nothing ever dies.[11]

Amusement parks flourished in the two decades after the founding of Steeplechase Park (and other major parks) at Coney Island. An estimated 1,500 to 2,000 such parks existed by 1919, but by the 1920s they began a steady decline. Among the causes of this decline were the physical deterioration of many of the parks, the encroachment of urban development, racial conflict, and gang violence. Above all, amusement parks came to be seen as seedy and risque settings that were not deemed suitable for middle-class families with small children. It was in this context that the first Disney theme park was created in the 1950s, and one of its premises was the rooting out of all of the seediness of the earlier parks.

Of course, Disney World is not the only cathedral of consumption that is based on being squeaky clean. Blockbuster Video will not rent X-rated movies. Wal-Mart forces recording companies to alter offensive lyrics and CD covers. There are certainly exceptions to this. Las Vegas casinos offer topless (and sometimes bottomless) reviews, cruises implicitly promise a voyage that will include a week of sexual abandon, and there are proliferating sites on the Internet through which one can obtain hard-core pornographic material. However, in the main, the new means of consumption offer highly sanitized environments in which to purchase goods and services.

Transformed Relationships

The new means of consumption have, in various ways, dramatically altered the nature of the social relationships that take place within them. Instead of interacting with other people, those who use the cathedrals of consumption are more likely to interact with the cathedrals themselves and with the goods and services offered by them. The attraction is often the cathedral itself. At least initially, the consumer interacts with the setting, be it a fast food restaurant, a mall, a cruise ship, an amusement park, or a casino. Such settings, as we have seen, have become destinations, and it is to these icons that people have been drawn.

In some settings such as the cybermall there are no human beings; the only interaction possible is with the specific consumption sites.

In other cases, such as the superstore or hypermarket, the staff has been reduced to the bare minimum so that there is little opportunity to interact with human employees. In any case, the draw is the cathedral, its commodities and the attractions within it; visitors generally want to interact with them. Once inside Disney World, the goal is to interact with as many of the sites within it as possible. One does not want that relationship mediated by human beings who may destroy the magic of interacting with the icon. When we interact with human employees in the cathedrals of consumption, we expect them to be part of the attraction and to interact in a way that is consonant with the attraction, or at least does not disturb the enchantment.

Another factor in the change in human relationships is the tendency of at least some of the means of consumption to lull consumers into a dream-like state in which they "float" through these settings largely oblivious to other humans around them. This is best reflected in the so-called "zombie effect" associated with shopping malls. Those who spend a lot of time surfing the cybermalls are even more likely to be unaware of those around them. Casinos seek to immerse gamblers so deeply in the games they are playing that they are not only oblivious to those around them, but also of where they are and how much time is passing.

There is little "genuine" human interaction in the new means of consumption. And because the new means of consumption have invaded the home, we may be increasingly less likely to engage in authentic human interaction even in our homes. The new means of consumption are transforming the nature of social relationships. In those increasingly ubiquitous settings we are more and more likely to interact with inhuman structures and sites and with people constrained to behave in a nonhuman fashion. Add this to the nonhuman interaction that characterizes our relationship with the television and movie screen and one is forced to wonder about the future of "social" relationships.

I would like to return to an issue raised in Chapter 5. I discussed David Chaney's distinction between the spectacular society and society of the spectacle. Chaney contended that in the earlier spectacular society spectacles tended to involve spectators, and in today's society spectacles tend to be put on *for* the audience. Today's consumers are seen as more passive observers of the spectacles taking place around them than as active participants in them. There is certainly much truth to this as exemplified by the parades, fireworks, and rides at Disney World; the extravaganzas both inside and outside Las Vegas casinos; and the shows put on by the cruise lines (to say nothing of the ships themselves).

However, there are reasons to question this perspective. Most notable is the development of new means of consumption that require the active participation of the consumer. These are the settings in which the actor is both consumer and producer. Although such active participation takes place in various settings such as fast food restaurants, it perhaps best describes the new dematerialized means of consumption. The consumer is an active participant in any form of consumption that takes place on the Internet. In buying a book on Amazon.com, the consumer is very active in accessing it, reading reviews, selecting books, ordering them, entering payment information, and perhaps writing reviews of recently read books.

More generally, there is the move toward the centrality of entertainment in the means of consumption. Some of this is quite passive (e.g., watching a movie in a multiplex in the mall), but much of it requires the active participation of the consumer. No entertainment would take place if the consumer did not play the games or don the virtual reality gear at Sega World. Gambling requires that participants be actively involved, and in the case of the slot machine to produce the game totally on their own.

Transformed Consciousness

Not only have social relationships been transformed by the revolution in the means of consumption, but so have people's "habits of mind." For example, when people today think of a vacation or outing, they very often think about spending it at or near one or more of the new cathedrals of consumption. In part, this is a result of the absence of viable alternatives. If an older person wants to walk indoors in a safe environment, or a young couple wants to take their child for a ride in a carriage on a rainy day, what alternatives are there to the shopping mall? More generally, if people want to shop, the demise of the local small store means that they have to go to one of the chains found in the mall. More important, the cathedrals of consumption have, as we have seen, become reenchanted and this makes them an irresistible attraction to many people. As a result of the absence of alternatives, the enchantment and the rationality, the cathedrals of consumption rank high in people's consciousness.

This means that when people do take one of these outings or vacations, consumption is increasingly central to their thinking. Even if people go to the mall to walk, the thought of consumption is, at the minimum, in the back of their minds. Even if it is not, once they are there, such thinking comes immediately to the fore in the presence of all those attractive sites for consumption. More generally, people engage in day-to-day activities with the thought of doing at least some of them in and around the new means of consumption. Thinking about extraordinary activities like vacations is also shaped by the cathedrals of consumption and the desire to consume. As we have seen, for many people a vacation is a trip to a mega-mall or a discount mall. Such trips are undertaken with the goal of consuming goods and services. More traditional vacations have always been, at least in part, about consuming sites, sounds, and local handicraft. The new means of consumption such as Las Vegas, Disney World, and cruise ships have further commercialized vacations with the result that people are more likely to set out with the mind-set that they are going to consume, to spend lots of money on a wide variety of attractions, souvenirs, and products of all types. In sum, our thinking about both our day-to-day activities as well as our vacations is permeated with thoughts about consumption induced, at least in part, by the cathedrals of consumption.

These habits of the mind are being extended to a variety of settings that we have not tended to think about in this way in the past. We are thinking about more and more places as settings to be consumed and as locales in which we can consume. For example, we are increasingly inclined to think about universities, hospitals, churches, and museums in this way. We see ourselves as consuming them and being able to consume things in them. Furthermore, when we think about them, we have the model of the most glittering new means of consumption in mind. We expect them to look and function more like shopping malls, for example. Furthermore, we expect other settings that have always been means of consumption to resemble the new means of consumption. The best example is baseball stadiums, which have always been about consuming the game, food, and souvenirs, but are now expected in addition to be glittering shopping malls and amusement parks. Another is the home that many think of now as a means of consumption. Overall, we think of more and more settings as cathedrals of consumption.

Most generally, the cathedrals of consumption are important contributors to the fact that many of us think about consumption much of the time; consumption pervades our consciousness. When we are not actively consuming, we are often thinking about it and what we can obtain when we do. Of course, the cathedrals of consumption are not the only, and perhaps not even the most important, contributor to this way of thinking. It is likely that advertising, most of it about the cathedrals of consumption and the goods and services offered by them, is the more important contributor to this mind set. What sets the new means of consumption apart is that they not only help to create this way of thinking, but they provide the outlets where it can be translated into action, resulting in the purchase of the desired goods and services. Ultimately, the most important point to be made is that the new means of consumption are playing a major role in transforming our thinking (and action) so that more and more of our lives revolves around consumption.

Production? Consumption? Or Both?

This book has sought to make a contribution to overcoming the productivist bias in the social sciences by focusing on consumption in general, and the means of consumption in particular. This analysis was put in the context of the overall shift from production to consumption. However, one of the things that this work indicates is that it is increasingly difficult to sustain a clear distinction between production and consumption, especially in the contexts analyzed

For one thing, as we saw in a previous section, consumers are often busily producing that which they consume. For their part, the service workers in the new means of consumption are hardly production workers in the conventional sense of the term. Rather, they are more likely to operate in collaboration with consumers in order to produce an "experience." The dealers at Las Vegas card tables can be seen as "producing" a game, but it is more accurate to see them as collaborating with gamblers in the production of a game that is simultaneously being consumed. The people in the Mickey Mouse or Snow White costumes at Disney World are engaged with visitors in the simultaneous creation of a Disneyesque experience. The same could be said of the waiters in eatertainment, the salespeople in retailtainment, and the staff of the entertainment director of a cruise ship.

There are still workers who clearly and unequivocally produce things, and there are instances in which people are pure consumers. However, in the new means of consumption there is an increasing trend toward being unable to clearly distinguish between them. In the new world of consumption, especially as it is increasingly dominated by entertainment, it will make less sense to distinguish between production and consumption.

Iron Cage, Minicages, or Wide-Open Spaces?

Weberian theory leads to the view that the cathedrals of consumption, when taken together, create a rationalized iron cage from which it is difficult, if not impossible, to escape. This is a totally commodified world in which it would be futile, or nearly so, to hope to find a space in which one is free from commercial pressures. Supportive of this view is the proliferation of the new means of consumption, especially their spread into the home, so that even there one is unable to avoid opportunities and pressures to consume.

A second view, more traceable to theories of Michel Foucault, is that instead of an overarching iron cage, what we have is a great number of minicages.[12] Each cathedral of consumption is a minicage and when consumers are in one of them, they are constrained. Following Foucault's notion of the "carceral archipelago," we can think of each of the new means of consumption as an island fortress that is part of a larger archipelago. Using this metaphor, the consumer is free to hop from island to island (from mall to mall, for example), but on each of the islands the consumer is constrained.

There is a third view associated with rational choice theory. It argues that consumers are free to move in and out of the cathedrals of consumption as they wish. And when they find themselves in one of the cathedrals, they can decide for themselves whether or not to consume. More generally, they can decide to avoid any and all of the cathedrals; they are free to totally avoid consumption if they wish.

Which one of these views is most accurate? There are clearly elements of truth in each of them, but the evidence in this book suggests that the most apt metaphor is the idea of the cathedrals of consumption as a series of minicages forming a "consumer archipelago." There is, at least at the present, no iron cage from which there is no escape. Consumers are free to leave each island of consumption, though great control is exerted over them while they are on each island. Consumers can, and do, decide not to visit the islands of consumption and, when they do, they are free not to consume, but we must not forget the enormous forces brought to bear on them to visit cathedrals of consumption and to consume while they are there.

The idea of a consumer archipelago seems to imply a very different view than that of a black hole. However, the two views are compatible in that all of the various islands have to do with consumption. Whatever the degree of compatibility of these perspectives, they along with the iron cage imagery all communicate a sense of the increasing ubiquity of the cathedrals of consumption and, more generally, of consumption.

High and Low Culture

Social scientists, especially those associated with a postmodern perspective, have come to reject the long-held distinction between high and low culture.[13] This analysis of the cathedrals of consumption tends to support the view that it is increasingly difficult to clearly distinguish the two.

In the main, the cathedrals discussed in this book are associated with what has generally been considered low culture. However, one of the key implications of this book is that those who control the means of consuming "high culture" are being forced to emulate the cathedrals of consumption. And if the settings associated with high culture are to survive and to thrive, they must increase the pace and level of that emulation.

I have touched on various ways in which settings we usually associate with high culture—museums, schools, universities, concert halls—have come to take on more and more trappings of the cathedrals of consumption: Museums have high tech, interactive displays, encompass shopping malls, and have opened outlets in conventional malls; universities have theme dorms, food courts in student unions, and offer virtual courses in virtual universities that are largely indistinguishable from cybermalls. As a result of such changes, it becomes increasingly difficult to distinguish between high- and low-culture settings; the distinction between them grows increasingly meaningless.

There is grave risk associated with this convergence. Will the means of consuming high culture lose their traditional customer base if they look too much like shopping malls and theme parks? It is certainly possible to go too far in this. Some of the elite means of consumption already have. For example, there is an aquarium in Auckland, New Zealand (Kelly Tarltons), with a Disneyesque ride that takes visitors past a display of live penguins, but ends with a tacky, quite fake orca-like whale rising out of the depths of the sea. One would certainly have cause to worry if a university adopted, say, an old English theme and had its professors play the role of Oxford dons replete with flowing robes and full academic regalia.

Although it is certainly possible to go too far, those in charge of the means of consuming high culture have no choice but to study the successful cathedrals of consumption and to adopt those methods that will work for them without totally compromising their distinctive characteristics. Consumers want many of the same things from the means of consuming high culture as they get at the shopping mall, the fast food restaurant, and Disney World. The means of consuming high culture cannot afford to continue to lag far behind the "lower brow" cathedrals of consumption. If they do, they will find themselves in danger of losing a large portion of their clientele. The challenge is how to give consumers of high culture what they seem to want without totally surrendering the characteristics that have made high culture settings distinctive.

Dealing with Hyperconsumption

If Americans are hyperconsumers, if they spend too much on consumption (and Chapter 2 offered much evidence that they do), then is there anything to be done about it? This book suggests that if change is needed, it is needed at the level of the cathedrals that are luring consumers with ever more reenchanted settings and then leading them to spend more than they should. Another culprit at the structural level is the advertising industry that is also devoted to luring people into hyperconsumption. Yet another guilty party at this level is the credit card industry and its determined efforts to lure people into debt. But consumers also certainly bear some responsibility. What is stopping them from reducing their trips to the cathedrals of consumption, refusing to read or listen to so many advertisements, and destroying their credit cards? However, given the powerful forces that exist at the structural level, change by consumers cannot succeed without significant changes in the cathedrals of consumption, advertising, and the credit card industry.

In a recent book that focuses on the "overspent American," Juliet Schor falls into the trap of blaming consumers (a version of "blaming the victim") for overspending because of their "upscaling," or choosing reference groups that earn much more, and therefore are able to consume much more, than they do. She argues that the answer to this problem lies almost exclusively in changing individual consumers. She makes the case for the need to choose reference groups that consume less and for "downshifting" where people work less, earn less, and spend less: "Downshifters are opting out of excessive consumerism, choosing to have more leisure and balance in their schedules, a slower pace of life, more time with their kids, more meaningful work, and daily lives that line up squarely with their deepest values."[14]

Schor offers nine principles designed to deal with the problem of overspending. Virtually all of them focus on things consumers should do such as controlling desire, imposing voluntary restraints on themselves, sharing more with others, becoming more educated consumers, and avoiding shopping for therapeutic reasons. The only structural response mentioned by Schor is governmental action to restrain spending by, for example, taxing expensive commodities more than mid- or lower-range versions of the same commodities. I do not disagree with the courses of actions outlined by Schor, but they are likely to fail unless there is a parallel effort to change the cathedrals of consumption, advertisers, credit card companies, and other structural entities that play such a large role in hyperconsumption and overspending. Of course, that is not going to be easy because they have a vested interest in continuing their current ways and, if anything, finding new ways of promoting hyperconsumption.

Fun

One of the reasons that most consumers are not likely to heed Schor's call is that those who control the cathedrals of consumption have devoted themselves to making consumption fun. Consumption has less and less to do with obtaining goods and services and more to do with entertainment. In fact, the means of consumption are increasingly learning from, and becoming part of, show business. The cathedrals of consumption can be seen as great stage sets that are constructed to lure consumers and extract their money. Employees are increasingly actors who may well be in costume and speak scripted lines. Consumers are made to feel part of the show, at least for the time they are in the cathedral.

This show business analogy obviously best fits Disney's operations, because its movie and theater businesses so clearly inform, and interpenetrate with, its cathedrals of consumption. The great casino–hotels of Las Vegas and the enormous cruise ships are also clearly stage sets in which consumers can act out their fantasies (or is it the fantasies of the designers of these settings?), at least for a short period of time. Eatertainment and retailtainment are also all about the creation of sets where consumers can eat their food or buy their commodities in fantastic theatrical settings. Even the fast food restaurant has the quality of a movie set with its unnatural cleanliness, its clowns, its marquee-like menu, and so on. In terms of the extensions of the new means of consumption, the new baseball stadiums look like stage sets from the movie *The Natural*, supplemented by city skylines as a backdrop (Cleveland and Baltimore), restored warehouses (Baltimore, again), artificial rock formations (Anaheim), and enormous scoreboards (virtually everywhere). Luxury gated communities have such a manicured perfection that residents might feel as if they are living on the set of a movie and that they are actors in it.

Several times in this book I have mentioned the shopping malls Ontario Mills, Sawgrass Mills, Potomac Mills, which are the creation of the Mills Corporation, the leader in turning malls into settings for fun. As the chief executive of the corporation put it, "Shopping is really entertainment-based."[15] He is, for example, very excited about the Bass Pro Shop in the Gurnee Mills mall near Chicago, "Before you ever walk in the store, there's a trout stream. . . . When you walk in the store . . . it's like Sherwood Forest with trees and leaves and branches."[16] Is the consumer on the stage set of the movie, *Robin Hood*? Or *A River Runs Through It*?

How can we expect people to become "downshifters" if they are increasingly part of show business and are having so much fun playing their parts? Consumers can give up things, especially superfluous things (and much of what we consume is superfluous), but can they be expected to give up having fun? Having a role in the movie that is their lives? As long as the economy is good, and consumer's basic needs are satisfied, they are going to demand more entertainment. Many of these stage sets may come crashing down in a deep recession or depression, but they will be back, bigger and better, with the next upturn in the economy.

The Disenchanted

In spite of all of the spectacle, all the stuff, and the great fun, there are people who have become disenchanted with the cathedrals of consumption. Most of those who are able to gain access to the cathedrals of consumption and afford what they have to offer can be said to be enchanted by them. However, there are those who have the money and the access but who have concluded, often on the basis of past experience, that what the means of consumption have to offer does not bring meaning and happiness, or at least not as much as they seem to promise. As a result, such people may either give up their efforts to participate in the new means of consumption or, if they continue to take part, do so minimally. In either case, they can be said to have become disenchanted with the new means of consumption and with what they have to offer.

A much large group of the disenchanted are those who lack access to the cathedrals of consumption, or even if they gain access, can afford few if any of the goods and services offered by them. They may still long for that access, and for the possibility of becoming bewitched, but they are disillusioned by their past, and likely future, failures. In the next section I will focus on this group, especially those who on the basis of their race, class, or gender are likely to have become disillusioned.

RACE, CLASS, GENDER, AND THE
CATHEDRALS OF CONSUMPTION

The new means of consumption have, in general, succeeded in making consumption not only more fun, but also more democratic. More goods and services are available to more people than ever before. Pizza is now readily deliverable to the vast majority of doorsteps in the United States and, increasingly, in many parts of the world that not long ago had never even heard of pizza. The luxury of a Caribbean cruise is now available to far more Americans because of the existence of many more ships and costs that are, at least relative to what they once were, low. There is no question that the new means of consumption have contributed to the democratization of consumption.

However, democratization does *not* mean that all goods and services are equally available to all people. Not everyone has access, or at least equal access, to our prized cathedrals of consumption and their cornucopia of goods and services. There *is* discrimination in the new means of consumption. (Although I will focus on discrimination in the new means of consumption, they are far from the only aspects of the consumer world that discriminate. For example, advertisers increasingly target certain groups, usually the affluent, and in the process ignore others.[17])

Race

All of the new means of consumption are barred legally from discriminating on the basis of race (as well as gender). It is clear, nonetheless, that in general one is far more likely to see members of the White majority than minority groups members in most of the new means of consumption. This may be mainly a by-product of income differences because minorities are likely to earn far less than majority group members. Whatever the cause, minorities tend to be underrepresented as consumers[18] in most of the new means of consumption.

However, there is considerable variation in their degree of representation. For example, because of lower average income, minorities may well be overrepresented in the chains of fast food restaurants with their comparatively low-priced meals. The same is likely to be true of a number of other new means of consumption such as discount chains such as Kmart. On the other end of the spectrum, minorities are likely to be underrepresented at higher-end means of consumption such as Disney World, cruise ships, and Las Vegas casinos. Undoubtedly one of the most extreme and most obvious examples of discrimination on the basis of race (and class) is the elite gated community. These enclaves tend to be segregated on the basis of race, and typically that means that Blacks and other racial minorities are largely excluded.[19] In fact, many, though certainly not all, buyers of homes in most elite gated communities are attracted by the racial homogeneity. There are likely to be a few minority group homeowners, but the chances are that they will be from the same upper social classes as the White majority. Racial homogeneity may not be the primary motivation of White homeowners, but it is a major factor in being attracted to, and remaining in, gated communities. Although the racial exclusion in luxury gated communities is not overt, it is certainly a powerful factor in creating and maintaining residential segregation.

Racial exclusion is also a by-product of the economics of living in elite gated communities. The cost of purchasing housing in such communities is high. On top of that, there are a variety of fees— grounds maintenance, the cost of belonging to the golf and tennis clubs, as well as the other costs associated with such a lifestyle. Given the relatively small numbers of minority group members in the upper-classes, it is not surprising that they are dramatically underrepresented in elite gated communities.

Hilton Head, South Carolina, is well-known for a number of things, including its elite property developments known, ironically, as "plantations." Included are such gated communities as Shipyard Plantation, Port Royal Plantation, Wexford Plantation, Colleton River Plantation, and Hilton Head Plantation. The lack of Blacks in these developments led one local historian to comment, "It used to be you couldn't get off the plantations. Now you can't get on."[20]

The success of Hilton Head has led to efforts to develop in a similar fashion more of the islands off the South Carolina coast. As a result, it has been argued that "the . . . coast is increasingly becoming a walled resource."[21] Much attention has focused on Daufuskie Island, which is inhabited mainly by the Gullah people. These descendants of freed slaves have preserved to a large degree their language and West African culture. In order to colonize this island with elite walled communities, developers are interested in inducing or forcing the Gullah to leave.

And once forced out, minorities (and the poor) are not only unable to live in these communities, but the gates and guards effectively prevent minorities from even visiting them. In some cases, local associations permit pedestrian visitors, but they charge a fee that effectively excludes minorities and the poor. In some senses such a system is more discriminatory than a complete ban on anyone other than residents.

Hilton Head is far from the only locale in which one finds racial discrimination in gated communities. In Golden Beach, Florida, the 1990 census found a handful of Blacks in a town that was 85 percent White. Many of the households in Golden Beach had incomes in excess of $100,000 per year.[22]

Elite gated communities are only an extreme example of a more general phenomenon. Most of the cathedrals of consumption are controlled by White owners and patrons. The majority of shopping malls, mega-malls and superstores are dominated by White owners and, more important, White consumers. This is primarily a result of economic differences between the races, but it is also because such new means of consumption tend to be in locations that are not very accessible to Blacks and other minorities. Most minorities tend to be concentrated in large cities, but most malls, mega-malls, and superstores tend to be in suburbs or even in small towns (Wal-Mart, for example). The relative lack of automobiles hinders the efforts of minorities to get to these settings, especially given the inadequacies of public transportation in the United States. Even when they are able to get to the malls, Blacks often do not feel comfortable in those arenas that are dominated by Whites. According to an architect, "Black people do come, but they are not common. As a group, Blacks don't feel welcome."[23]

Most minorities go to schools that have fewer computers and they are less likely to have expensive computers in their homes. This has a wide variety of consequences, among them the fact that minorities are far less likely to have access to cybermalls and other ways of consuming on the Internet. A history professor has contended, "Where I live, shopping malls are white spaces. . . . So, probably, is cyberspace. When people converse there, they expect the other person to be white."[24]

Blacks tend to use the Internet in general, and cybermalls in particular, less than Whites. One reason is that Black-run and Black-oriented consumption sites are underrepresented on the Internet. The numbers are growing, however, and more such sites will help lead to greater Black participation in cybercommerce.[25] However, the cost of computers (only 22 percent of Blacks have home computers versus 34 percent of Whites) and Internet access are additional barriers to Black participation.

Social Class

It is worth recalling that many of the cathedrals of consumption are highly democratic, discriminating little, if at all, on the basis of social class. For example, the vast majority of franchised systems and many chains cater to all social classes and some are even more focally interested in the business provided by those with lower incomes. The goods and services that cathedrals of consumption offer tend to be sought out by those throughout the class system:

> It took the convergence of several trends—homogenization, mass communication and the arrival of a new, more visually sophisticated young professional class—to make design marketable in the way that it has

become today. Now, class distinctions are pretty much besides the point: the moment I realized that the Gap was truly a broad social and cultural phenomenon was when I heard Brooke Astor tell someone that it was her favorite place in New York to shop.[26]

It is clear from the preceding section that the new means of consumption are affected by social class, however, and a number of them are stratified, at least to some degree. Access to the credit that facilitates use of the new means of consumption is stratified. There is stratification among credit card users (green, gold, and platinum cards), but the most important distinction is between those who do and those who do not have credit cards. The middle- and upper-classes have virtually unlimited access to credit and debit cards and the lower-classes have limited access. And those who are poor may have even less access, or it may cost them more to gain access than it does the wealthier members of society.

Take the case of so-called "secured" credit cards. These cards are offered to people with poor credit ratings—those who may have become delinquent on previous credit card (or other) debt and even those who may at one time have been forced to declare bankruptcy. Such cards usually carry higher than normal fees and interest rates. Most important, they are called secured cards because the people to whom they are issued must deposit a sum of money with the credit card company, often equal to the credit limit of the account. In other words, secured card holders are allowed to borrow their own money at a high interest rate and with substantial fees. In favor of such an arrangement, it should be noted that those who demonstrate an ability to make payments and to handle their credit on secured accounts can eventually qualify for a regular credit card account. The secured card is a route for the poor (and others) to obtain the same kind of credit (if not nearly the same amount) available to the upper classes.

Although the middle- and upper-classes are far more able to pay their bills through debit or credit cards at little or no cost, the poor are likely to use so-called "poor people's banks" and, therefore, are subject to far higher fees in paying the same kinds of bills. Beyond that, the more affluent sectors of society enjoy the benefits of increasingly cashless business, whereas business in the poor areas continues to be done almost exclusively on a cash basis.[27] The more affluent members of society, especially those who pay their credit card bills in full each month, are able to gain access to free credit unavailable to the poor who pay immediately in cash.

To get access to money, the poor can try to get money from so-called "payday loan companies," pawn shops, or illegal loan sharks. However, the poor have also been targeted by large legitimate companies, such as Household Finance Co. (HFC), which are eager to grant loans to those who are deeply in debt to their credit card companies. Said an HFC manager, "I love to see five to 10 [credit cards] . . . we target them first."[28] Unsecured loans often carry interest rates of 18 to 20 percent, and even go as high as 30 percent or more in the case of some smaller loans. HFC ends up with a lot of bad loans, but that is considered part of the business, and the company is very profitable. In any case, HFC's major clients are from the lower-middle- and lower-classes, and they end up paying far higher rates for loans than those in the middle- and upper-social-classes.

On the surface, home shopping television would seem not to differentiate on the basis of social class. After all, it is available to everyone with access to cable or satellite television. However, home shopping television networks clearly target the lower-classes. For one thing, they tend to offer poor quality, glitzy goods such as costume jewelry and imitation gems that are sold as "luxury" items. Such goods are described as "merchandise that caters to the need to look like you have more than you do. . . . The home shopping hosts are marketing the pearly gates of upper-class heaven. They just happen to be faux pearl."[29] And the home shopping networks use hosts and hostesses who emphasize their class character and the possibilities of upward mobility.

And then there is Ivana Trump, perhaps the ultimate emblem of eighties excess-as-success, a woman, her co-host Bobbi reminds us, "who knows what it is to roll down Rodeo Drive and go shopping." In her pink silk "House of Ivana" outfit, girlish blonde curls, and what looks like tens of thousands of dollars of plastic surgery, she comes on HSN to share her designs and her secrets (and plug her new book). She is holding out a hand from the Beautiful People to the Little People.

That women are unnervingly grateful for these nuggets from Park Avenue, Palm Beach, and Hollywood lives is a poignant reminder of just how central an issue class continues to be in American life. "You can afford anything, Ivana," one caller says, "and due to you, people like me —I'm a nurse—can too. We live vicariously through you."[30]

This is not to say that there are not new means of consumption that cater to those at the upper end of the class spectrum. Dolce and Gabbana is a small worldwide chain that, among other things, sells dresses that cost $2,000, or more. Such price tags are clearly out of the reach of all but the wealthiest members of society. Furthermore, such shops tend to be in the poshest of locales, where poor people are likely to be intimidated and therefore avoid. Adding to the effect on differentiation is the fact that the stores are internally stratified on a class basis:

> Despite . . . talk about warmth and inclusiveness (. . . "We want the person who buys cologne to have the Dolce & Gabbana experience as much as the woman who buys the $2,000 dress"), the most distinctive feature of the store may be the upstairs V.I.P. room, for the large celebrity clientele and any groups that need special attention (like a wedding party). "There's a need for celebrities to be able to come and shop with a little bit of privacy". . . . The V.I.P. room will allow entourages to sample the complete collections without having to mix with the regular folk, but it doesn't have a separate entry, which means that customers will get glimpses on the way in and out.[31]

Shopping malls tend to be stratified, as well, on a class basis. Malls range all the way from the most prosaic of strip malls to high end malls such as Riverside Square Mall in Hackensack, New Jersey, which targets families with incomes above $100,000. Shoppers there are apt to spend $143 a visit as compared to the national average of $71. Upscale malls are likely to have more elegant stores (e.g., Neiman

Marcus), fancier restaurants, more elaborate landscaping, and lusher furnishings. Says one retailing consultant of entering such elite malls, "It's a daunting experience, like crossing the border and having to show your credit card."[32]

Actually, the creation of elite malls is at least as much about discouraging teenagers as it is about attracting some social classes rather than others. It is therefore a form of age discrimination. They spend lots of money, but teenagers are seen as discouraging adults from shopping out of fear of rowdyism and violence. Elite malls tend to discourage movie theaters, food courts, and video game arcades—in other words teenage attractions.

Some malls are also stratified internally. The Ontario Mills mall has an upscale area known as Off Rodeo Drive Beverly Hills, which includes boutiques such as Dolce & Gabbana, Moschino, and Calvin Klein. There are discounted goods in these elite shops, but they are out of reach of most consumers. For example, a Donna Karan men's leather jacket is sold at half price: $1,022. The average expenditure at the Donna Karan boutique is about $700. However, the mall also has shops for middle- and even lower-class shoppers, including Marshall's, Burlington Coat Factory, J.C. Penney catalog outlet, and Bed, Bath & Beyond®. According to the mall's general manager, "The thing that sets Mills apart is that we serve everybody, from bottom to top."[33]

Just as they tend to be predominantly White, elite gated communities tend to be enclaves of the rich.[34] Amitai Etzioni had the following to say on this issue: "I don't approve of setting up gates and barriers for class purposes . . . in the best of all possible worlds, with no crime, I might say, take down the gates. But in the world we live in, upper middle-class people don't want to rub shoulders with other classes of people. They haven't wanted to for 200 years."[35] Former Secretary of Labor Robert Reich sees elite gated communities as part of a more general process of the "secession of the successful."[36] Such communities, and the secession they imply, threaten to further enhance the already enormous class divide that separates Americans from one another. Unlike racial discrimination, discrimination on the basis of class is not against the law. Nevertheless, it has a number of deleterious effects on the lower-classes and on society as a whole.

For example, members of elite gated communities tend to focus on the needs of their local community to the exclusion of a concern for the larger society. Paying high fees, in effect taxes, in their local communities, members of these communities are apt to vote against new taxes that support the needs of the larger society. Faced with high and often escalating fees, residents are likely to be devoted chanters of the "no new taxes" mantra. Given the success of such efforts, luxury gated communities grow increasingly luxurious as the larger society, especially its infrastructure, grows increasingly impoverished.

One sees stratification on the basis of class *within* some gated communities. For example, the five villages of Lakewood Ranch, Florida, are divided into neighborhoods that target specific groups—those who are first-time buyers, older people who are looking for a smaller home after their children have grown, wealthy retirees, and so forth. Prices begin at about $90,000 and rise to more than $400,000. These housing differences and differences in price serve to segregate the community on the basis of social class.[37] Those with more money are able to afford the larger homes that are on the lakefront or line the golf course.

Walt Disney's town of Celebration does not keep out the middle- and lower-classes, but it does have a considerable spread in terms of housing prices. The well-to-do are able to build expensive "estate homes." Then there are three levels of predesigned homes, priced from $130,000. There are also apartments that are available for rent for as little as $600 a month.[38] Like Disney World itself (about three-fourths of adult visitors are highly paid professionals, managers, or technicians[39]), Celebration is skewed in the direction of the upper-middle-class.

As our cities have developed what Bender calls "City Lite," the poor have tended to be excluded.[40] A good example is the reinvigoration of Times Square, which has been discussed several times throughout this book. The poor, who could afford the movie theaters and hot dog stands that used to dominate Times Square, are being driven out, and the area is being taken over by the well-to-do. Such processes are leading to even more segregation on the basis of class within our cities.

Las Vegas is a highly stratified world. In general, the hotels on the Strip are the higher-status hotels, whereas downtown Las Vegas and the Fremont Street area are generally the province of lower-middle-class visitors to Vegas. On the Strip, Mirage Resorts runs a high-end casino–hotel, the Mirage, as well as nearby Treasure Island for a less affluent crowd. Mirage Resorts recently completed the Bellagio, a more luxurious hotel than the Mirage. One of Bellagio's distinguishing characteristics is hundreds of millions of dollars in fine art, especially French impressionism.[41] Within many Las Vegas casinos there are roped-off areas for high rollers and games and slots are stratified on the basis of the size of the wager permitted. If one gambles (and loses) enough, one may even have a blackjack table and dealer reserved for personal use.[42]

For the truly affluent, the high rollers, or, as they are called, the "whales," there is a whole other Las Vegas. These are people who are apt to bet $100,000 or more, to have lines of credit of several million dollars, and to lose enough to account for 20 percent of a casino's winnings. Among many other "perks," these gamblers are accorded first-class airplane tickets and limousines for their use while they are in Las Vegas. In 1995, the Las Vegas Hilton built three penthouse suites for the "whales." Each suite has a swimming pool, a media room, and "24-hour butlers trained by the man who also educates butlers for England's royal family."[43] And the cost of all these amenities to the "whales" themselves? Zero! In the terminology of Las Vegas, they are "comped." The richer you are and the more you gamble (and lose), the less you pay in Las Vegas. Drinks are free to the gamblers from the lower-middle-class, although they are likely to get well brands whereas higher-stakes gamblers will get premium brands. If lower-class gamblers get free food, it will likely to be at the buffet, whereas the high roller may be comped at one of the elegant restaurants on premises. Small stakes gamblers are responsible for the cost of their rooms and transportation to, from, and in Las Vegas.[44]

Because of the costs involved, cruise ships exclude the poor and many of those in the lower-class. On board, there is considerable stratification based on things such as cabin placement (those that offer a view of the water are more desirable and expensive) and size. There is even stratification between cruise lines. Seabourn, partially owned by Carnival, offers small, yacht-like ships accommodating about 200 passengers in 106 suites at a cost of about $1,000 per person, per day. Passengers are provided with, among other things, 24-hour a day room service (with all the caviar one desires) and cooks will go so far as to prepare a passenger's own recipes. The average household income of Seabourn passengers is approximately $200,000 per year. In contrast, the much larger ships of the Carnival line cater to passengers with average family incomes of as little as $30,000 per year. "If Seabourn is delivering an expensive and exclusive vacation for the affluent, Carnival is offering a scaled down experience for the mass market."[45] Although Seabourn is part of the elite "luxury class" of cruise ships, Carnival is part of the much lower ranking "contemporary" category. However, there is an even lower "budget" category for those passengers who stand even lower in the stratification system.

Conspicuous Inconspicuousness

One of the most enduring theories of the relationship between social class and consumption is Thorstein Veblen's theory of conspicuous consumption.[46] At the turn of the twentieth century, Veblen argued that the motivation to consume a variety of goods (services were of little interest in Veblen's day, but the same idea would apply) is not subsistence, but to create the basis for invidious distinctions among people. The possession of such goods would lead to higher status for those who possess them. In deciding what goods to consume, people are ultimately emulating the behavior of the leisure class at the pinnacle of the stratification system. The tastes of that class eventually work their way down the stratification hierarchy so that most people end up emulating the acquisitions of the class immediately above them in the stratification system.

Several points about Veblen's thesis are worth making based on this analysis of the new means of consumption. First, writing at the peak of the industrial revolution when services paled in significance in comparison to goods, Veblen made a distinction between conspicuous consumption and conspicuous leisure that is no longer viable. Veblen argued that leisure, or the nonproductive use of time, was an early way of making invidious distinctions among people. That is, people conspicuously wasted time in order to elevate their social status. In the more modern era, people consumed conspicuously, that is wasted goods rather than time, in order to create such distinctions. Buying expensive goods when far less expensive commodities would accomplish the same objectives is an example of waste in the realm of goods.

However, the importance of new means of consumption that focus on leisure (casinos, cruises, theme parks, eatertainment, retailtainment), indicates that much of modern consumption has as much to do with leisure as it does with goods; both are commodities bought and sold in the marketplace. It is certainly *not* the case that conspicuous consumption has replaced conspicuous leisure, or that the latter is only characteristic of some earlier age. In fact, with the increasing importance of amusements and fun, leisure may once again be in the process of gaining ascendancy over the consumption of goods. A more contemporary view would be to see *both* conspicuous leisure and conspicuous consumption as bases of commodity consumption. A cruise and a gambling junket are as much commodities as a Mercedes Benz and a mink coat.

A second point is that people do not simply consume commodities, they also consume the means of consumption. Another basis of invidious distinction is the places in which one consumes. As was discussed earlier, the means of consumption are stratified and participating in those that have high status yields higher prestige for the individual. Shopping at Nordstrom's (and, given the importance of signs in a postmodern world, leaving with that shopping bag with the Nordstrom's logo) yields higher status than shopping at J.C. Penney. In Las Vegas, staying at the Bellagio confers higher status than staying at the Holiday Inn. Veblen saw property as trophies, but it is now the shopping bags, t-shirts, and kitsch that carry the labels and logos of Nordstrom's and Bellagio, to say nothing of Hard Rock Cafe and Planet Hollywood, that are our new trophies.

This remarkable trend toward wearing all manner of clothing (and many other things) with labels prominently displayed cries out for comment. Subtlety has clearly all but disappeared when it comes to displaying the signs associated with the goods we consume. Most of us do not seem confident that those around us can "read" the clothes we wear. We leave nothing to doubt; we literally wear the labels on our sleeves. The paradox is that although we no longer seem to trust one another as readers of signs, the fact is that we have all become much more sophisticated and sensitive readers of those signs. Wearing labels seems like overkill, but this is just fine as far as merchants are concerned because in the past they had to pay for this kind of advertising (e.g., people walking the streets wearing "sandwich boards"). In fact, this is yet another example of getting the customer to do unpaid work for which employees in the past had to be recompensed.

The most important point to be made on the basis of this analysis of the new means of consumption is that although there is certainly conspicuous consumption today, what defines much of consumption, at least as far as the new means are concerned, is a kind of *conspicuous inconspicuousness*. With the boom in chains of many of the new means of consumption, the vast majority of people are consuming in the same settings and coming home with many of the same goods or experiencing much the same service. Labels such as Wal-Mart, Target, the Gap, Princess Cruise Line, Walt Disney, Hard Rock Cafe, and McDonald's adorn the packages and the commodities of the vast majority of people. Most of us are consuming in essentially the same places and buying essentially the same things. There is certainly some effort at creating invidious distinctions ("We went on that Destiny cruise or to Disney World, you didn't"), but there is also a dem-onstration of the fact that we are consuming like everyone else; we are inconspicuous in our consumption patterns.

This may indicate a shift in the sensibilities of at least some of us. In the past we may have wanted to distinguish ourselves from others, but it may be that we are now more interested in demonstrating our commonality with the vast majority of other people. It also may be that people do not want to stick out too much from the crowd. Perhaps in this era of perceived high crime, most people prefer to be largely indistinguishable, at least in their public consumption and appear-ance, rather than easily distinguished from others.

However, this is probably too psychologistic an explanation. The fact is that people are sporting the same labels at least in part because of the domination of the means of consumption that have generally succeeded in driving smaller and local competitors out of business. All of those Wal-Marts, McDonald's, Bed, Bath and Beyonds, and Princess Line cruise ships mean that most of us consume in the same places offering more or less the same selection of goods and services. To a large extent, we are forced into conspicuous inconspicuousness; the cathedrals of consumption and their commodities are increasingly our best, and in many cases our only, option.

What of the modern parallel of Veblen's leisure class? Aren't they still engaging in conspicuous consumption? The answer is clearly yes. They can still afford the one-of-a-kind vacation, the designer dress, or the custom-made shoes. In consuming such things they are making an invidious distinction between themselves and those below them in the stratification system. However, it is interesting to note that even in the leisure class we see an increasing amount of inconspicuous consumption and for many of the same reasons noted previously. Many are less interested in sticking out from the crowd because, among other reasons, they fear that they would be more likely to become crime victims. More important, we are witnessing the expan-sion of chains of the elite means of consumption such as Valentino's, Gucci, and the like. The result is that the elites, wherever they may be, are also increasingly likely to consume in the same settings and purchase many of the same things. The elites find it more difficult to distinguish themselves from other members of the upper-class. Further, although frequenting the highest status means of consumption may set them apart from classes below them in the stratification system, it is increasingly difficult in this age of low-priced "knock-offs" of high-priced goods to distinguish between those who carry Gucci bags and those who carry the copies. "Original" and copy are made even more indistinguishable by the fact that they are both simulations. Gucci bags are simulations and the knock-offs are simulations of those simulations.

Veblen argued that no class, not even the poorest, forgoes all conspicuous consumption. This is even truer of inconspicuous consumption. Even the poorest of the poor can afford a t-shirt with a Caesar's Palace logo from the half-price rack at Wal-Mart or a hamburger in a bag sporting McDonald's golden arches. Even the street person can fish such things out of the local trash can. Many of the poor spend inordinate amounts on such inconspicuous consumption and, in the process, may ignore essential needs and purchases. This tends to support Veblen's view that people will endure a quite shabby private life in order to have the public symbols they deem desirable.

Gender

Prior to the 1850s, women were rare in the marketplace for consumer goods. If they did appear there, it was under the control of their fathers or husbands. The coming of innovations such as the department store helped to liberate women from this control. A century or more ago, "the great metropolitan department stores were first established and set themselves up not merely as merchants but also as veritable bazaars, bringing women out of their houses and into the public realm for the first time."[47] One of Elizabeth Cady Stanton's rallying cries in 1854 was "GO OUT AND BUY."[48]

Today, of course, many, perhaps most, of the new means of consumption cater to women. For a variety of reasons, women do the bulk of the purchasing and as a result they are targeted by the means of consumption. For example, one estimate is that 80 percent of the audience of home shopping television is female. Most of them are middle-aged and beyond, but the television hosts will certainly also target younger women:

> "Summer's coming up," says the no-nonsense marketer of a nail buffing kit. "That means beach weather, that means sandals, ladies. Do you want to show your toenails the way they look right now? . . . If you're not picking up our kit today, you're a loser."[49]

In addition to catering to women, there is a kind of retrogressive character to home shopping television as it seemingly beckons women back to an earlier time and to earlier means of consumption:

> In its evocation of Tupperware parties, the kaffeeklatsch, Mary Kay cosmetics saleswomen stopping by your home—all traditions that have fallen, or are falling, by the wayside—home shopping hearkens back to the past in another way: It speaks to women as they were before women's liberation. Callers are "honey" and "dear." "That executive look" is just another fashion statement. Women lunch, they shop, they entertain, they go on cruises, they have craft parties. Femininity sells. Dolls, cooed over by hosts as if they were children, are very popular.
>
> Watching this throwback to another era, it's easy to forget that for many women, the underbelly of that era was a gnawing sense of dissatisfaction. But that's the idea: to banish both the dark side of history and the bright side of real life from living rooms. For a woman like Dorothy from North Carolina, who says, "I watch home shopping from the time I get up until my husband comes home from work," home shopping channels affirm, indeed encourage, her choice to wile away her days with them. "I hope you're going to stay with us for the whole show," hosts implore callers.[50]

Some of the cybermalls and other Web sites are also targeting women who would be more likely to be home during the day, use their services, and in the process make purchases. There is, for example, the recently redesigned Web site oriented to parents and families: Disney's Family.com. (yet another example of the seemingly insatiable desire of Disney to be a presence in virtually every conceivable means of consumption). "Family-related sites are hot because they attract women—in the minority on the Internet but usually in charge of the household budget."[51] The sites are interactive and provide information on health and nutrition issues, advice on raising children and ideas for family-oriented activities. There may also be things like a recipe library that, based on a person's selections, creates a shopping list. Some of these Web sites do charge, or will soon start charging, fees and, of course, there are the revenues from advertisements.

Of course athletic stadiums and many other means of consumption are dominated by and cater to males. Price Club and the other warehouse stores seem to cater to men who like the smaller selection and the possibility of coming home with a bargain-priced trophy.[52] Video games and centers that are based on such games are oriented mainly toward males. Take the following description:

> Inside, the predominantly male feel is confirmed with words and phrases like: "Apache longbow," "destroy your enemy," "driving like a maniac," "footie games," "wages of war," "mercenaries," "shooting everyone with your phaser," "space battles," "krush, kill n destroy" and "don't just hurt 'em, eradicate 'em."[53]

When females are present in such settings, they tend to serve more as observers or "cheerleaders."

Boys, especially of high school age and beyond, are more likely to use computers than girls. One of the reasons for this may lie in the fact that far less software is written for girls than boys, though this is changing somewhat.[54] Males are more than twice as likely to be on-line than females, although projections are that the gap will narrow dramatically in the next few years because providers are beginning to offer women more sites; more girls will gain computer experience in school; more women will use computers at work and bring that experience to the use of home computers; the seniors market will grow and seniors are overwhelmingly female; women will be increasingly willing to pay for time-saving computer-based services (e.g., supermarket shopping); women are likely to become more engaged in home-based businesses that also will give them more involvement with the computer and the Internet; and women more frequently manage home finances (home banking via computer is on the rise).[55]

There is a mixed picture as far as women and consumption are concerned, but it is clear that women fare "better" than minorities and the poor (many of both, of course, are women) in the new means of consumption. On the one hand this is clearly welcome, but on the other it means that women also have a better chance of being major contributors to our consumerist society and becoming themselves hyperconsumers.

DISENCHANTED ENCHANTMENT:
WHERE ARE WE HEADED?

Although some see signs of a waning of the consumer society,[56] and others argue for the need for such a trend,[57] there is no evidence in this analysis of any such decline. As this book has argued, there appears to be a major expansion of consumerism underway in the United States and many other parts of the world. As long as the current economic boom continues in the United States (and many other nations with advanced economies), consumerism will continue to expand.

The same is even more true of the cathedrals of consumption. Virtually all of the specific means discussed in this book will continue to expand as will the means of consumption in general. The new means of consumption are enchanted, and they are in various ways quite spectacular, but above all they are highly effective selling machines. As effective as they are, through the process of "creative destruction" today's means of consumption will eventually be supplanted by even newer means that are infinitely more enchanted, spectacular, and effective as selling machines.[58] Just as the Sands in Las Vegas succumbed to New York, New York, the latter will eventually be replaced. The future will bring with it unimagined palaces of consumption filled to capacity with a cornucopia of goods and services. And they will be incredibly effective selling machines that will bring with them an even further escalation of the consumerism that already is such a dominant reality in the contemporary world.

It is difficult to anticipate anything other than the continued growth of consumption and expansion of the cathedrals that service consumers, but there are some self-destructive trends that may threaten this expansion. The postmodern processes of reenchantment have generally been depicted throughout these pages as the salvation of the new means of consumption in the sense that they have allowed them to overcome the problems associated with disenchantment and to be attractive to ever-larger numbers of consumers. However, the implosion of the means of consumption into the home threatens the existence of many other means of consumption. Just as movie theaters were threatened by the arrival of television and later the VCR and video rentals, contemporary shopping malls, chain stores, super-stores, and so on are endangered by the increasing ability to shop at home through home shopping television, cybermalls and shops, and the ubiquitous mail order catalogs. The latter are likely to grow in the coming years and other mechanisms for shopping at home are apt to come into existence. All of this is likely to come at the expense of some of the contemporary cathedrals of consumption. In fact, the latter have already been changing, becoming reenchanted, in response to this threat.

The point is that implosion, like most everything else about postmodernity, is both an opportunity and a danger. Some cathedrals of consumption have become reenchanted as a result of implosion, and others (e.g., cybermalls) have been made possible by it. However, still others are endangered by it and may well disappear. The increase in consumption shows no signs of ebbing, let alone disappearing. People will need to get what they want somewhere. The landscape formed by the cathedrals of consumption is constantly changing, but though it may encompass a different set of settings, it will still be filled with cathedrals.

It is likely that many of the means of consumption of the future will be more dematerialized, more ephemeral than those that predominate today. The new means of consumption have tended to be architectural settings—malls, fast food restaurants, hotels, casinos, cruise ships, theme parks, and so on. They have tended to be physical locations to which the consumer must travel, often over long distances. But the newest means of consumption take more dematerialized forms as we receive them through our television sets or computers. This gives them a great advantage—they can come to us rather than requiring that we go to them. It is far more efficient to stay at home and shop, play the stock market, gamble, and the like than it is to venture out to the material cathedrals of consumption.

It seems unlikely that people will come to do all, or even most, of their purchasing at home. People will continue to need to go out, to be with other people (even if they do not interact with them very much). No matter how effective and seductive the dematerialized means of consumption that find their ways into our homes, most people are still likely to require a variety of things that they cannot provide. In order to obtain these kinds of things, large numbers of people will leave their television and computer screens for the more material settings.

Another self-destructive aspect of the cathedrals of consumption is the ever-escalating need for spectacle. No matter how astonishing, consumers grow accustomed to extravaganzas. In order to attract their attention, let alone their business, the next spectacle must be even more spectacular than the last. Also contributing to this escalation is the competition among the cathedrals of consumption, each trying to put on an extravaganza that is more astonishing than that of its competitors. Of course, most of the costs are passed on to the consumers. More problematic is the need to keep coming up with extravaganzas that are innovative and spectacular enough to satisfy increasingly bored consumers.

At the same time, many of the spectacles discussed have little to do with the intentional actions of those who lead today's cathedrals. Various unforeseeable developments in the future will impel the cathedrals in the direction of being increasingly spectacular. For example, technological advances of various types will undoubtedly create innumerable possibilities for spectacle unimaginable today. Unforeseen implosions of various types will have a similar effect. Spectacles will also derive from further compression of time and space, as well as from as yet undreamt of uses of both.

Wary of grand narratives in this era of postmodern social theory, one must be ever-attuned to the possibility of developments that might disrupt or even derail the seemingly inevitable development of the means of consumption. For example, we could, I suppose, come to the collective realization that true happiness does not await us in the cathedrals and their goods and services. We could look elsewhere for satisfaction—family, work, the noncommodified realms of nature. Or the consumer could, perhaps even unwittingly, lure the means of consumption into disaster through unsupportable expansion or a level of indebtedness that could help to bring the economy down.[59]

However, the alternatives to consumption all seem like retrogressions into a past that is not likely to be resuscitated. As far as the economy may plunge in the midst of the deepest of recessions or depressions, it will recover and the consumer, as well as the means of consumption needed to help generate and satisfy the needs of the consumer, are likely to enjoy a rebirth that will make them even more central than they are today. Those who worry about consumer society, consumerism, the cathedrals of consumption, and the increasingly dizzying array of commodities have genuine concerns and many battles to fight, but the most immediate issue is how to live a more meaningful life within a society increasingly defined by consumption.

NOTES

1. Yiannis Gabriel and Tim Lang. *The Unmanageable Consumer: Contemporary Consumption and Its Fragmentation*. London: Sage, 1995.

2. Jean Baudrillard. *The System of Objects*. London: Verso, 1968/1996.

3. The focus is on the macrostructures in which consumption takes place and *not* microlevel consumers and their actions. To put it another way, the focus is on structures and *not* on consumers as agents.

4. For a discussion of some older means of consumption see Ray Oldenburg. *The Great Good Place*. New York: Paragon House, 1989; David Nasaw. *Going Out: The Rise and Fall of Public Amusements*. New York: Basic Books, 1993.

5. The issue of whether there is really anything "new" about the new means of consumption will be discussed at length in Chapter 7.

6. It is interesting to note how many of the new means of consumption have their roots in the 1950s. This is undoubtedly traceable to the increasing affluence of American society as well as the growth of facilitating means of consumption relating to transportation—automobiles, highways, jet planes, and so on.

7. DisneySea, at a cost of $2.5 billion, is currently under construction by Tokyo Bay.

8. Stephen M. Fjellman. *Vinyl Leaves: Walt Disney World and America*. Boulder, CO: Westview, 1992; Alan Bryman. *Disney and His Worlds*. London: Routledge, 1995.

9. Judith A. Adams. *The American Amusement Park Industry: A History of Technology and Thrills*. Boston: Twayne, 1991, p. 111.

10. John F. Kasson. *Amusing the Million: Coney Island at the Turn of the Century*. New York: Hill and Wang, 1978, p. 44.

11. Coney Island *did* have some structure and Disney World *does* offer some respite from the structures people encounter in their daily lives.

12. John F. Kasson. *Amusing the Million: Coney Island at the Turn of the Century*. New York: Hill and Wang, 1978, p. 50.

13. Michael Sorkin. "See You in Disneyland," in Michael Sorkin (ed.). *Variations on a Theme Park*. New York: Hill and Wang, 1992, p. 231.

14. Bruce Handy. "It's Only a Day Away: Tomorrowland Gets an Update. Too Bad Tomorrow Has Gone Out of Style." *Time* June 1, 1998, p. 66; for an even more acid critique, see William Booth. "Planet Mouse: At Disney's Tomorrowland, the Future Is a Timid Creature." *Washington Post*, June 24, 1998, pp. D1, D8.

15. This innovation represents the coming of the "thrill ride" to Epcot and the erosion of the distinction between Disney World and Epcot, which was supposed to be about educating the public and raising important issues about the future. It is reflective of the trend toward the fact that more and more things need to be entertaining. See Gene Sloan. "For the Future, Epcot Turns to the Present." *USA Today*, August 6, 1997, p. 6D.

16. Sharon Zukin. *Landscapes of Power: From Detroit to Disney World*. Berkeley: University of California Press, 1991.

17. Charles V. Bagli and Randy Kennedy. "Disney Wished Upon Times Sq. and Rescued a Stalled Dream." *New York Times*, April 5, 1998, pp. 1, 32.

18. Everett Evans. "'Sleaziest Block in America' Transformed Into Family-Friendly Heart of New York." *Houston Chronicle*, March 8, 1998, p. 1, Travel.

19. Although I am calling them *structures,* these settings are increasingly taking a dematerialized form as, for example, the case of cybermalls or home shopping television. For a general discussion of dematerialization in the realm of consumption, see Don Slater. *Consumer Culture and Modernity*. Cambridge: Polity Press, 1997.

20. Stuart Ewen. *Captains of Consciousness*. New York: McGraw-Hill, 1976; Roland Marchand. *Advertising the American Dream*. Berkeley: University of California Press, 1985; Jib Fowles. *Advertising and Popular Culture*. Thousand Oaks, CA: Sage, 1996; Adam Lury. "Advertising: Moving Beyond Stereotypes," in Russell Keat, Nigel Whiteley, and Nicholas Abercrombie (eds.). *The Authority of the Consumer*. London: Routledge, 1994, pp. 102–115.

21. Richard S. Tedlow. *New and Approved: The Story of Mass Marketing in America.* New York: Basic Books, 1990.

22. A recent study of changing tastes in food in Great Britain concluded that little could be said about the issue because data are sparse and inconclusive (and this is even more true of tastes in consumer goods in general). The author was able to say much more that is definitive about the production of food as well as the means of consumption that make that food available to consumers. See Alan Warde. *Consumption, Food and Taste.* London: Sage, 1997.

23. Stuart Ewen. *All Consuming Images: The Politics of Style in Contemporary Culture.* New York: Basic Books, 1988.

24. Gilles Lipovetsky. *The Empire of Fashion: Dressing Modern Democracy.* Princeton: Princeton University Press, 1994.

25. Campbell offers an even broader sense of this process "involving the selection, purchase, use, maintenance, repair and disposal of any product or service." Campbell's use of the term *shopping* (selection and purchase of goods and services) is closer to our sense of this process, but it does not apply well to our interest in theme parks, cruise lines, and casinos; we usually do not think of people as "shopping" in these settings. See Colin Campbell. "The Sociology of Consumption," in Daniel Miller (ed.). *Acknowledging Consumption: A Review of New Studies.* London: Routledge, 1995, pp. 102, 104.

26. See, for example, Pasi Falk and Colin Campbell (eds.). *The Shopping Experience.* London: Sage, 1997; Hoh-Cheung Mui and Lorna H. Mui. *Shops and Shopkeeping in Eighteenth-Century England.* London: Routledge, 1989; Alison Adburgham. *Shops and Shopping: 1800-1914.* London: George Allen and Unwin Ltd., 1964.

27. This extension to museums makes it clear that it is increasingly difficult to distinguish between "high" and "low" culture.

28. This means, among other things, that the exchange need not necessarily be completed. That is, something like "window shopping" would be part of our concern, even if no purchase takes place. See Anne Friedberg. *Window Shopping: Cinema and the Postmodern.* Berkeley: University of California Press, 1993.

29. Juliet B. Schor. *The Overspent American: Upscaling, Downshifting, and the New Consumer.* New York: Basic Books, 1998.

30. Corrigan has recently described an earlier means of consumption, the department store, in a similar way: "It is not an exaggeration to see department stores as similar to cathedrals: they attracted people to worship at the temple of consumption." See Peter Corrigan. *The Sociology of Consumption.* London: Sage, 1997, p. 56.

31. Bill Keller. "Of Famous Arches, Beeg Meks and Rubles." *New York Times,* January 28, 1990, section 1, p. 12.

32. Bob Garfield. "How I Spent (and Spent and Spent) My Disney Vacation." *Washington Post,* July 7, 1991, p. B5.

33. Alexander Moore. "Walt Disney World: Bounded Ritual Space and the Playful Pilgrimage Center." *Anthroplogical Quarterly* 53(1980):207–218.

34. David Streitfeld. "A Story that Speaks Volumes." *Washington Post,* September 24, 1997, p. D2.

35. William Severini Kowinski. *The Malling of America: An Inside Look at the Great Consumer Paradise.* New York: William Morrow, 1985, p. 218.

36. Ira G. Zepp, Jr.. *The New Religious Image of Urban America: The Shopping Mall as Ceremonial Center,* 2nd ed. Niwot: University Press of Colorado, 1997; see also Alexander Moore. "Walt Disney World: Bounded Ritual Space and the Playful Pilgrimage Center." *Anthropological Quarterly* 53(1980):207–218.

37. I will have a lot more to say about atriums, and the contribution of the architect John Portman, in Chapter 6.

38. Zepp also discusses Disneyland, baseball stadiums, and airports in these terms. All of these means of consumption will be discussed in this book.

39. This is not impossible because it could be argued that this is exactly what takes place in thousands of churches and synagogues on the sabbath.

40. Thomas S. Dicke. *Franchising in America: The Development of a Business Method, 1840-1980.* Chapel Hill: University of North Carolina Press, 1992, pp. 2–3.

41. Thomas S. Dicke. *Franchising in America: The Development of a Business Method, 1840–1980.* Chapel Hill: University of North Carolina Press, 1992.

42. There are two basic types of franchising arrangements. The first, *product franchising,* is a system in which "a manufacturer markets its output almost entirely through highly specialized retailers who, in turn, rely on the manufacturer for most of the products they sell." McCormick harvesting machines and Singer sewing machines involved product franchising and, most important, to this day so does the sale of new automobiles. The second, *business-format franchising,* "is where the outlet itself—together with a comprehensive package of services to support it—is the product." The fast food franchises are the best example today of business-format franchising, but this type has expanded into many other types of retail businesses since the 1950s. See Thomas S.

Dicke. *Franchising in America: The Development of a Business Method, 1840–1980*. Chapel Hill: University of North Carolina Press, 1992, p. 3.

43. David Seagal. "In Hopes of a Chain Reaction." *Washington Post,* April 30, 1997, pp. C11, C19.

44. Richard Gibson. "Fast-Food Spinoff Enters Pepsi-Free Era." *Wall Street Journal,* October 7, 1997, pp. B1, B2.

45. David Handelman. "The Billboards of Madison Avenue." *New York Times,* April 6, 1997, section 6: 50ff.

46. Although an important and growing means of consumption, catalogs are in the early phases of a long-term transformation that will end with the dominance of on-line, Internet catalogs.

47. Sonia Csencsits. "Limited Time, Travel Turn Attention to Handy Catalogs." *The Morning Call (Allentown),* February 23, 1997, p. B1ff.

48. There were precursors (e.g., arcades) to the modern shopping mall in Europe in the late 1700s and 1800s.

49. Margaret Crawford. "The World in a Shopping Mall," in Michael Sorkin (ed.). *Variations on a Theme Park.* New York: Hill and Wang, 1992, p. 20.

50. John Holusha. "The Key to the Mall? That's Entertainment." *New York Times,* February 9, 1997, section 9, p. 1.

51. Peter A. McKay and Maryann Haggerty. "Entertaining New Mall Ideas." *Washington Post,* June 19, 1998, pp. F1, F10.

52. Laura Bird. "Huge Mall Bets on Formula of Family Fun and Games." *Wall Street Journal,* June 11, 1997, pp. B1, B12.

53. "The Outlet as Destination for Those Who Love a Sale." *New York Times Travel,* April 5, 1998, pp. 12, 24.

54. Frank DeCaro. "Looking for an Outlet." *New York Times,* April 6, 1997, section 6, p. 70ff.

55. Frank DeCaro. "Looking for an Outlet." *New York Times,* April 6, 1997, section 6, p. 70ff.

56. Danielle Reed. "A Tale of Two Leaves: Outlet Shopping . . . " *Wall Street Journal,* October 17, 1997, p. B12.

57. Marc Fisher. "Naming Your Price." *Washington Post,* June 30, 1997, p. C2.

58. Gary Gumpert and Susan J. Drucker. "From the Agora to the Electronic Shopping Mall." *Critical Studies in Mass Communications* 9(1992):186–200.

59. Linda Castrone. "The 'Couch Potato' Medium: College Class Analyzes Infomercials' Huge Appeal." *Rocky Mountain News,* December 17, 1996, p. 3D.

60. Some traditional advertisements do this, as well.

61. Mike Mills. "A Pentagon Plan Became the Internet: The Network Was Born From a Divide-and-Conquer Strategy for Communications Security." *Washington Post,* July 2, 1996, p. A6ff.

62. David Bank. "What Clicks?" *Wall Street Journal,* March 20, 1997, pp. R1, R4.

63. "More Surfers Shop Online." *New Media Age,* January 16, 1997, p. 15.

64. Richard Tompkins. "Wal-Mart Plans Big On-line Expansion." *Financial Times,* March 27, 1997, p. 33. There have also been failures. Shopping 2000, a cyberclone of a traditional mall with fifty-eight storefronts, failed because it was too cumbersome.

65. Diane Cyr. "Web Winners . . . and Losers Strive to Make Sense of Selling on the Internet." *Catalog Age,* October 1, 1996, p. 1ff.

66. Elizabeth Corcoran. "What Intuit Didn't Bank On." *Washington Post,* June 22, 1997, p. H5.

67. David Streitfeld. "King of the Booksellers' Jungle: Amazon.com Proved that Readers and the Internet Can Click." *Washington Post,* July 10, 1998, pp. A1, A20.

68. Beth Berselli. "Gamblers Log on to Deal Themselves In." *Washington Post,* August 19, 1997, pp. A1, A8.

69. Beth Berselli. "Gamblers Log on to Deal Themselves In." *Washington Post,* August 19, 1997, p. A1.

70. Wal-Mart has recently run into some resistance to expanding its economic base. See Jessica Hall and Jim Troy. "Wal-Mart, Go Home! Wal-Mart's Expansion Juggernaut Stumbles as Towns Turn Thumbs Down and Noses Up." *Warfield's Business Record,* July 22, 1994, vol. 9, section 1, p. 1ff.

71. "Winning the Grocery Game." *Consumer Reports,* August 1997, pp. 10–17.

72. "Winning the Grocery Game." *Consumer Reports,* August 1997, pp. 10–17.

73. Some trace it much further back to the founding of FAO Schwartz in New York in the 1860s

74. Richard Panek. "Superstore Inflation." *New York Times,* April 6, 1997, section 6, p. 66ff.

75. Rodney Ho. "Health-Care Superstores Experience Growing Pains." *Wall Street Journal,* May 12, 1997, pp. B1, B2.

76. Joseph Pereira. "New Sneaker Superstores Aim to Step on Their Competition." *Wall Street Journal,* March 19, 1997, pp. B1, B5.

77. Richard Panek. "Superstore Inflation." *New York Times,* April 6, 1997, section 6, p. 66ff.

78. Stanley Cohen and Laurie Tayor. *Escape Attempts: The Theory and Practice of Resistance in Everyday Life*, 2nd ed. London: Routledge, 1992.

79. John Urry. "The 'Consumption' of Tourism." *Sociology* 24(1990): 23–35.

80. Bob Dickinson and Andy Vladimir. *Selling the Sea: An Inside Look at the Cruise Industry*. New York: John Wiley and Sons, 1997.

81. Bob Dickinson and Andy Vladimir. *Selling the Sea: An Inside Look at the Cruise Industry*. New York: John Wiley and Sons, 1997, p. 111.

82. Nancy Keates. "Cruise-Ship Delays Leave Guests High and Dry." *Wall Street Journal,* October 24, 1997, p. B8.

83. Robert J. Martin. "Historical Background," in International Gaming Institute. *The Gaming Industry: Introduction and Perspectives.* New York: John Wiley and Sons, 1996, pp. 3–48.

84. Kenneth Labich. "Gambling's Kings: On a Roll and Raising Their Bets." *Fortune,* July 22, 1996, p. 82.

85. Hank Burchard. "High-Rollin' on the River." *Washington Post,* December 14, 1997, p. E1.

86. Linton Weeks and Roxanne Roberts. "Amusement Mall." *Washington Post,* December 7, 1996, p. C1.

87. Linton Weeks and Roxanne Roberts. "Amusement Mall." *Washington Post,* December 7, 1996, p. C5.

88. Margaret Webb Pressler. "Putting a New Tag on Retailing." *Washington Post,* June 13, 1995, D1.

89. Mitchell Pacelle. "Skeletons, Subs and Other Restaurant Themes Do Battle." *Wall Street Journal,* May 21, 1997, p. B1.

90. David Wolitz. "Hard Rock Absurdity." *San Francisco Daily Online!* August 15, 1996.

91. Hard Rock Cafe Web site.

92. Thorstein Veblen. *The Theory of the Leisure Class: An Economic Study of Institutions.* New York: Modern Library, 1899/1934, p. 36.

93. Planet Hollywood Web site.

94. "Whatever You Call It, The Theme Concept Spells Success." *Discount Store News,* February 3, 1997, p. 13.

95. David Sweet. "To Maximize On-Field Product, Try Hitting Ball out of Park Often." *Wall Street Journal,* May 8, 1998, p. B1.

96. David J. Kennedy. "Residential Associations as State Actors: Regulating the Impact of Gated Communities on Nonmembers." *Yale*

Law Journal 105(1995):761–793; Mike Davis. *City of Quartz: Excavating the Future in Los Angeles.* New York: Vintage Books, 1992, p. 246.

97. Arthur G. Powell, Eleanor Farrar, and David K. Cohen. *The Shopping Mall High School: Winners and Losers in the Educational Marketplace.* Boston: Houghton Mifflin, 1985.

98. Debbie Goldberg. "A Room for Every Lifestyle." *Washington Post-Education Review,* October 26, 1997, pp. 1, 8.

99. George Ritzer. "McUniversity in the Postmodern Consumer Culture." *Quality in Higher Education* 2(1996):185–199.

100. Rene Sanchez. "Colleges Turning Virtual Classrooms into a Reality." *Washington Post,* March 27, 1997, pp. A1, A18.

101. Christine Laine and Frank Davidoff. "Patient-Centered Medicine: A Professional Evolution." *The Journal of the American Medical Association* 275(January 10, 1996):152ff.

102. Anita Sharpe. "Medical Entrepreneur Aims to Turn Clinics into a National Brand." *Wall Street Journal,* December 4, 1996, p. A1.

103. Anita Sharpe. "Medical Entrepreneur Aims to Turn Clinics into a National Brand." *Wall Street Journal,* December 4, 1996, p. A1.

104. As well as theme parks, see Margaret J. King. "The Theme Park Experience: What Museums Can Learn from Mickey Mouse." *Futurist* 25(1991):24–31.

105. Ada Louise Huxtable. *The Unreal America: Architecture and Illusion.* New York: New Press, 1997, p. 85.

106. Margaret Crawford. "The World in a Shopping Mall," in Michael Sorkin (ed.). *Variations on a Theme Park.* New York: Hill and Wang, 1992, p. 30.

107. Claudia Dreifus. "Talking Shop." *New York Times,* April 6, 1997, section 6, p. 83ff.

108. Joshua Harris Prager. "Out of Ideas: Give a Goat or a Seaweed Body Wrap." *Wall Street Journal,* December 23, 1997, pp. B1, B11.

109. Gustav Niebuhr. "Where Shopping-Mall Culture Gets a Big Dose of Religion." *New York Times,* April 16, 1995, pp. 1, 14; Linda Perlstein. "The Rock of Ages Tries the Rock of Youth." *Washington Post,* July 18, 1998, p. A3.

110. Gustav Niebuhr. "Where Shopping-Mall Culture Gets a Big Dose of Religion." *New York Times,* April 16, 1995, p. 1.

111. Gustav Niebuhr. "Where Shopping-Mall Culture Gets a Big Dose of Religion." *New York Times,* April 16, 1995, p. 14.

112. James Barron. "A Church's Chief Executive Seeks the Target Audience." *New York Times,* April 18, 1995, p. A20.

Chapter 2

1. Stuart Ewen. *Captains of Consciousness*. New York: McGraw-Hill, 1976.

2. As I will discuss in more detail later, credit cards are not a means of consumption, but they do facilitate their use by consumers.

3. There is a substantial literature on shopping, but it is only a part of our concern and does not well describe the relationship between consumers and many of the new means of consumption, especially cruise ships, casinos, theme parks, eatertainment centers, and so on.

4. Ellen Goodman. "Zapping Christmas." *Washington Post*, December 20, 1997, p. A21.

5. Michael F. Jacobson and Laurie Ann Mazur. *Marketing Madness: A Survival Guide for a Consumer Society*. Boulder, CO: Westview Press, 1995.

6. In this, they are much like the tobacco companies and their efforts to hook teenagers on cigarettes.

7. Gary Cross. *Kids' Stuff: Toys and the Changing World of American Childhood*. Cambridge, MA: Harvard University Press, 1997.

8. Gary Cross. "The Plight before Christmas: How the Toy Market Outgrew Grown-Ups." *Washington Post*, December 21, 1997, p. C1.

9. George Ritzer. *Expressing America: A Critique of the Global Credit Card Society*. Thousand Oaks, CA: Pine Forge Press, 1995.

10. And the facilitating means themselves need facilitators. For example, wider scale credit card use on the Internet awaits greater trust in the reliability of methods of encryption.

11. David Hilzenrath. "Change Is Good, They Bet." *Washington Post-Washington Business*, October 21, 1996, p. 12.

12. Ann Smart Martin. "Makers, Buyers, and Users." *Wintherthur Portfolio* 28(1993):141–157.

13. A number of other experts trace the origins of mass consumption in the United States to the 1920s, the shift from a mentality of scarcity to one of abundance and the rise of modern advertising.

14. William Leach. *Land of Desire: Merchants, Power, and the Rise of a New American Culture*. New York: Pantheon Books, 1993, p. 3.

15. Susan Strasser has analyzed the new means of consumption in turn-of-the-century America in the context of a larger discussion of the creation of a mass market for consumer goods. See Susan Strasser. *Satisfaction Guaranteed: The Making of the American Mass Market*. New York: Pantheon Books, 1989.

16. William Leach. *Land of Desire: Merchants, Power, and the Rise of a New American Culture*. New York: Pantheon Books, 1993, p. 269.

17. Rosalind Williams. *Dream Worlds: Mass Consumption in Late Nineteenth-Century France*. Berkeley: University of California Press, 1982.

18. Americans are not the only ones obsessed with consumption. For a discussion of the Japanese case, see John Clammer. *Contemporary Urban Japan: A Sociology of Consumption*. Oxford: Blackwell, 1997.

19. Juliet B. Schor. *The Overworked American: The Unexpected Decline of Leisure*. New York: Basic Books, 1991, p. 109.

20. Clammer also uses the term *hyperconsumption* to describe contemporary Japanese consumption; see John Clammer. *Contemporary Urban Japan: A Sociology of Consumption*. Oxford: Routledge, 1997, p. 54.

21. Stephen E. Lankenau. *Native Sons: A Social Exploration of Panhandling*, Doctoral Dissertation, College Park, MD, 1997.

22. Given this focus on consumption, I have opted not to discuss the situation confronting the millions of people who work in or on behalf of the cathedrals of consumption. This is an important issue, worthy of a book of its own.

23. Robert Manning and Brett Williams. *Credit Card Nation: America's Dangerous Addiction to Consumer Debt*. New York: Basic Books, 1996.

24. Robert J. Samuelson. "Shades of the 1920s?" *Washington Post*, April 22, 1998, p. A23.

25. Juliet B. Schor. *The Overspent American: Upscaling, Downshifting, and the New Consumer*. New York: Basic Books, 1998, p. 20.

26. George Ritzer. *Expressing America: A Critique of the Global Credit Card Society*. Thousand Oaks, CA: Pine Forge Press, 1995.

27. The Japanese have managed to engage in hyperconsumption while remaining largely opposed to debt and reliant on a cash economy. See John Clammer. *Contemporary Urban Japan: A Sociology of Consumption*. Oxford: Routledge, 1997.

28. Jacob N. Schlesinger. "Are Lenders Letting Optimism Go Too Far?" *Wall Street Journal*, April 20, 1998, p. A1.

29. Juliet B. Schor. *The Overspent American: Upscaling, Downshifting, and the New Consumer*. New York: Basic Books, 1998, pp. 20–21.

30. Marc Fisher. "Naming Your Price." *Washington Post*, June 30, 1997, p. C2.

31. See Marc Fisher. "Naming Your Price." *Washington Post*, June 30, 1997, pp. C1, C2, for a discussion of at least one exception to this.

32. Another recent innovation designed to increase consumption is mechanisms built into products that demonstrate to consumers that it is time to replace them. Examples include razors with strips that fade indicating that the blade needs to be replaced, beer cans with brewing dates designed to encourage consumers to discard stale beer (even though beer can last for years), and toothbrushes with blue bristles that fade, indicating that it is time to replace the brushes. See Dana Canedy "Where Nothing Lasts Forever." *New York Times,* April 24, 1998, pp. C1, C3.

33. Malcolm Gladwell. "The Science of Shopping." *New Yorker,* November 4, 1996, pp. 66–75.

34. Margaret Crawford. "The World in a Shopping Mall." in Michael Sorkin (ed.). *Variations on a Theme Park.* New York: Farrar, Strauss and Giroux, 1992, p. 13.

35. Marc Fisher. "Where Hunters Gather." *Washington Post Magazine,* September 3, 1995, p. 20.

36. Albert B. Crenshaw. "How Direct-Mail Marketers Are Pushing the Envelope." *Washington Post,* March 17, 1996, pp. H1, H5.

37. "Winning the Grocery Game." *Consumer Reports,* August 1997, pp. 10–17.

38. Of course, consumers do not always buy, or buy as much as they are "supposed" to. Furthermore, consumers may actively resist and rebel against the new means of consumption. They may also use the cathedrals in ways unanticipated by those who designed and manage them.

39. Emile Zola. *Au Bonheur des Dames.* Lausanne, Switzerland: Edihons Rencontre, n.d.

40. Kevin Sullivan. "Barbie Doll: Japan's New Look." *Washington Post,* December 16, 1996, p. A20.

41. George Ritzer. *The McDonaldization Thesis: Explorations and Extensions.* London: Sage, 1998.

42. I am taking a position that is opposed by most globalization theorists as well as Featherstone, who argues against this idea and who sees a shift away from the United States in particular and the West in general. See Mike Featherstone. *Consumer Culture and Postmodernism.* London: Sage, 1991, pp. 127, 142.

43. However, there are limits to this, as Mars Inc. candy makers discovered in Russia, where its America-oriented ads, as well as a general return to "Russianness," led to a backlash and renewed interest in "real Russian chocolate." See Christian Caryl. "We Will Bury You . . . with a Snickers Bar." *U.S. News and World Report,* January 26, 1998, pp. 50, 52; see also Daniel Williams. "Advertisers Cash in on Things Russian." *Washington Post,* June 12, 1998, p. A16.

44. Edwin McDowell. "Bazaar; Megamalls; Dropping in to Shop." *The Orange County Register,* August 4, 1996, p. D4.

45. Richard F. Kuisel. *Seducing the French: The Dilemma of Americanization.* Berkeley: University of California Press, 1993.

46. John Vidal. *Counter Culture vs. Burger Culture.* London: Macmillan, 1997.

47. McDonald's sued two members of Greenpeace for passing out leaflets critical of the company. The trial ran for more than two years, becoming the longest running trial in the history of Great Britain. The judge's decision in mid-1997 was generally seen as a partial and pyrrhic victory for McDonald's. The case became the rallying cry for a large number of individuals and groups critical of McDonald's on a wide variety of grounds.

48. Jane Perlez. "A McDonald's? Not in Their Medieval Square." *New York Times,* May 23, 1994, p. A4.

49. Of course, with capitalism now triumphant throughout virtually the entire world, the conditions (e.g., hyperexploitation) may be being put into place to allow for the reemergence of a radical alternative to capitalism.

50. McDonald's Corp. *The Annual: McDonald's Corporation Annual Report.* Chicago: Author, 1996.

51. Judith H. Dobrzynski. "The American Way." *New York Times,* April 6, 1997, section 6, p. 79ff.

52. Jim Fox. "Category Killers Mount Major Canadian Invasion; US Retailers in Canada." *Discount Store News,* vol. 34, July 17, 1995, p. 44ff.

53. David Horovitz. "Big Macs Challenge the Cuisine of the Kibbutz." *The Irish Times,* July 21, 1995, p. 8.

54. Michael Freeman. "Cubicov Zirconiumich: US-Produced Russian Home Shopping Show 'TV Style'." *Mediaweek,* vol. 5, June 5, 1995, p. 12ff.

55. Robert Muraskin. "Hungary to Shop, American Style." *Washington Post,* November 29, 1996, p. B12.

56. Keith B. Richburg. "Attention, Shenzen Shoppers!" *Washington Post,* February 12, 1997, p. C14.

57. As well as theme parks: In addition to DisneySea now under construction, Universal Studios will build a new park in Western Japan. See Mary Jordan. "Universal Studios to Build a Theme Park in Japan." *Washington Post,* May 10, 1998, p. A26.

58. Sandra Sugawara. "D.C. Developer Sounds the Call of the Supermall for Japan." *Washington Post-Real Estate,* August 3, 1996, pp. E1, E4.

59. Mai Hoang. "The Americanization of Vietnam." *Washington Post,* May 11, 1997, p. A25.

60. Kevin Sullivan. "Saigon Goes to the Superbowl: American-Style Mall Draws Young, Newly Affluent Vietnamese." *Washington Post,* June 6, 1997, p. A29.

61. Jonathan Friedland. "Can Yanks Export Good Times to Latins?" *Wall Street Journal,* March 6, 1997, p. A11.

62. Jonathan Friedland. "Can Yanks Export Good Times to Latins?" *Wall Street Journal,* March 6, 1997, p. A11.

63. Dana Thomas. "La Mall Epoque." *Washington Post,* January 3, 1997, p. D6.

64. Dana Thomas. "La Mall Epoque." *Washington Post,* January 3, 1997, p. D6.

65. Dana Thomas. "La Mall Epoque." *Washington Post,* January 3, 1997, p. D6.

66. Jeff Kaye. "Invasion of the Discounters: American-Style Bargain Shopping Comes to the United Kingdom." *Los Angeles Times,* May 8, 1994, p. D1ff.

67. Peter Jones. "Factory Outlet Shopping Centres and Planning Issues." *International Journal of Retail & Distribution Management,* vol. 23, January 1995, p. 12ff.

68. Jeff Kaye. "Invasion of the Discounters: American-Style Bargain Shopping Comes to the United Kingdom." *Los Angeles Times,* May 8, 1994, p. D1ff.

69. Jonathan Friedland. "Can Yanks Export Good Times to Latins?" *Wall Street Journal,* March 6, 1997, p. A11.

70. Jonathan Friedland. "Can Yanks Export Good Times to Latins?" *Wall Street Journal,* March 6, 1997, p. A11.

71. John Clammer. *Contemporary Urban Japan: A Sociology of Consumption.* Oxford: Routledge, 1997, p. 72.

72. Judith H. Dobrzynski. "The American Way." *New York Times,* April 6, 1997, section 6, p. 79ff.

73. Gabriel Escobar and Anne Swardson. "From Language to Literature, a New Guiding Lite." *Washington Post,* September 5, 1995, p. A1ff.

74. Justin Arenstein. "Tourism Boom Expected for Mpumalanga." *Africa News,* May 27, 1997.

75. James L. Watson (ed.). *Golden Arches East: McDonald's in East Asia.* Stanford, CA: Stanford University Press, 1997.

76. Mary Yoko Brannen. "'Bwana Mickey': Constructing Cultural Consumption at Tokyo Disneyland," in Joseph Tobin (ed.). *Remade in*

Japan: Everyday Life and Consumer Taste in a Changing Society. New Haven: Yale University Press, 1992, pp. 216–234; John Van Maanen. "Displacing Disney: Some Notes on the Flow of Culture." *Qualitative Sociology* 15(1992):5–35.

77. Thomas L. Friedman. "Big Mac II." *New York Times,* December 11, 1996, p. A21.

78. Kenneth J. Cooper. "It's Lamb Burger, Not Hamburger, at Beefless McDonald's in New Delhi." *Washington Post,* November 4, 1996, p. A14.

Chapter 3

1. It is increasingly difficult to separate them. In many of the new means of consumption consumers produce their own consumption. For example, by pouring their own drinks or making their own salad, consumers are helping to produce their own meals.

2. Adam Smith. *The Wealth of Nations.* New York: Modern Library, 1789/1994.

3. Karl Marx. *Capital: Volume Two.* New York: Vintage Books, 1884/ 1981, p. 471.

4. Karl Marx. *Capital: Volume Two.* New York: Vintage Books, 1884/ 1981, p. 471.

5. Karl Marx. *Capital: Volume Two.* New York: Vintage Books, 1884/ 1981, p. 479.

6. Karl Marx. *Capital: Volume Two.* New York: Vintage Books, 1884/ 1981, p. 479.

7. Smith (1789/1994, p. 938) does not make this error, labeling what Marx calls the means of consumption "consumable commodities." Marx, like Smith, is really dealing with consumer goods and not with the kinds of structures that are discussed in this book as the means of consumption.

8. However, as we have already seen and will have occasion to examine further, there is a sense in which we "consume" means of consumption such as the fast food restaurant.

9. As the reader will see, I will waffle a bit on whether the consumer is, like the worker, exploited.

10. Georg Simmel. *The Philosophy of Money.* Rosalind H. Williams. *Dream Worlds.* Berkeley: University of California Press, 1982:95; London: Routledge and Kegan Paul, 1907/1978, p. 477; Sharon Zukin. *Landscapes of Power: From Detroit to Disney World.* Berkeley: University of California Press, 1991.

11. Jean Baudrillard. *The Consumer Society*. London: Sage, 1970/1998.

12. Sheila Rothenberg and Robert S. Rothenberg. "The Pleasures of Paris." *USA Today* (Magazine), March 1993, p. 38ff.

13. Baudrillard also discusses the credit card, which is an important example of what has been termed "facilitating means."

14. Mike Gane. *Baudrillard's Bestiary: Baudrillard and Culture*. London: Routledge, 1991, p. 65.

15. Paul Baran and Paul M. Sweezy. *Monopoly Capital: An Essay on the American Economic and Social Order*. New York: Monthly Review Press, 1966.

16. Juliet B. Schor. *The Overspent American: Upscaling, Downshifting, and the New Consumer*. New York: Basic Books, 1998, p. 20.

17. Juliet B. Schor. *The Overspent America: Upscaling, Downshifting, and the New Consumer*. New York: Basic Books, 1998.

18. Ira Chinoy and Charles Babington. "Low-Income Players Feed Lottery Cash Cow." *Washington Post,* May 3, 1998, pp. A1, A22; Charles Babington and Ira Chinoy. "Lotteries Lure Players with Slick Marketing." *Washington Post,* May 4, 1998, pp. A1, A10.

19. Harry Braverman. *Labor and Monopoly Capital: The Degradation of Work in the Twentieth Century*. New York: Monthly Review Press, 1974; Richard Edwards. *Contested Terrain: The Transformation of the Workplace in the Twentieth Century*. New York: Basic Books, 1979.

20. Cited in Hans Gerth and C. Wright Mills (eds.). *From Max Weber*. New York: Oxford University Press, 1958, p. 128.

21. Or at least less. In fact, because the three types of authority are also "ideal types," each appears, at least to some degree, in all particular cases of the exercise of authority.

22. Max Weber. *Economy and Society*, 3 vols. Totowa, NJ: Bedminster Press, 1921/1968, p. 223.

23. Max Weber. *Economy and Society*, 3 vols. Totowa, NJ: Bedminster Press, 1921/1968, p. 1156.

24. Max Weber. *The Protestant Ethic and the Spirit of Capitalism*. New York: Scribner's, 1904–5/1958, p. 54.

25. However, as we will see, there is an important trend toward less objective, dematerialized means of consumption.

26. The idea of a "neon cage" has recently been employed by Lauren Langman to analyze one of the new means of consumption—the shopping mall. Langman takes a Marxian, rather than a Weberian, view of malls, but he nonetheless sees them as isolated structures in which everything—from temperature to merchant displays to people—is

controlled. To his credit, Langman also sees malls as producers of fantasies and dream-like states. See Lauren Langman. "Neon Cages: Shopping for Subjectivity," in Rob Shields (ed.). *Lifestyle Shopping: The Subject of Consumption*. London: Routledge, 1992, pp. 40–82.

27. Mark A. Schneider. *Culture and Enchantment*. Chicago: University of Chicago Press, 1993, p. ix.

28. Hans Gerth and C. Wright Mills. "Introduction," in Hans Gerth and C. Wright Mills (eds.). *From Max Weber*. New York: Oxford University Press, 1958, p. 51.

29. Mark A. Schneider. *Culture and Disenchantment*. Chicago: University of Chicago Press, 1993, p. ix.

30. Mark A. Schneider. *Culture and Disenchantment*. Chicago: University of Chicago Press, 1993, p. xiii.

31. It appears also in his writings on law. Weber argues, "Inevitably, the notion must expand that the law is a rational technical apparatus . . . and devoid of all sacredness of content." In other words, law grows increasingly disenchanted. Max Weber, *Economy and Society*, 3 vols. Totowa, NJ: Bedminster Press, 1921/1968, p. 895.

32. Max Weber. "Science as a Vocation," in Hans Gerth and C. Wright Mills (eds.). *From Max Weber*. New York: Oxford University Press, 1958, p. 139.

33. Colin Campbell. *The Romantic Ethic and the Spirit of Modern Consumerism*. Oxford: Blackwell, 1989.

34. Colin Campbell. *The Romantic Ethic and the Spirit of Modern Consumerism*. Oxford: Blackwell, 1989.

35. This is so at least in the form of being emotional about not showing emotion.

36. Colin Campbell. *The Romantic Ethic and the Spirit of Modern Consumerism*. Oxford: Blackwell, 1989, p. 153.

37. Of course, they are successful to varying degrees. Some consumers may find a cathedral of consumption quite enchanting, whereas others will fail to see its enchanting qualities. Most, of course, will stand somewhere in between.

38. Mark A. Schneider. *Culture and Disenchantment*. Chicago: University of Chicago Press, 1993, p. x.

39. Although Williams's work is discussed in this section, her research does not fit comfortably under the heading of neo-Weberian theory. However, she is dealing with the issue of enchantment.

40. Rosalind Williams. *Dream Worlds: Mass Consumption in Late Nineteenth-Century France*. Berkeley: University of California Press, 1982, pp. 70–71.

41. Michael B. Miller. *The Bon Marché: Bourgeois Culture and the Department Store, 1869–1920*. Princeton: Princeton University Press, 1981.

42. Michael B. Miller. *The Bon Marché: Bourgeois Culture and the Department Store, 1869–1920*. Princeton: Princeton University Press, 1981, p. 68.

43. Michael B. Miller. *The Bon Marché: Bourgeois Culture and the Department Store, 1869–1920*. Princeton: Princeton University Press, 1981, p. 71.

44. Colin Campbell. *The Romantic Ethic and the Spirit of Modern Consumerism*. Oxford, Blackwell, 1989, p. 227.

45. George Ritzer. *Postmodern Social Theory*. New York: McGraw-Hill, 1997.

46. Zygmunt Bauman. *Intimations of Postmodernity*. London: Routledge, 1992.

47. Eva Illouz. *Consuming the Romantic Utopia*. Berkeley: University of California Press, 1997, p. 13.

48. Jean Baudrillard. *The Consumer Society*. London: Sage, 1970/1998.

49. Pauline Marie Rosenau. *Post-Modernism and the Social Sciences: Insights, Inroads, and Intrusions*. Princeton: Princeton University Press, 1992, p. 6.

50. Jean Baudrillard. *The Mirror of Production*. St. Louis: Telos Press, 1973/1975, p. 83.

51. Jean Baudrillard. *Symbolic Exchange and Death*. London: Sage, 1976/1993.

52. Clammer offers a powerful critique of Baudrillard by demonstrating the continued importance of the gift, and thereby symbolic exchange, in contemporary Japan. See John Clammer. *Contemporary Urban Japan: A Sociology of Consumption*. Oxford: Blackwell, 1997.

53. The reader might want to think of other aspects of the American society from this point of view. For example, this helps us understand the popularity of the television show and movie "The X-Files."

54. Zygmunt Bauman. *Postmodern Ethics*. Oxford: Basil Blackwell, 1993, p. 33.

55. Jean Baudrillard. *Fatal Strategies*. New York: Semiotext(e), 1983/1990, p. 51.

56. Illouz does much the same thing; see Eva Illouz. *Consuming the Romantic Utopia*. Berkeley: University of California Press, 1997, p. 17.

Chapter 4

1. William Severini Kowinski. *The Malling of America: An Inside Look at the Great Consumer Paradise.* New York: William Morrow, 1985, p. 61.

2. Mark Marymount. "A Sound Idea: Music Catalogs Hit All the Right Notes for Some Shoppers." *Chicago Tribune-Your Money,* April 5, 1995, p. 1ff.

3. Sandra S. Vance and Roy V. Scott. *A History of Sam Walton's Retail Phenomenon.* New York: Twayne, 1994, p. 135.

4. Robert Bryce. "Merchant of Death." *Texas Monthly,* June 1996, p. 58ff.

5. Dean Takahashi. "Little Caesar's Plans 'Big! Big!!' Pizzas, While Keeping the Price Structure the Same." *Wall Street Journal,* September 2, 1997, p. B10.

6. Philip Elmer-DeWitt. "Fat Times." *Time,* January 16, 1995, pp. 60–65.

7. "Loose slots" are those that pay out the most frequently.

8. Although, as we will see, Disney World is also in a sense a shopping mall oriented to getting people to spend far more than they do on their daily pass.

9. G. Bruce Knecht. "Book Superstores Bring Hollywood-Like Risks to Publishing Business." *Wall Street Journal,* May 29, 1997, pp. A1, A6.

10. Kmart Web site.

11. Marc Fisher. "Where Hunters Gather." *Washington Post Magazine,* September 3, 1995, pp. 31–32. Used with permission.

12. Christina Binkley. "A Day with a High Roller." *Wall Street Journal,* May 1, 1998, p. W1.

13. Margaret Webb Pressler. "2 with Reservations at the Gourmet Table." *Washington Post,* April 24, 1998, pp. FI, F4.

14. Richard Gibson. "Popular Pizza Chain's Gimmick is Taste." *Wall Street Journal,* April 28, 1997, pp. B1, B10.

15. Richard Gibson. "Popular Pizza Chain's Gimmick Is Taste." *Wall Street Journal,* April 28, 1997, pp. B1, B10.

16. George Ritzer. *The McDonaldization Thesis: Explorations and Extensions.* London: Sage, 1998.

17. Robin Leidner. *Fast Food, Fast Talk: Service Work and the Routinization of Everyday Life.* Berkeley: University of California Press, 1993, pp. 45–47.

18. David Wolitz. "Hard Rock Absurdity." *San Francisco Daily Online!* August 15, 1996.

19. Paul Goldberger. "The Sameness of Things." *New York Times,* April 6, 1997, section 6, p. 56ff.

20. Paul Goldberger. "The Sameness of Things." *New York Times,* April 6, 1997, section 6, p. 56ff.

21. Wal-Mart exercises the usual kinds of control McDonaldized systems have over customers, as well as one that is fairly unique. It censors the words and images on CDs sold in its stores. Some disks are marked: "Sanitized for your protection." Customers are not allowed to decide for themselves whether they want to listen to the forbidden lyrics or view the proscribed images. See "American Survey." *The Economist,* November 23, 1996, pp. 27–28.

22. Sandra S. Vance and Roy V. Scott. *A History of Sam Walton's Retail Phenomenon.* New York: Twayne, 1994, p. 93.

23. Margaret Crawford. "The World in a Shopping Mall," in Michael Sorkin (ed.). *Variations on a Theme Park.* New York: Farrar, Straus and Giroux, 1992, p. 14.

24. William Severini Kowinski. *The Malling of America: An Inside Look at the Great Consumer Paradise.* New York: William Morrow, 1985, p. 359.

25. William Severini Kowinski. *The Malling of America: A Look at the Great Consumer Paradise.* New York: William Morrow, 1985, p. 349.

26. William Severini Kowinski. *The Malling of America: A Look at the Great Consumer Paradise.* New York: William Morrow, 1985, p. 354.

27. William Severini Kowinski. *The Malling of America: An Inside Look at the Great Consumer Paradise.* New York: William Morrow, 1985, p. 343.

28. William G. Staples. *The Culture of Surveillance: Discipline and Social Control in the United States.* New York: St. Martin's Press, 1997.

29. David Dillon. "Fortress America: More and More of Us Are Living Behind Locked Gates." *Planning* 60 (1994):8ff.

30. Karen E. Klein. "Code Blues: Rules that Govern Life in Homeowners Associations Are Being Challenged in Court by Angry Owners." *Los Angeles Times,* March 5, 1995, pp. K1ff.

31. Cited in William G. Staples. *The Culture of Surveillance: Discipline and Social Control in the United States.* New York: St. Martin's Press, 1997, p. 64.

32. Judith A. Adams. *The American Amusement Park Industry: A History of Technology and Thrills.* Boston: Twayne, 1991, p. 111.

33. Michel Foucault. *Discipline and Punish: The Birth of the Prison.* New York: Vintage, p. 216.

34. Mike Davis. *City of Quartz.* London: Verso, 1990.

35. Michel Foucault. *Discipline and Punish: The Birth of the Prison.* New York: Vintage, p. 298.

36. John O'Neill. "The Disciplinary Society: From Weber to Foucault." *British Journal of Sociology* 37(1986):42–60.

37. Erving Goffman. *Asylums.* Garden City, New York: Anchor Books, 1961, p. xiii.

38. Louis A. Zurcher, Jr. "The Sailor aboard Ship: A Study of Role Behavior in a Total Institution." *Social Forces* 53(1965):389–400.

39. Gary Gumpert and Susan J. Drucker. "From the Agora to the Electronic Shopping Mall." *Critical Studies in Mass Communication* 9(1992):186–200.

40. Laura Billings. "Click on Triple Rinsed Mesclun." *New York Times,* April 6, 1997, section 6, p. 34ff.

41. Although in other contexts rationality and reason are often used interchangeably, they are here employed to mean antithetical phenomena.

42. Cited in Sandra S. Vance and Roy V. Scott. *A History of Sam Walton's Retail Phenomenon.* New York: Twayne, 1994, p. 126.

43. Rene Sanchez. "Colleges Turning Virtual Classrooms into a Reality." *Washington Post,* March 27, 1997, pp. A1, A8.

44. Laura Esquivel. *Like Water for Chocolate.* New York: Doubleday, 1992, pp. 10–11.

45. Laura Esquivel. *Like Water for Chocolate.* New York: Doubleday, 1992, p. 39.

46. Laura Esquivel. *Like Water for Chocolate.* New York: Doubleday, 1992, pp. 241–242.

47. As we will see, great spaces, large sizes, and the like can have, or be made to appear to have, a magical character.

48. Ada Louise Huxtable. *The Unreal America: Architecture and Illusion.* New York: New Press, 1997, p. 61.

49. Christina Binkley. "Starless Nights in the 'New' Las Vegas." *Wall Street Journal,* May 9, 1997, p. B1.

50. This can be traced to the first Ferris Wheel at the 1893 Chicago Exposition, and perhaps even before that. But whatever its origins, we are amazed by the new technologies.

Chapter 5

1. Teena Hammond. "Inland Empire Focus: Entertaining the Shopper." *The Business Press/California,* September 23, 1996, p. 1.

2. James Bernstein. "Retailers: Let Us Entertain You, Too." *Newsday,* October 20, 1996, p. F8ff.

3. Mike Featherstone. *Consumer Culture and Postmodernism.* London: Sage, 1991, p. 103.

4. Michael B. Miller. *The Bon Marché: Bourgeois Culture and the Department Store, 1869–1920.* Princeton: Princeton University Press, 1981, p. 173.

5. William Leach. *Land of Desire: Merchants, Power, and the Rise of a New American Culture.* New York: Pantheon, 1993.

6. Guy Debord. *The Society of the Spectacle.* New York: Zone Books, 1967/1994.

7. Guy Debord. *The Society of the Spectacle.* New York: Zone Books, 1967/1994, p. 16.

8. Guy Debord. *The Society of the Spectacle.* New York: Zone Books, 1967/1994, p. 16.

9. Guy Debord. *The Society of the Spectacle.* New York: Zone Books, 1967/1994, p. 26.

10. Guy Debord. *The Society of the Spectacle.* New York: Zone Books, 1967/1994, p. 26.

11. David Chaney. *Fictions of Collective Life.* London: Routledge, 1993.

12. M. M. Bakhtin. *Rabelais and His World.* Cambridge: MIT Press, 1968; P. Stallybrass and A. White. *The Politics and Poetics of Transgression.* London: Methuen, 1986.

13. I will have occasion in the final chapter to criticize another of Chaney's distinctions between spectacular society and the society of the spectacle.

14. Although we often talk in this book as if the cathedrals of consumption act, it is clearly the case that it is those people who design, control, and work in them who take the actions. We must be wary of reifying the new means of consumption.

15. On the importance of crowds to consumption, see John Clammer. *Contemporary Urban Japan: A Sociology of Consumption.* Oxford: Blackwell, 1997.

16. William N. Thompson, J. Kent Pinney, and John A. Schibrowsky. "The Family that Gambles Together: Business and Social Concerns." *Journal of Travel Research* 34(1996):70–74.

17. Kenneth Labich. "Gambling's Kings: On a Roll and Raising Their Bets." *Fortune,* July 22, 1996, p. 82.

18. Rick Bragg. "Las Vegas Is Booming after City Reinvention." *New York Times,* May 4, 1997, p. 22.

19. Neil Postman. "The Las Vegasizing of America." *National Forum,* Summer 1982, p. 6.

20. Hugh Hart. "Dave & Buster's Offers Fun by Day for the Whole Family." *Chicago Tribune,* April 4, 1997, p. 73.

21. Rainforest Cafe Web site.

22. Glenn Collins. "Egg McMuffins, Priced to Move." *New York Times,* April 4, 1997, p. C1.

23. Doris Hajewski. "Gurnee Mills Aiming to Give Shoppers Fun Time." *Milwaukee Journal Sentinel, Business,* March 12, 1997, p. 1.

24. Paul Goldberger. "The Store Strikes Back." *New York Times,* April 6, 1997, section 6, p. 45ff.

25. Paul Goldberger. "The Store Strikes Back." *New York Times,* April 6, 1997, section 6, p. 45ff.

26. Paul Goldberger. "The Store Strikes Back." *New York Times,* April 6, 1997, section 6, p. 45ff.

27. Roxanne Roberts. "High-Browse Fun." *Washington Post,* April 3, 1997, p. C1.

28. Roxanne Roberts. "High-Browse Fun." *Washington Post,* April 3, 1997, p. C8.

29. Roxanne Roberts. "High-Browse Fun." *Washington Post,* April 3, 1997, p. C8.

30. Paul Goldberger. "The Store Strikes Back." *New York Times,* April 6, 1997, section 6, p. 45ff.

31. Ann Carrns. "Skyscrapers Try to Top Same Old Thrill." *Wall Street Journal,* April 11, 1997, p. B1.

32. Jean Baudrillard. *Simulations.* New York: Semiotext(e), 1983, p. 4.

33. Jean Baudrillard. *Simulations.* New York: Semiotext(e), 1983, p. 15.

34. Jean Baudrillard. *Simulations.* New York: Semiotext(e), 1983, p. 23.

35. Unfortunately, for lovers of simulations, it has recently been closed, but there are many others to choose from at a Disney theme park.

36. Christina Binkley. "Gambling on Culture: Casinos Invest in Fine Art." *Wall Street Journal,* April 15, 1998, p. B10.

37. Ada Louise Huxtable. *The Unreal America: Architecture and Illusion.* New York: New Press, 1997, pp. 64, 65.

38. Ada Louise Huxtable. *The Unreal America: Architecture and Illusion.* New York: New Press, 1997, p. 3. Unlike Baudrillard, Huxtable does have a sense of the real as, for example, "an architecture integrated into life and use" (p. 3).

39. Ada Louise Huxtable. "Living with the Fake and Liking It." *New York Times,* March 30, 1997, section 2, p. 1. Used with permission.
40. Ada Louise Huxtable. "Living with the Fake and Liking It." *New York Times,* March 30, 1997, section 2, p. 40. Used with permission.
41. Ada Louise Huxtable. *The Unreal America: Architecture and Illusion.* New York: New Press, 1997, p. 50.
42. Ada Louise Huxtable. *The Unreal America: Architecture and Illusion.* New York: The New Press, 1997, p. 101.
43. Robin Leidner. *Fast Food, Fast Talk: Service Work and the Routinization of Everyday Life.* Berkeley: University of California Press, 1993.
44. Alfred Schutz. *The Phenomenology of the Social World.* Evanston, IL: Northwestern University Press, 1932/1967.
45. Amy Waldman. "Lonely Hearts, Classy Dreams, Empty Wallets: Home Shopping Networks." *Washington Monthly* 27(June 1995):10ff.
46. Of course, the real Old West has been filtered for so long through the simulations of movies and television shows that it is difficult to even have a glimmer of what it "really" was.
47. Norman K. Denzin. *The Cinematic Society: The Voyeur's Gaze.* London: Sage, 1995.
48. DIVE! Website.
49. Don Kaplan. "Retail Hot Spots: New Retail Centers Differentiate Themselves from Megamalls." *Daily News Record,* February 10, 1997, p. 22.
50. This is the site, by the way, of the haunted hotel in the classic horror novel cum-movie, *The Shining.*
51. Don Kaplan. "Retail Hot Spots: New Retail Centers Differentiate Themselves from Megamalls." *Daily News Record,* February 10, 1997, p. 22.
52. Mark Gottdiener. *The Theming of America.* Boulder, CO: Westview, 1997, p. 147.
53. David Littlejohn. "They Took Manhattan—to the Desert." *Wall Street Journal,* January 21, 1997, p. A16.
54. William Booth. "At Disney's Tomorrowland, The Future Is a Timid Creature," *Washington Post,* June 24, 1998, pp. D1, D8.
55. Peter Carlson. "At Animal Kingdom, a Disney Critic Smells a Rat." *Washington Post,* June 24, 1998, p. D7.
56. "United Artists Opens 'Virtual Theme Park' in Denver." *Tour & Travel News,* November 18, 1996.
57. Alexander Stille. "Virtual Antiquities Could Help Real Icons Stand Test of Time." *The Washington Post,* December 25, 1995.

58. Sam Walker. "Hair Salons, Hot Tubs and . . . Oh, Yeah, Basketball." *Wall Street Journal,* March 27, 1998, p. W6.

59. Mark Gottdiener. *The Theming of America: Dreams, Visions, and Commercial Spaces.* Boulder, CO: Westview Press, 1997.

60. *Ossi* was the easterners slang term for East German citizens.

61. Cited in Benjamin R. Barber. *Jihad vs. McWorld.* New York: Times Books, 1995, p. 133; italics added.

62. Kathy M. Newbern and J. S. Fletcher. "Leisurely Cruise the Caribbean." *The Washington Times,* August 27, 1995. All is not lost; the McDonald's built on the island was forced (by lack of business) to close after six months.

63. Susan Carey. "Ersatz Isles Lack Local Color, but the Bathrooms Shine." *Wall Street Journal,* February 16, 1996, pp. B1, B5.

64. Susan Carey. "Ersatz Isles Lack Local Color, but the Bathrooms Shine." *Wall Street Journal,* February 16, 1996, p. B1.

65. Susan Carey. "Ersatz Isles Lack Local Color, but the Bathrooms Shine." *Wall Street Journal,* February 16, 1996, p. B1.

66. Susan Carey. "Ersatz Isles Lack Local Color, but the Bathrooms Shine." *Wall Street Journal,* February 16, 1996, p. B1; italics added.

67. Susan Carey. "Ersatz Isles Lack Local Color, but the Bathrooms Shine." *Wall Street Journal,* February 16, 1996, p. B5. They probably would if they were simulated.

68. Ada Louise Huxtable. *The Unreal America: Architecture and Illusion.* New York: New Press, 1997, p. 82.

69. Shelby Grad. "Irvine with a Down Home Side? It's All in the Master Plan." *Los Angeles Times, Orange County Edition,* July 8, 1996, p. B3.

70. Russ Rhymer. "Back to the Future: Disney Reinvents the Company Town of Celebration, FL." *Harper's Magazine,* October 1996, p. 65ff.

71. Mike Williams. "Living with the Magic Kingdom." *The Atlanta Journal and Constitution,* September 29, 1996, p. 14ff.

72. Russ Rhymer. "Back to the Future: Disney Reinvents the Company Town of Celebration, FL." *Harper's Magazine,* October, 1996, p. 66. Used with permission.

73. Russ Rhymer. "Back to the Future: Disney Reinvents the Company Town of Celebration, FL." *Harper's Magazine,* October 1996, p. 67. Used with permission.

74. Russ Rhymer. "Back to the Future: Disney Reinvents the Company Town of Celebration, FL." *Harper's Magazine,* October 1996, p. 68. Used with permission.

75. Russ Rhymer. "Back to the Future: Disney Reinvents the Company Town of Celebration, FL." *Harper's Magazine,* October 1996, p. 75. Used with permission.

Chapter 6

1. Like much else to do with the cathedrals of consumption, implosions are not new, although they have accelerated in recent years. For example, a century and a half ago the department store was created as a result of the implosion of boundaries separating a wide range of specialty shops.

2. Jean Baudrillard. *Simulations.* New York: Semiotext(e), 1983, p. 57.

3. Malcolm Waters. *Globalization.* London: Routledge, 1996.

4. Umberto Eco. *Travels in Hyperreality.* San Diego: Harcourt Brace Jovanovich, 1986.

5. Peter McKay and Maryann Haggerty. "Entertaining New Mall Ideas." *Washington Post,* June 19, 1998, pp. F1, F10.

6. Anne Friedberg. *Window Shopping: Cinema and the Postmodern.* Berkeley: University of California Press, 1993, p. xi.

7. Laura Bird. "Huge Mall Bets on Formula of Family Fun and Games," *Wall Street Journal,* June 11, 1997, pp. B1, B12.

8. Laura Bird. "Huge Mall Bets on Formula of Family Fun and Games," *Wall Street Journal,* June 11, 1997, p. B12.

9. Michael Pretes. "Postmodern Tourism: The Santa Claus Industry." *Annals of Tourism Research* 22(1994):1–15.

10. Reuters. "American Express, America Online Hook Up." *The Washington Post,* January 31, 1995, p. D3.

11. "Fast Food Speeds Up the Pace." *Time,* August 26, 1985, p. 60.

12. Christina Brinkley. "Huge Casino Project Does the Unthinkable: It Rattles Las Vegas." *Wall Street Journal,* December 4, 1997, pp. A1, A10.

13. This may even be more true of the Japanese.

14. Andy Dworkin. "Jurassic Jostling: Two Giant Malls Threaten to Steal Others' Thunder." *The Dallas Morning News* July 24, 1996, p. 1D.

15. Edwin McDowell. "Bazaar: Megamalls; Dropping in to Shop." *The Orange County Register,* August 4, 1996, p. D4.

16. Edwin McDowell. "Bazaar: Megamalls; Dropping in to Shop." *The Orange County Register,* August 4, 1996, p. D4.

17. Rachel Spevack. "Nike in N.Y.: In the Starting Blocks." *WWD,* October 29, 1996, p. 4ff.

18. Naedine Joy Hazell. "The Sailings Grow in Popularity, Cruises and More, Seagoing Vacations Enhanced with Country Music, Irish Culture, Cigar Smoking" *Hartford Courant,* September 15, 1996, p. F1.

19. Judith Evans. "Catering to the Quick Food Fix." *Washington Post-Business* May 19, 1997, pp. 12–13.

20. Margaret Webb Pressler. "Retailing's Quick Fix." *Washington Post,* June 13, 1998, pp. D1, D3.

21. Richard Panek. "Superstore Inflation." *New York Times,* April 6, 1997, section 6, p. 66ff.

22. Richard Panek. "Superstore Inflation." *New York Times,* April 6, 1997, section 6, p. 66ff.

23. Lori Lincoln. "Scenes from a Mall." *Business Traveler,* June 1998, p. 51.

24. Margaret Webb Pressler. "Retailers, Restaurants Aim to Grab Some of Travelers' Time." *Washington Post,* July 16, 1997, p. F12.

25. Lori Lincoln. "Scenes from a Mall." *Business Traveler,* June 1998, pp. 48–51.

26. Lori Lincoln. "Scenes from a Mall." *Business Traveler,* June 1998, pp. 48–51.

27. Sam Walker. "Hair Salons, Hot Tubs and . . . Oh, Yeah, Baseball." *Wall Street Journal,* March 27, 1998, pp. W1, W6.

28. Sam Walker. "Hair Salons, Hot Tubs and . . . Oh, Yeah, Baseball." *Wall Street Journal,* March 27, 1998, p. W6.

29. Sam Walker. "Hair Salons, Hot Tubs and . . . Oh, Yeah, Baseball." *Wall Street Journal,* March 27, 1998, p. W6.

30. Dave Kindred. "Luxurious New Ballparks Monuments to Greed." *Atlanta Journal and Constitution,* March 23, 1997, p. 03G.

31. Paul Newberry. "Stadium Pace Has Questions." *Chatanooga Free Press,* February 12, 1997, p. H8.

32. Michelle Hiskey. "The Ballpark: It's Entertaiment." *The Atlanta Journal and Constitution,* March 23, 1997, p. 02G.

33. Michelle Hiskey. "The Ballpark: It's Entertaiment." *The Atlanta Journal and Constitution,* March 23, 1997, p. 02G.

34. I. J. Rosenbergh. "No Mickey Mouse Operation: Braves are Going to Disney World." *Atlanta Journal and Constitution* February 24, 1997, p. 01C. Disney owns the Anaheim Angels and its Edison Stadium has recently been refurbished, including a Disneyesque simulated rock formation beyond the centerfield fence.

35. Peter Applebome. "Franchise Fever in the Ivory Tower." *New York Times Educational Life Supplement,* April 2, 1995, section 4A, p. 16; cited in Mark Gottdiener. *The Theming of America.* Boulder, CO: Westview Press, 1997, p. 91.

36. Anne Friedberg. *Window Shopping: Cinema and the Postmodern.* Berkeley: University of California Press, 1993, p. xii.

37. "Latest Mall of America Offering: College Classes." *The Orlando Sentinel,* March 12, 1997, p. A12. Another example of implosion involves plans to open the Meaning Store at Mall of America, which will minister to the spiritual and religious needs of mall customers. See Norman Draper. "A Shop for New 'Meaning' at the Mall of America." *Star Tribune* (Minneapolis, MN), July 3, 1996, p. 1A.

38. Arthur G. Powell, Eleanor Farrar, and David K. Cohen. *The Shopping Mall High School: Winners and Losers in the Educational Marketplace.* Boston: Houghton Mifflin, 1985.

39. Arthur G. Powell, Eleanor Farrar, and David K. Cohen. *The Shopping Mall High School: Winners and Losers in the Educational Marketplace.* Boston: Houghton Mifflin, 1985, p. 8.

40. Arthur G. Powell, Eleanor Farrar, and David K. Cohen. *The Shopping Mall High School: Winners and Losers in the Educational Marketplace.* Boston: Houghton Mifflin, 1985, p. 8.

41. Arthur G. Powell, Eleanor Farrar, and David K. Cohen. *The Shopping Mall High School: Winners and Losers in the Educational Marketplace.* Boston: Houghton Mifflin, 1985, pp. 8–9.

42. Arthur G. Powell, Eleanor Farrar, and David K. Cohen. *The Shopping Mall High School: Winners and Losers in the Educational Marketplace.* Boston: Houghton Mifflin, 1985, p. 10.

43. Carl Quintanilla. "Planning a Vacation? Give Some Thought to Spamtown USA." *Wall Street Journal,* April 30, 1998, p. A6.

44. Carl Quintanilla. "Planning a Vacation? Give Some Thought to Spamtown USA." *Wall Street Journal,* April 30, 1998, p. A1.

45. Jim Carlton. "A Vancouver Condo Irks the Neighbors, But Nobody Cares." *Wall Street Journal,* March 8, 1998, p. A1.

46. John M. Goshko. "New York Wrestles with King Kong-Size Retail Dilemma: Superstores." *Washington Post,* April 13, 1997, p. A3.

47. James T. Yenckel. "New York by Night: The New Times Square; The City Hasn't Dropped the Ball." *Washington Post-Travel* April 13, 1997, p. E6.

48. Gary A. Warner. "Times Square Now 'Great Whitewashed Way': Heart of New York Gets G-Rated Refurbishment." *The Arizona Republic,* July 27, 1997, p. T14ff.

49. See, for example, Scott Lash and John Urry. *Economies of Signs and Space*. London: Sage, 1994; Roger Friedland and Deirdre Boden (eds.). *NowHere: Space, Time and Modernity*. Berkeley: University of California Press, 1994.

50. Anthony Giddens. "A Reply to My Critics," in D. Held and J. B. Thompson (eds). *Social Theory of Modern Societies: Anthony Giddens and His Critics*. Cambridge: Cambridge University Press, 1989, pp. 249–301.

51. David Harvey. *The Condition of Postmodernity: An Inquiry into the Origins of Cultural Change*. Oxford: Blackwell, 1989, p. 284.

52. As such, they are an early example of making consumption "fun."

53. There is some evidence that these are experiencing something of a revival. See Jacqueline L. Salmon. "Break out the Tupperware: Home Is Where the Sell Is." *Washington Post*, March 24, 1997, pp. A1, A12.

54. Caroline E. Mayer. "Telemarketers Just Beginning to Answer Their Calling." *Washington Post*, August 31, 1997, p. H1.

55. Being on-line has brought with it yet another type of intrusion into the home—"spam," or unwanted junk e-mail often designed to lure viewers into buying goods or services.

56. Amy Waldman. "Lonely Hearts, Classy Dreams, Empty Wallets: Home Shopping Networks." *Washington Monthly* 27(June 1995):10ff. Used with permission.

57. Murray Melbin. "Night as Frontier." *American Sociological Review* 43(1978), pp. 3-22.

58. As Juliet Schor has pointed out, the validity of this assertion depends on one's point of comparison.

59. Linton Weeks. "In U.S., Nighttime Is the Right Time." *Washington Post*, July 20, 1997, p. A1.

60. Linton Weeks. "In U.S., Nighttime Is the Right Time." *Washington Post*, July 20, 1997, p. A16.

61. This also goes for credit cards as facilitating means.

62. Colin Campbell. *The Romantic Ethic and the Spirit of Modern Consumerism*. Oxford: Blackwell, 1987.

63. College students without jobs are often offered credit cards, however. Modern "bankers" eager to get as many credit cards issued as possible ask, Why should the lack of a job be an impediment to obtaining credit?

64. It is true that the merchant must pay the credit card companies a small fee (2 to 4 percent, in general) on each transaction; a fee that would not be incurred in a cash transaction. However, it is also the case that

many transactions take place that would not have were it not for credit cards.

65. Larry Fox and Barbara Radin Fox. "Floating a Loan." *Washington Post*, March 16, 1997, p. E4.

66. Michelle Wong. "Virtual Inventory." *Star Tribune* (Minneapolis, MN), August 6, 1996, p. 1D.

67. Some of the other new means of consumption also serve to render time zones less relevant, or even irrelevant. If one is watching HSN or QVC, or shopping by catalog, it does not matter whether it is 9 a.m. on the East Coast or 6 a.m. on the West Coast. If one is shopping on the Internet, it is of no consequence whether one is doing it in the United States or at the same time in Australia, which is more or less a day later.

68. Linton Weeks. "In U.S., Nighttime Is the Right Time." *Washington Post*, July 20, 1997, pp. A1, A16.

69. It is interesting to note that these first three very different worlds are literally next door to one another on the Las Vegas Strip.

70. Gary Dretzka. "Disney Joins Pay-for-Play Players." *Chicago Tribune*, March 31, 1997, p. C1ff.

71. Kevin McManus. "Jeepers a Joy, At Least for Kids." *The Washington Post*, February 2, 1996, p. N51.

72. Dave McNary. "New High-Tech Arcades Aim to Redefine Theme Parks." *Pittsburgh Post-Gazette*, May 3, 1997, p. D8.

73. William Kowinski. *The Malling of America: An Inside Look at the Great Consumer Paradise*. New York: William Morrow, 1985, pp. 216–217.

74. William Kowinski. *The Malling of America: An Inside Look at the Great Consumer Paradise* New York: William Morrow, 1985, p. 218.

75. Although the opportunity to see and explore huge spaces may draw us to the mall, once there it is also necessary to break this huge expanse up into manageable spaces so that the consumer is impressed, but not overwhelmed, by the physical confines of the mall. The malls usually have wings, often anchored by a department store. Customers are simultaneously led to believe that they are in physically manageable settings and that they are in a much larger, nearly infinite shopping space to explore later or at some future date. The sense conveyed is that outside of a manageable wing is a seemingly infinite space yet to be explored.

76. Edwin McDowell. "Sailings Worldwide: Not Just Cruise Ships Anymore." *New York Times,* February 2, 1997, section 5, p. 13ff.

77. Larry Fox and Barbara Radin Fox. "Your Destiny Awaits." *Washington Post*, December 8, 1996, p. E4.

78. It is worth remembering that it characterized the early arcades.

79. Edward William Henry, Jr. *Portman: Architect and Entrepreneur.* Doctoral Dissertation, University of Pennsylvania, 1985, p. 162.

80. John Portman and Jonathan Barnett. *The Architect as Developer.* New York: McGraw-Hill, 1976, pp. 74–76.

81. John Portman and Jonathan Barnett. *The Architect as Developer.* New York: McGraw-Hill, 1976, p. 10.

82. Edward William Henry, Jr. *Portman: Architect and Entrepreneur.* Doctoral Dissertation, University of Pennsylvania, 1985, p. 202.

83. Richard Panek. "Superstore Inflation." *New York Times,* April 6, 1997, section 6, p. 66ff.

84. "American Survey." *The Economist,* November 23, 1996, pp. 27–28.

Chapter 7

1. Ada Louise Huxtable. *The Unreal America: Architecture and Illusion.* New York: The New Press, 1997, pp. 51–2.

2. Jean-Francois Lyotard. *The Postmodern Condition: A Report on Knowledge.* Minneapolis: University of Minnesota Press, 1979/1984.

3. Jean Baudrillard. *Simulations.* New York: Semiotext(e), 1983.

4. Jean Baudrillard. *The Transparency of Evil: Essays on Extreme Phenomena.* London: Verso, 1990/1993, p. 122.

5. John F. Kasson. *Amusing the Million: Coney Island at the Turn of the Century.* New York: Hill and Wang, 1978, p. 60.

6. Judith A. Adams. *The American Amusement Park Industry.* New York: Twayne, 1991, p. 44.

7. Although, in the early Disney cartoons Mickey Mouse looked less harmless and was somewhat more daring in his actions.

8. Michael Sorkin. "See You in Disneyland," in Michael Sorkin (ed.). *Variations on a Theme Park.* New York: Hill and Wang, 1992, p. 223.

9. Judith A. Adams. *The American Amusement Park Industry.* New York: Twayne, 1991, p. 44.

10. Judith A. Adams. *The American Amusement Park Industry.* New York: Twayne, 1991, p. 45.

11. William Booth. "At Disney's Tomorrowland, The Future Is a Timid Creature." *Washington Post,* June 24, 1998, p. D8.

12. Michel Foucault. *Discipline and Punish: The Birth of the Prison.* New York: Vintage, 1975/1979.

13. Pierre Bourdieu. *A Social Critique of the Judgment of Taste.* Cambridge, MA: Harvard University Press, 1984.

14. Juliet B. Schor. *The Overspent American: Upscaling, Downshifting, and the New Consumer.* New York: Basic Books, 1998, p. 22.

15. Peter A. McKay and Maryann Haggerty. "Entertaining New Mall Ideas." *Washington Post,* June 19, 1998, p. F1.

16. Peter A. McKay and Maryann Haggerty. "Entertaining New Mall Ideas." *Washington Post,* June 19, 1998, p. F10.

17. Joseph Turow. *Breaking up America: Advertisers and the New Media World.* Chicago: University of Chicago Press, 1997.

18. They may be overrepresented as workers, often poorly paid, in many of these settings.

19. David J. Kennedy. "Residential Associations as State Actors: Regulating the Impact of Gated Communities on Nonmembers." *Yale Law Review* 105(1995):761–793.

20. Peter Applebome. "Tourism Enriches an Island Resort, But Hilton Head Blacks Feel Left Out." *New York Times,* September 2, 1994, p. 18.

21. David J. Kennedy. "Residential Associations as State Actors: Regulating the Impact of Gated Communities on Nonmembers." *Yale Law Review* 105(1995):761–793.

22. Larry Keller. "On Golden Beach." *Sun-Sentinel* (Fort Lauderdale), February 4, 1996, sunshine section, p. 12ff.

23. Ira G. Zepp. *The New Religious Image of Urban America: The Shopping Mall as Ceremonial Center.* Niwot: University Press of Colorado, 1997, p. 147.

24. Quentin Hardy. "School of Thought: The Unbearable Whiteness of Being." *Wall Street Journal,* April 24, 1997, p. A1ff.

25. Tamara Holmes. "Seeing a Future with More Blacks Exploring the Internet." *USA Today,* February 20, 1997, p. 5D.

26. Paul Goldberger. "The Sameness of Things." *New York Times,* April 6, 1997, section 6, p. 56ff.

27. Jack Weatherford. "The Plastic Curtain." *Washington Post,* February 18, 1997, p. A13.

28. Jeff Bailey. "HFC Profits Nicely by Charging Top Rates on Some Risky Loans." *Wall Street Journal,* December 11, 1996, p. A1.

29. Amy Waldman. "Lonely Hearts, Classy Dreams, Empty Wallets: Home Shopping Networks." *Washington Monthly* 27(June 1995):10ff. Used with permission.

30. Amy Waldman. "Lonely Hearts, Classy Dreams, Empty Wallets: Home Shopping Networks." *Washington Monthly* 27(June 1995):10ff. Used with permission.

31. David Handelman. "The Billboards of Madison Avenue." *New York Times,* April 6, 1997, section 6, p. 50ff.

32. Louise Lee. "To Keep Teens Away, Malls Turn Snooty." *Wall Street Journal,* October 17, 1996, p. B6.

33. Carol Emert. "The Disneyland of Malls." *The San Francisco Chronicle,* April 11, 1997, p. A1ff.

34. For a fictional treatment of the class differences (and class warfare) in and around one of these communities, see T. Coraghessan Boyle. *The Tortilla Curtain.* New York: Viking, 1995.

35. David Dillon. "Fortress America: More and More of Us Are Living Behind Locked Gates." *Planning* 60(1994):8ff.

36. Robert B. Reich. "Secession of the Successful." *New York Times,* January 20, 1991, section 6, p. 16ff.

37. Tom Matrullo. "Times A-Changin': Like with Everything Else, Baby Boomers Have Very Different Ideas Compared to Earlier Generations about What Retirement and Retirement Communities Should Be." *Sarasota Herald-Tribune,* October 14, 1996, business section, p. 1ff.

38. Russ Rhymer. "Back to the Future: Disney Reinvents the Company Town Celebration, FL." *Harper's Magazine,* October 1996, p. 65ff. Used with permission.

39. Judith A. Adams. *The American Amusement Park Industry: A History of Technology and Thrills.* Boston: Twayne, 1991, p. 146.

40. Thomas Bender. "City Lite: Today's City Is More a Theme Park for Tourists than a Civic Center Where Values and Experiences Are Shared. Does Our Future Lie in a Gritty, Organic Center for Culture and Urbanity, or in a Crabgrass Utopia?" *Los Angeles Times,* December 22, 1996, p. M1ff.

41. Joel Achenbach. "2009: A Magician's Odyssey." *Washington Post,* April 21, 1997, p. D4.

42. Christina Binkley. "A Day with a High Roller." *Wall Street Journal,* May 1, 1998, pp. W1, W8.

43. Joe McGowan. "Hooking the High Rollers." *Fortune,* July 22, 1996, p. 84.

44. John M. Stefanelli and Andrew Nazarechuk. "Hotel\Casino Food and Beverage Operations," in International Gaming Institute. *The Gaming Industry: Introduction and Perspectives.* New York: John Wiley and Sons, 1996, p. 134.

45. Bob Dickinson and Andy Vladimir. *Selling the Sea: An Inside Look at the Cruise Industry.* New York: John Wiley and Sons, 1997, p. 113.

46. Thorstein Veblen. *The Theory of the Leisure Class: An Economic Study of Institutions.* New York: Modern Library, 1899/1934.

47. Paul Goldberger. "The Store Strikes Back." *New York Times,* April 6, 1997, section 6, p. 45ff.

48. Cited in Anne Friedberg. *Window Shopping: Cinema and the Postmodern.* Berkeley: University of California Press, 1993, p. 58.

49. Amy Waldman. "Lonely Hearts, Classy Dreams, Empty Wallets: Home Shopping Networks." *Washington Monthly* 27(June 1995).10ff. Used with permission.

50. Amy Waldman. "Lonely Hearts, Classy Dreams, Empty Wallets: Home Shopping Networks." *Washington Monthly* 27(June 1995):10ff. Used with permission.

51. Barbara Kantrowitz. "Modem Moms." *Newsweek,* December 16, 1996, p. 72ff.

52. Marc Fisher. "Where Hunters Gather." *Washington Post Magazine,* September 3, 1995, pp. 31–32.

53. Joe Armstrong. "A Lost Boyhood of Violent Computer Games." *The Irish Times,* March 10, 1997, p. 8.

54. "Gender Differentiates Web Activity." *Jupiter Communications, Digital Kids Report,* March 1, 1997.

55. "Women Online: Will They Bring Their Kids?" *Jupiter Communications, Digital Kids Report,* September 1, 1996.

56. Yiannis Gabriel and Tim Lang. *The Unmanageable Consumer: Contemporary Consumption and Its Fragmentation.* London: Sage, 1995.

57. Juliet B. Schor. *The Overspent American: Upscaling, Downshifting, and the New Consumer.* New York: Basic Books, 1998.

58. The concept of creative destruction is traceable to Joseph Schumpeter. *Capitalism, Socialism, and Democracy,* 3d ed. New York: Harper and Brothers, 1950, pp. 81–86.

59. These are what Baudrillard calls "fatal strategies." See Jean Baudrillard. *Fatal Strategies.* New York: Semiotext(e), 1983/1990.

INDEX